Settling Disputes

SECOND EDITION

Settling Disputes

Conflict Resolution in Business, Families, and the Legal System

Linda R. Singer

Westview Press

BOULDER • SAN FRANCISCO • OXFORD

Copyright © 1990, 1994 by Linda R. Singer

Published in 1994 in the United States of America by Westview Press, Inc., 5500 Central Avenue, Boulder, Colorado 80301-2877, and in the United Kingdom by Westview Press, 36 Lonsdale Road, Summertown, Oxford OX2 7EW

Library of Congress Cataloging-in-Publication Data
Singer, Linda R.
    Settling disputes : conflict resolution in business, families, and the legal system / Linda R. Singer. — 2nd ed.
        p. cm.
    Includes bibliographical references and index.
    ISBN 0-8133-8655-1— ISBN 0-8133-8656-X (pbk.)
    1. Dispute resolution (Law)—United States.   I. Title.
KF9084.S57   1994
347.73'9—dc20
[347.3079]   94-17711
                                                                                CIP

Printed and bound in the United States of America

The paper used in this publication meets the requirements of the American National Standard for Permanence of Paper for Printed Library Materials Z39.48-1984.

10   9

Contents

Figures

Preface to
the Second Edition

Significant changes have taken place since the first publication of *Settling Disputes*, as alternative dispute resolution (ADR) increasingly has become part of the mainstream. Most dramatic have been the developments in the courts, in the federal and local governments, and in business. As a result, I have changed or updated much of the first edition.

My own professional life now is spent mediating large commercial, public, and employment disputes, with some time devoted to one-on-one mediations, lawyering, and teaching. Thus I am particularly grateful to Susan Horn, who ably assisted me in revising and updating the book, and to my law partner and agent, Gail Ross, who, as always, encouraged me to find the time to keep the book current.

Throughout the years, many colleagues and friends have shared with me their visions and their concerns about settling disputes. I could not possibly thank them all by name. I will mention only one here: my husband, comediator, coteacher, and closest colleague, Michael Lewis.

I also want to thank all the people who responded to the first edition and let me know that it had changed the way they practice their professions or handle their own disputes. I hope that this version of the book continues to inspire them and others like them.

Linda R. Singer

1

Origins and Growth of the Dispute Settlement Movement

A QUIET REVOLUTION IS TAKING PLACE in the methods Americans have available to them for dealing with conflict. Innovations, almost all of them fewer than fifteen years old, are being developed not only to settle disputes out of court, but to supplement or replace the processes used by legislatures to budget funds, by businesses to manage employees, by therapists to treat families, and by diplomats to respond to global crises. There also are new institutions and new methods for resolving conflicts, such as those between neighboring families or countries, that once could be dealt with only by fighting it out with lawyers, with fists, or with armies.

From the beginning, America has been a nation of fighters, with a tradition of every man—and sometimes woman—for himself. Our culture is permeated with the language of sports—and of war. Perhaps it is our history of bountiful land and ever-expanding frontiers. Perhaps it is the perceived opportunity to get rich within a single generation, unaided by family or community. Whatever the explanation, our tradition of individualism also has spawned a history of confrontation. Except for countries actively undergoing revolution, the United States has the highest incidence of violent crime in the world.

The way we deal with lawbreakers also reflects our frontier and individualistic heritage. Except for the former Soviet Union and South Africa, we lock up more people, for longer periods of time, than any other country in the world.

Our civil as well as our criminal courts have been heavily used throughout our history. The public perception of a litigation explosion is not new. De Tocqueville wrote 150 years ago, "Scarcely any political question arises in the United States that is not resolved, sooner or later, into a judicial question."[1]

Early Americans distrusted lawyers. The Fundamental Constitutions of Carolina termed pleading a case for a fee "a base and vile thing." Yet there are many more lawyers in the United States today than in any other country, both in absolute numbers and relative to the size of our total population. While the United States accounts for about 5 percent of the world's population, we have at least 35 percent of the world's lawyers.[2] According to a speech by Harvard Law School Dean Robert Clark, the percentage of the U.S. gross national product devoted to legal services more than doubled between 1988 and 1993.[3] Historian Jerold Auerbach has written, "Five hundred years from now, when historians sift through twentieth-century artifacts, they doubtless will have as little comprehension of American legal piety as most Americans now display toward medieval religious zeal. The analogy is illuminating: the courtroom is our cathedral, where contemporary passion plays are enacted."[4]

Several developments have contributed to the public perception of a litigation explosion. Although the actual number of cases filed in state courts has grown only in proportion to population, both the number and complexity of disputes brought to court have increased during this century. Federal legislation designed to regulate business, to ensure civil rights, and, more recently, to protect the public from hazardous products and polluted air and water all have contributed to a significant increase in the business of our federal courts. Whatever the reason, the number of civil suits filed in federal courts alone has nearly tripled since 1970. This trend has been exacerbated by the sharp upturn in the criminal matters brought to federal courts, which in many parts of the country makes it difficult to have civil claims heard at all.

The nature of the disputes litigated also has changed, from a predominance of private business and property cases to personal injury accident claims and cases involving products liability, domestic relations, criminal law, and government regulatory actions. With the creation of products such as asbestos insulation, Bendectin, and Agent Orange, which have the potential of injuring huge numbers of people, and the invention of legal techniques (especially class actions) for bringing large numbers of cases involving accident victims or injured workers or consumers to court at a time, court battles affect the lives of many more people than they once did. They also require greater technical expertise. Demand for expert witnesses has increased markedly; witness brokers and clearinghouses can locate experts willing to testify on almost any subject. Despite the proliferation of new types of lawsuits, some of them with far-reaching implications, preliminary data from an ongoing study of federal litigation between 1971 and 1991 indicate that contract disputes among Fortune 1000 companies constituted the largest category of lawsuits filed in federal court.[5]

When Americans must use the system—for example, to handle corporate conflicts over substantial sums or personal problems such as accidents, discrimination, or divorce—court or administrative action displaces our power over our own disputes. The legal process distorts reality; not only speed and economy but the real issues in dispute and the treatment of disputants by the professional dispute resolvers escape our control. Even top corporate managers feel as if their business problems take on a legal life of their own once they turn them over to lawyers and courts.

Despite the well-documented flaws in the system, which have attracted increased attention in recent years, it would be shortsighted to overlook the system's enormous benefits in establishing critical principles—principles many of us consider vital to our individual freedoms. Over the past forty years, for example, the courts have served as the last resort for racial and other minorities whose interests do not command a majority vote. Schools and workplaces have been desegregated; blacks and women have made political, economic, and social gains; public institutions, such as prisons and mental hospitals, have received far greater scrutiny. Courts also have improved the environment, increased safety in the workplace, and deterred manufacturers from injuring consumers through negligence or fraud. For example, the flood of litigation to compensate workers exposed to asbestos undoubtedly brought about safer handling—and eventual banning—of the insulation material sooner than would otherwise have been the case.

But all lawsuits do not involve important legal principles. In a large urban court, it can take years for even the simplest case to come to trial. Lengthy, complex procedures, both costly and time-consuming, make the courts appear to be exclusively the province of the rich, the patient, and the hearty. As early as 1926, Judge Learned Hand confessed, "I must say that, as a litigant, I should dread a lawsuit beyond anything else short of sickness and death."

Costs and delays, coupled with occasional multimillion-dollar verdicts (and, some charge, trial lawyers' and insurance companies' greed), have caused the rates of liability coverage for doctors, lawyers, car owners, and even architects to skyrocket. Yet awards made to the injured who use the courts to obtain compensation also are consumed by these same costs and delays. According to a study of the costs of compensating accident victims through litigation, victims receive only 45 cents in net compensation for every dollar spent on a lawsuit by the parties, their insurance companies, and the public.[6]

Even administrative agencies, established to cope with such widespread, immediate problems as employment discrimination or consumer fraud in a faster, more accessible way than courts, have become courtlike, with long waits, complex procedures, and trial-like proceedings. Our large and complex society no longer can be run like a New England town meeting. The enactment of legislation and regulations, even at the local level, is so remote that it is completely removed from the lives of most Americans.

Even if our legal system of justice were more efficient, it would not satisfy some participants' most critical interests. The emphasis of courts and other traditional forums on pronouncing right and wrong and naming winners and losers necessarily destroys almost any preexisting relationship between the people involved. Whether the parties are a divorcing husband and wife who must continue to share the parenting of their children, businesses that want to retain their customers and suppliers, or employers and employees who want to keep their jobs, it is virtually impossible to maintain a civil relationship once people have confronted one another across a courtroom.

At the same time that use of the official system for resolving disputes is so forbidding, other traditional methods of settling conflict have lost much of their effectiveness. In a nation where moving from neighborhood to neighborhood, city to city, and job to job has become the norm, the mediating roles once played by the extended family, by churches, and by respected citizens in small towns persist only in a few homogeneous, cohesive communities. For Orthodox Jews in New York and residents in Chinatown in San Francisco, dispute resolution by rabbis or by community elders still remains a possibility. For the rest of us, such traditions, if they ever existed at all, belong to the distant past.

Then what do we do when we have a complaint of nonpayment on a bill or a contract, mistreatment on our jobs, or pollution of our air? Most of us recoil from fighting. Except for large corporations, hiring a lawyer seems far beyond our means: According to a survey by the American Bar Association, approximately 1 percent of the U.S. population receives 95 percent of the country's legal services.[7]

So, in the words of legal anthropologist William Felstiner, most of us "lump it."[8] We take out our frustrations on family and friends. We may even write occasional letters to our representatives in Congress. But generally we do nothing at all. The less money we have, the less likely we are to complain—whether directly to sellers or to third parties such as newspapers or television, consumer complaint centers, or civil courts. The costs, the stresses, and the inaccessibility of ways to resolve conflict other than through the polar alternatives of fight or flight cause some of us to drop out or to seek extreme techniques to make our points.

No less a member of the legal establishment than Derek Bok, former president of Harvard University and former dean of the Harvard Law School, described our system for resolving disputes as "strewn with the disappointed hopes of those who find [it] too complicated to understand, too quixotic to command respect, and too expensive to be of much practical use."[9] Harvard law professor Laurence Tribe adds that the results do not justify the costs: "Too much law, too little justice; too many rules, too few results. ... "[10]

The Move Toward Alternatives

Against this backdrop, new methods of settling disputes are emerging both in and out of courts, in businesses, in diplomacy, and in communities. Diverse though they are, the innovations have a number of characteristics in common:

- They all exist somewhere between the polar alternatives of doing nothing or of escalating conflict.
- They are less formal and generally more private than ritualized court battles.
- They permit people with disputes to have more active participation in and more control over the processes for solving their own problems than do traditional methods of dealing with conflict.
- Most of the new methods have been developed in the private sector, although courts and administrative agencies now are borrowing and adapting some of the more successful techniques.

The movement by now has earned its own awkward acronym: "ADR," for "alternative dispute resolution." It draws on the history of tightly knit religious and immigrant ethnic groups, beginning with the Puritans in the 1600s and including the Dutch in New Amsterdam, the Jews on Manhattan's East Side, the Scandinavians in Minnesota, and the Chinese on the West Coast. All of these groups resolved differences within the community through mediation by ministers or elders.

The movement also draws on our commercial history. In settings such as the maritime, securities, fur, and silk industries, where firms dealt regularly with one another on an ongoing basis, businesses and trade associations early established private channels for resolving their differences. Commercial arbitration was born in 1768, when the New York Chamber of Commerce set up its own way of settling business disputes according to trade practice rather than legal principles.

This trend reached the personal level as well. George Washington put an arbitration clause in his will to resolve disputes among his heirs. Abraham Lincoln, while practicing law, arbitrated a boundary dispute between two farmers.

More recently, labor unions and employers developed an entire system of resolving work-related disputes as an alternative to violence or costly strikes. Although Congress authorized the secretary of labor to appoint

"commissioners of conciliation" as early as 1913 when it created the
United States Department of Labor, authority in U.S. industrial society before World War II, to quote labor arbitrator George Nicolau, was "unilat-
eral and unreviewable." Workers resorted to direct action to challenge
management's authority, which was "personal, arbitrary, and virtually
unrestrained."[11] Violent seizures of property, sit-downs, and bloody
strikes were common. Characterized as unlawful, these actions more often than not were met with force by private security guards, state police,
or the National Guard.

In the 1930s and early 1940s, several states and a few cities initiated
publicly sponsored mediation services to settle labor-management disputes. During World War II, when Congress determined that industrial
strife was too costly to the war effort to be tolerated, the War Labor Board
was born. Grievance procedures, binding arbitration, and other innovations for solving industrial disputes became the norm throughout most of
the United States. In 1947 Congress created an independent agency to settle labor disputes: the Federal Mediation and Conciliation Service.

The still-evolving history of resolving conflict in nonunionized corporations and in urban communities, prisons, schools, and universities reflects many of the same events. Yet only in dealing with conflicts between
unionized labor and management have we actually developed well-de-
fined institutions for resolving disputes, a set of laws that help to achieve
settlement, a cadre of professional dispute settlers (negotiators, mediators, and arbitrators), and the resulting expectation that disputes will be
settled peacefully and fairly.

In the early 1970s, when I was one of a small group of lawyers working
to develop ways of resolving disputes between prisoners and their keep-
ers, the history of labor and management was our chief inspiration. Despite the obvious differences between captive prisoners and unionized
employees, we managed to create models of settling disputes that applied
mediation and arbitration to a markedly different setting. Some of the
same methods are being used today in corporations, in universities, and
in public schools and are being discussed as essential components of a re-
vamped health-care system. A few years later, those of us who were involved in creating the first "neighborhood justice centers," where community volunteers help people to settle their own disputes, looked both to
our experience with various types of organizations and to the traditional
roles of clergy and village elders in tightly knit communities. The pioneers
in settling environmental and government-related disputes built on these
experiences and took additional inspiration from New England town
meetings.

Some of these disparate efforts to develop new methods of dealing
with conflict began to coalesce in April 1976, when Warren E. Burger, then

chief justice of the Supreme Court, convened the Roscoe E. Pound Conference on the Causes of Popular Dissatisfaction with the Administration of Justice in Saint Paul. (In 1906, speaking in Saint Paul to the Minnesota legislature, Pound already had voiced concern about the irrelevance of the legal system to the problems of most Americans.) Expressing the fear that "we may well be on our way to a society overrun by hordes of lawyers, hungry as locusts, and brigades of judges in numbers never before contemplated," and that "we have reached the point where our systems of justice—both state and federal—may literally break down before the end of this century,"[12] Burger invited an unusual mixture of people to reconsider Pound's wisdom.

The meeting attracted members of the judicial establishment who were concerned about the volume of litigation in general and the presence of cases with which courts were growing increasingly uncomfortable: environmental litigation, class actions, cases brought to reform public institutions, and so-called minor disputes involving small amounts of money. Also present at the meeting were a few veterans of the civil rights movement, together with public interest lawyers concerned about increasing people's access to the legal system and the fairness of procedures. These strange bedfellows were joined by academics intent on developing better solutions to increasingly complex scientific or social problems. Absent from the conference, but active throughout the early development of the field, were the peace groups and grassroots community organizers, intent on empowering communities and enabling people to resolve their own conflicts.

The Pound Conference served to spark the interest of the legal establishment in alternative ways of settling disputes. But the different, and sometimes conflicting, values and goals of its participants have remained alive as the movement has gathered force. Not surprisingly, these differences have resulted in a diversity of settlement philosophies and techniques. For example, corporate minitrials coexist, sometimes uncomfortably, with community dispute centers as part of the same overall movement. The unusual alliance that makes up the ADR movement also has produced tensions among those who advocate the use of the same processes: There is no consensus on whether the primary benefits of settlement devices are the savings of time and money, the increase in the parties' participation, or the achievement of better results.

Since the Pound Conference, the proliferation of techniques for settling disputes and the emergence of new institutions and professionals to use them have constituted a major phenomenon of social change. In a varied and often unorganized way, discrete efforts are evolving into a new system for handling conflict.

1. Corporate executives are signing up for training courses in negotiation to learn to deal directly with their employees, customers, and competition. They also are attending seminars in mediation. Business school offerings are changing to reflect executives' different orientation. More than half of all business schools now offer courses in ADR. Although managers may have the power to order subordinates to take certain courses of action, they often find it more effective to reach consensus, whether by negotiating or mediating among employees who disagree with their bosses or with one another. High success rates and participant satisfaction have made these skills essential for managers and a permanent part of their job descriptions.

When faced with disputes with consumers or other corporations, business executives increasingly insist that their lawyers reduce cost, delay, and bruised feelings by settling cases through negotiation, mediation, or minitrials. Businesses can bind themselves and those who deal with them to specific methods of resolving future disputes by including agreements to mediate and/or arbitrate in their contracts; some will not sign a contract unless it contains such a provision. As a result of such devices, the number of federal lawsuits over alleged breaches of contract, which peaked at over 10,000 in 1987, dropped 30 percent to just over 7,000 in 1991.[13]

Businesses also have begun to use corporate ombudspeople, mediators, or peer review panels to attempt resolution of complaints by employees or customers. Even the U.S. Senate has implemented a multistep dispute resolution program to resolve complaints of employment discrimination.

Insurance companies used ADR to handle claims arising from Hurricane Andrew and the devastating fire that destroyed much of Oakland, California. As a result, an estimated $20 million will be saved in transaction costs related to Hurricane Andrew victims alone, not to mention the months or years that otherwise would have separated them from much-needed compensation.

In response to their clients' demands, a growing number of law firms are appointing ADR coordinators; a few have separate departments of settlement or negotiation that operate independently of the firm's litigators. Led by Colorado, several states have adopted new ethics rules for lawyers, which strongly encourage or require them to advise their clients of alternatives to litigation. Profit-making dispute settlement firms, such as Judicial Arbitration and Mediation Service, Endispute, and ADR Associates, have sprung up to take advantage of the business market.

2. Troubled families used to go to court or to therapists. Now they can go to mediation—with the same therapists, with lawyers, or with community volunteers. The idea is to use the third party, who has no power to

make decisions, to help settle disputes between husbands and wives, between parents and children, and, increasingly, between divorcing spouses. Some psychiatrists report that the emphasis of their entire practice has shifted from therapy to dispute settlement.

Following this trend, a number of jurisdictions require divorcing couples to try mediation before the courts will resolve their disputes for them. The proponents of mandatory mediation believe that the open communication and resolve-it-yourself nature of mediation make the process ideal for handling divorce settlements, especially where couples have children. Opponents caution that mediation probably works best when the parties engage in it voluntarily.

3. Approximately 350 neighborhood justice centers have been created throughout the United States in the past fifteen years, in sites ranging from storefronts to public schools and courthouses. These centers, sometimes called mediation services or "community boards," use community volunteers to settle landlord-tenant conflicts, neighborhood disputes, family rifts, and disputes involving the education of handicapped children. Some of them mediate between criminal defendants and their victims, either as an alternative to trial or as part of the sentence. In New York City alone, over 14,000 such disputes are handled through mediation each year.

4. Growing numbers of enforcement agencies, such as the Equal Employment Opportunity Commission and local consumer protection departments, require complaining employees and consumers to participate with businesses in settlement attempts presided over by the agency, before claims are investigated. The EEOC contracted with the Center for Dispute Settlement in Washington, D.C., to conduct a successful experiment with offering outside mediators to complainants and employers in an attempt at early settlements of selected charges filed in Washington, D.C., Philadelphia, Houston, and New Orleans. Some businesses have gone a step further and hired private mediators to help them settle disputes with dissatisfied current or former employees either before or after they are brought to enforcement agencies or courts. In Maryland, the state attorney general's office recruits citizen volunteers to arbitrate complaints against businesses instead of prosecuting them.

5. In the United States, 95 percent of the law schools, as well as rapidly increasing numbers of schools of business, planning, and public policy, offer some alternative dispute resolution courses as part of their curricula. Publishers of law school textbooks now include ADR in publications on civil procedure, contracts, torts, and family law. Of the practicing lawyers, judges, and law teachers who sign up for Harvard Law School's Program of Instruction for Lawyers each June, more than half choose the oversubscribed offerings in mediation or negotiation. ADR has become a perma-

nent part of the curriculum at the National Judicial College. Corporate lawyers recently were invited to learn about new ways of resolving cases on board a ship cruising around the Hawaiian islands. Most of them settle for the increasing numbers of ADR offerings in seminars offered by local bar associations or professional dispute resolvers.

6. Growing numbers of high schools and junior high schools across the country are developing courses in conflict resolution. Students are applying their new knowledge to resolving other students' disputes, including the fistfights that once would have guaranteed suspension. Working in teams with newly trained teachers, they also settle differences between students and teachers. Some have mediated conflicts between teenagers and their parents.

7. Congress in late 1990 passed the Administrative Dispute Resolution Act, which requires all federal agencies to develop policies on the use of ADR, appoint an ADR specialist, and provide appropriate employees with training in ADR.[14] Spurred by the legislation, and by a 1991 executive order requiring federal agencies that litigate to use negotiation or third-party settlement techniques in appropriate cases when the federal government is involved in litigation, several federal agencies have developed programs that use a variety of ADR methods to handle disagreements with employees, contractors, taxpayers, or regulated businesses.

8. Increasingly, federal agencies, state public utility commissions, and even local sanitation departments are issuing new regulations through what they call "negotiated rulemaking." In this new process, representatives of opposing special interest groups from industry, consumer, and environmental organizations sit down with one another and with the agencies involved and negotiate government regulations. The negotiating committee that devised the penalties prescribed for violation of the Clean Air Act by the manufacturers of diesel engines, for example, included representatives of competing manufacturers, operators and importers of diesel engines, environmentalists, state agencies, the Environmental Protection Agency, and the Office of Management and Budget. A statute, enacted in 1990, specifically authorized federal agencies to employ this process.[15]

9. In a related process, called "negotiated investment strategies," local, state, and federal officials negotiate with private interests over the allocation of government money for social services and public works projects. Resulting agreements have distributed the state budget for providing social services in Connecticut, established priorities for funding public works in Saint Paul, and provided government aid for industrial growth in Gary, Indiana.

10. The Civil Justice Reform Act, also passed in 1990, requires all federal district courts to create advisory committees to consider ways of reducing

the cost and delay of civil litigation.[16] The legislation specifically directs each committee to consider the use of ADR to reduce cost and delay. As a result of the committees' work, many (if not most) federal courts are instituting some sort of mediation, arbitration, or early neutral evaluation programs (many of them mandatory) to assist litigants in what is hoped will be earlier, less costly resolution of their cases.

11. Lawyers, therapists, retired judges, and entrepreneurs with no particular professional identity are hanging out shingles as mediators or judges for hire. Large numbers of students, together with professionals tired of other careers, are trying to build new careers in dispute resolution. They are helped by the public attention being generated by such events as court-sponsored "Settlement Weeks," when all judicial business stops to allow judges and volunteer mediators to help parties to settle cases, and statewide "Dispute Resolution Weeks," the first of which was proclaimed by the governor of Texas in 1985.

12. In 1978 President Jimmy Carter spent thirteen days at Camp David as a mediator between Menachem Begin and Anwar el-Sadat. (For the last ten days, Begin and Sadat never spoke to each other, although their cottages were only about one hundred yards apart.) Carter's unusual efforts produced the first comprehensive agreement between Egypt and a Jewish nation for more than two thousand years. Carter's efforts were preceded by Henry Kissinger's and later followed by Philip Habib's and then James Baker's shuttle diplomacy—a marked departure from traditional State Department procedures but one being used increasingly and in the most high-stake situations.

Fifteen years after the historic Camp David agreement, perhaps an even greater breakthrough in the Middle East was achieved with an agreement between Israel and the Palestine Liberation Organization (PLO). The negotiations, held in secret, were particularly tricky because neither group recognized the other's right to exist and it was a longstanding policy on both sides not to negotiate with the other.

Again an intervener offered critical assistance. Terje Rod Larsen, head of a Norwegian institute researching conditions in the Israeli-occupied territories, met Yossi Beilin, then an opposition Labor member of the Israeli Parliament, at an academic meeting in Tel Aviv in April 1992. Larsen offered to put Beilin in touch with senior Palestinian officials. Although the timing would not be right until after the Israeli national elections in June, the two kept in touch through an Israeli university professor. After the elections Beilin became deputy foreign minister and Larsen traveled to Jerusalem to renew his offer.

The ensuing events read like a John Le Carré novel. Again the professor served as the point mart. As the *New York Times* later described the first meeting:

On a December morning, the 49-year-old professor walked into the Gallery
Lounge of the modern Forte Crest St. James's hotel central London. He was
to have breakfast with Mr. Larsen.
   But after a brief conversation, the Norwegian slid out of his seat and left
the room. In his place sat Ahmed Suleiman Khoury, a senior P.L.O. official
in charge of finances and better known by the nickname Abu Alaa.[17]

Technically, the professor was committing a crime, since Israeli law
prohibited private contacts with declared terrorists groups, including the
PLO. (The law soon was repealed.) The talks, limited to one aide on each
side in order to preserve secrecy, then moved to Norway, first to a medieval mansion, then to a country estate, then to a labor union hall north of
Oslo, to different Oslo hotels, and finally to the home of Norwegian foreign minister Holst. In contrast with Camp David, when the chief negotiators did not speak to each other for days on end, the negotiators lived together and dealt with each other face-to-face.

   Although Foreign Minister Holst was present at all the meetings, his intervention was much less active than President Carter's. More a convener
and facilitator than a mediator, he refrained from joining in the discussions unless there were problems. Although the final document reflected
the needs of both the Israeli government, which was elected on a peace
platform, and the PLO organization, which was short of cash and experi-
encing a leadership struggle, the role of the Norwegians in making it safe
for the parties to take the first steps toward exploring options for peaceful
coexistence seems to have been critical to their eventual accord.

   Years earlier, when such an accord could barely be imagined, Swedish
diplomats, working through an unofficial committee of American Jews,
had crafted a delicate arrangement under which Yasir Arafat met American preconditions for beginning negotiation with the Palestine Liberation
Organization. It is no accident that George Shultz's skills as a negotiator
were honed at the bargaining table with management and labor. In other
parts of the world, mediators from the United Nations in two cases and
the Catholic hierarchy in a third helped warring factions to agree to peace
formulas in Afghanistan, the Persian Gulf, and Nicaragua.

   13. ADR has spread from North America, England, and Australia to
Vietnam, South Africa, Russia, several Central European countries, Sri
Lanka, and the Philippines. These countries are developing innovative
conflict management programs, specific to their own cultures, in areas
ranging from civil dispute mediation to environmental protection.[18]
Countries also are using ADR to resolve disputes in their ongoing relations with one another. The U.S.-Canada Free Trade Agreement and the
North American Free Trade Agreement contain explicit dispute resolution procedures.

The Growth of Settlement Options

What do all these developments have in common? What unites the disparate cadre of volunteers and professionals, ranging from former housewives to retired judges, who crowd into meetings of the burgeoning International Society of Professionals in Dispute Resolution, which only a few years ago limited its membership to professional labor mediators and arbitrators? And what of the even more motley crowd of law and sociology professors, psychologists, and community organizers (complete with their sleeping bags) who gathered periodically at the National Conferences on Peacemaking and Conflict Resolution?

Settlements reached through negotiation, mediation, or arbitration promise faster results than do traditional legal, managerial, or bureaucratic processes—and at a fraction of the cost. There is some hard evidence to support these claims. Yet savings in cost and time are not the sole reason for much of the rapidly increasing enthusiasm for settling disputes. The core of the excitement lies in the reactions of disputants and dispute resolvers alike: People—from squabbling neighbors to corporate managers to Begin and Sadat—gain satisfaction from taking an active role in settling both their own and other people's conflicts. A national survey conducted by the Wirthlin Group, in which 80 percent of the respondents said they would choose mediation or arbitration over litigation, found that active participation in solving problems and the opportunity to reach a fair conclusion were even more important to disputants than savings in time and cost.[19]

Many disputants care about preserving relationships even where they differ. All of us care about controlling the outcome of our own disputes. Even corporate executives with high-priced lawyers are more satisfied with both the process and the results when they are actively involved in shaping outcomes than when their affairs are placed in the hands of outsiders.

Decisions produced by collaboration among those who must live with the results can be tailored to the parties' needs. A schedule for caring for their children that is devised by divorcing parents themselves, for example, is more likely to take account of their preferences and other commitments than is a schedule imposed by a judge or even negotiated by their own lawyers. The resolution of a dispute between two corporations over late delivery of equipment or failure to pay for parts or labor can include agreements about long-term supply or service arrangements; a court could award only money. In other words, the participants themselves, sometimes aided by a disinterested third party, are more apt to produce mutually satisfactory solutions to their own disputes than are outside decisionmakers.

Negotiated or mediated settlements also are far more likely to preserve any continuing relationship between the parties than is a court battle. For some disputants, their ongoing relationship provides the most persuasive reason to attempt various settlement efforts. This is so not only in disputes among family members or neighbors; a continuing relationship may be the critical consideration between an employee and employer or between a business and a customer or critical supplier. Concern for preserving their long-term relationship with customers, for example, has been one of the primary incentives motivating automobile manufacturers to develop accessible mediation and arbitration procedures for the buyers of new cars claimed to be defective.

Finally, there is growing evidence that people who reach agreements themselves are more likely to abide by them than are people who are told what to do, whether by a judge, a supervisor, or a therapist. They also may be more willing to renegotiate their agreement as circumstances change. This observation has implications for a broad range of people and problems, from fathers who refuse to pay child support to companies whose products poison the environment.

Of course, together with the many advantages, informal dispute settlement can have significant disadvantages. Negotiated settlements do not develop standards to govern the behavior of others involved in similar disputes in the future. They do not punish lawbreakers or cheaters (although negotiated agreements can provide penalties for a later breach). They often do not obviate the need for lawyers, whether to give advice or to participate in negotiations. Nor do they serve to equalize the bargaining power between participants, such as husbands and wives or corporations and their employees, who may have markedly different resources or sophistication. Indeed, serious controversy exists over whether informal settlement is appropriate for parties of significantly unequal power or whether it reinforces their differences and thereby produces unfair results.

This book is about the growth of settlement alternatives in families, in businesses, in neighborhoods, in government, and in the legal system. It will discuss the advantages and disadvantages of various processes from the points of view of potential participants and others affected by either the outcome or the costs of achieving it. It will help people involved in disputes analyze their own personalities and situations to determine whether face-to-face dispute resolution makes sense for them. Finally, it will serve as a guide to new possibilities for professionals who wish to become conflict resolvers or whose jobs in the law, business, or mental health are affected by the new options for settling disputes.

2

Techniques for Settling Disputes

INNOVATIONS TO SETTLE DISPUTES rely on a few basic techniques. Unfortunately, even professional dispute resolvers do not always refer to the same process when they use a particular word to describe it. Despite a common tendency, dating from the early development of the English language, to describe "mediation," "arbitration," and even "negotiation" interchangeably or, more recently, to refer to them all glibly as "ADR," these techniques represent distinct methods of dealing with conflict.

Techniques for settling disputes can be grouped along a spectrum (see Figure 2.1). In general, the farther a process is from the left of the spectrum, the higher the cost to the parties and the less control they have over the outcome. Two of the common ways of dealing with disputes do not appear on the chart at all. Often people simply walk away from grievances. Such avoidance is considered by some to be all too common in the United States and to result in uncounted costs in the form of lost business or ruined relationships. At the other extreme are those who resolve differences through weapons or fists. The emerging field of dispute resolution attempts to develop a broad array of options between these extremes.

When people affirmatively attempt to resolve conflicts (rather than walk away), the most typical way to do so is through negotiation, through which people try to settle their own disputes. As attempts at settlement progress along the spectrum, outsiders become involved in increasingly active ways, through mediation or some hybrid involving elements of predicting outcome. As outside participation increases, the disputing parties surrender more and more power to resolve their own disputes. Their surrender reaches its ultimate at the far right of the spectrum with adjudication, where outsiders are given the power to make binding decisions for the parties. Arbitration most often is conducted in private, through private decisionmakers. In other forms of adjudication, those decisions are public and are made by public bodies, namely courts or administrative agencies. (Legislatures also make binding, publicly enforceable decisions.) People who use one or more of the various techniques for set-

Unassisted Negotiation	Assisted Negotiation		Adjudication
	Mediation	Hybrids: Outcome Prediction	
	Conciliation	Neutral Evaluation	Arbitration
	Facilitation	Fact-Finding	Agency
	Regulatory-Negotiation	Ombuds and Complaint Programs	Court
		Minitrial	
		Summary Jury Trial	
		Nonbinding Arbitration	
		Med-Arb	

FIGURE 2.1   Techniques for Resolving Disputes

tling disputes generally attempt to preempt such decisionmaking through their own agreement.

The basic processes for settling disputes are negotiation, mediation, and adjudication.

Negotiation

Unassisted negotiation involves only the people (at least two but often many) enmeshed in a dispute. Through negotiation, they communicate with each other in an effort to reach agreement. We all negotiate daily— with spouses, with children, and with peers, supervisors, and employees.

Ideas about how to negotiate effectively only recently have begun to interest scholars and other observers. The resulting theories can be grouped into two principal schools of thought. In one, sometimes called "competitive" negotiation, the negotiators seek to maximize their own gains, generally at the expense of other parties. Exaggerating (even lying), flexing muscles, or threatening to walk away may be useful techniques for achieving this goal. This method, although used exclusively by some negotiators, may be appropriate only in one-shot, single-issue negotiations over limited resources, if it is useful at all.

In the other school, called "collaborative," "problem-solving," or "win-win" negotiation, the goal is to help all the parties meet their needs. This method is particularly appropriate where creative solutions are possible or where the parties will continue to deal with one another in the future. Thus their ongoing relationship, credibility, and trust are important.

Searching for joint gains should be distinguished from compromising, which requires that everyone give up something. The goal in collaborative negotiation is to find solutions that satisfy everyone's interests, not to leave everyone with less than was hoped for. "Splitting the difference" in compromise merely distributes the pain of losing—and often rewards the more unreasonable bargainer to boot.

Naturally, all questions cannot be solved through collaborative negotiation; if there is only one pie to divide, giving someone a bigger piece necessarily means that the others will be smaller. Yet in a surprisingly large proportion of negotiations, the pie can be enlarged before it is cut. In fact, most negotiations have elements of two processes, which a recent book on negotiations for managers calls "creating" and "claiming value."[1] This is especially true when the parties' relationships are continuing and there is more than one issue to be settled.

Roger Fisher, Bruce Patton, and William Ury's best-seller, *Getting to Yes*, together with several works on negotiation that followed, discusses basic techniques for problem-solving negotiation.[2] Among them are the following:

Distinguishing Interests from Positions. A critical negotiating skill is the ability to identify the negotiator's own as well as other parties' interests. In order to do this, interests, or underlying needs, must be separated from positions, the public stands the parties take concerning the issues in dispute. Parties should ask themselves—and one another—*why* they care about a particular issue. The answer may well reveal their underlying needs.

For example, if an employee asks for a raise, does she need the money? Or does she believe that she currently lacks the prestige her contributions should bring? Or does she consider herself unfairly treated as compared with other employees, who she believes do work of the same or less importance? Is the employer's position based on financial or equitable considerations? Do the parties have different views of the employee's performance or her value to the company?

Generally, each party to a negotiation will have several different interests, which need to be ranked in priority order. Once priorities are understood, it may be possible to devise trade-offs of issues that are unimportant to one party but critical to the other. Insurance company claims adjusters negotiating with accident victims, for example, should recognize that one victim may have an urgent need for immediate cash, while another, with sick leave or family support, is more concerned with long-term income and security in old age. Either may be willing to accept a smaller settlement if it is tailored to the particular need for quick payment or long-term security.

Creating Options to Satisfy Everyone's Interests. The most creative part of negotiation is developing options or trades for meeting the needs of the parties. Negotiations are most productive when parties feel comfortable inventing solutions without committing to them—at least not until all possible outcomes have been identified and evaluated.

In some cases, the parties can discover options that will resolve single issues in a way satisfactory to everyone. For example, if the employee's prestige is her priority, perhaps additional responsibilities or a new office or title can serve the purpose at a much lower cost than a significant raise. In a different example, a divorcing couple's house, which both of them want, can be sold and the proceeds divided to enable each of them to make a downpayment on a new house.

In other cases, the parties may be able to trade separate issues of different priorities to each. (One spouse keeps the house but gives up other property or support.) Because of the possibilities for tradeoffs, multi-issue disputes often turn out to be easier to resolve than single issues, which may allow less room for creative swaps.

Finding Mutually Acceptable Standards. If the parties can agree on standards, or neutral principles, to govern their settlement, agreement on substance will be easier. It also may seem fairer and less arbitrary. Examples of standards parties might agree to are laws, court decisions, technical specifications, or regulations; neutral appraisals of property to determine values; "blue book" prices for automobiles; and methods such as letting the person who does not cut the pie choose the first piece. (By using the pie-cutting method, which most of us learned as children, one of two people fighting over various items of property as part of dissolving a business or marriage can divide them into two shares and the other can select a share. Or the parties can agree to alternate choices.)

Recognizing Constraints. Every negotiator works within limits. For example, do all the parties have the authority to conclude a final agreement? Or does the agreement have to be ratified by someone else not at the table? Do parties have a deadline or a limited budget? Sometimes negotiators can collaborate to remove constraints; they might convince absent parties to ratify, extend deadlines, or increase budgets. Wherever possible, however, it is simpler to have the parties who must approve agreements participate in reaching them.

Understanding the Alternatives to Agreement. A negotiator's power in a particular negotiation depends on the attractiveness of the party's alternatives to agreement. The better the alternatives, the less the person needs to give up in order to secure settlement. If more than one alternative is possible (as in litigation, where a party may either win or lose), both the best and the worst alternatives, together with the costs of achieving them, are important. (Fisher and Ury coined the acronym "BATNA" to remind negotiators to remember their "best alternative to a negotiated agreement." Often it seems that the "WATNA," or "worst alternative to a negotiated agreement," is both more significant and more easily forgotten.)

A live issue during any negotiation is the various expectations of what will happen if the parties fail to settle. In this regard, it is important to remember that agreement is not always the best option in a particular situation. In some cases a party's "walk-away" alternative exceeds anything that can be gained through the negotiation. Of course, each of the parties can be expected to exaggerate the attractiveness of its own alternatives, while belittling those available to other participants.

Assisted Negotiation

Assisted negotiation involves outsiders to a dispute, who bring the parties together and, most of the time, help them to resolve their own disagreements. They may also attempt to predict the likely outcome if the dispute were to be adjudicated. All decisions remain in the hands of the parties themselves.

Mediation

In negotiation every party has a stake in the outcome. Negotiators often get locked into positions, insisting on receiving everything they want and refusing to make concessions. At that point they may find it helpful to bring in an outsider to assist in the negotiations. An impartial umpire may be able to get negotiations back on track in any number of ways:

- By soothing ruffled feelings
- By acting as a neutral discussion leader and ensuring that all the parties have ample opportunity to speak
- By helping to distinguish interests from positions
- By working with the parties to devise creative solutions for meeting their needs
- By earning enough of the parties' trust that they will share confidential information about their interests and alternatives
- By communicating selected information back and forth, often translating it from negative to positive language
- By serving as an agent of reality, helping the parties to be more realistic about their alternatives to agreement
- By occasionally providing an outside opinion on the merits of a dispute

- By keeping negotiations going when the parties are ready to give up
- By making a recommendation if the parties request it
- By acting as a scapegoat when things go wrong

Mediation, the principal form of third party assistance, involves an outsider to the dispute, who lacks the power to make decisions for the parties. The mediator meets with the parties, often both separately and together, in order to help them reach agreement.

The most efficient trade-offs require an exchange of information. Yet parties may be reluctant to divulge information unless they trust one another—a rare occurrence in a stalled negotiation. A mediator attempts to gain the trust of all the parties so that they will confide in the mediator about their priorities, possible options for settlement, and their alternatives to agreement—critical information that they often do not wish to share. In this way the mediator may discover areas of agreement when the parties' lack of trust in one another or fear of appearing weak or excessively eager to settle may prevent them from revealing their true interests or "bottom lines" to one another.

The mediator also may help the parties to devise creative solutions or to communicate a proposal without the necessity of attributing it to one of the parties. The latter technique can help to avoid the psychological phenomenon of "reactive devaluation," which causes people to think less of suggestions if they are made by their adversaries. ("What does he know that I don't?" or "If he's offering that much, there must be more.")[3]

Unlike third parties who decide or even recommend, mediators have no need either to judge guilt or innocence or to decide who is right or wrong. Mediators often do raise questions about parties' predictions of successful resolution through adjudication, however. In this way they can help negotiators to weigh possible agreements against various eventualities if there is no settlement. At best, mediators can help the parties to focus on remedies for the future rather than on punishment or revenge or who is responsible for an event in the past.

This variety of ways in which a mediator can help parties reach settlements and mediation's high success rate have led one mediator to suggest a rule of "presumptive mediation," which holds that unless compelling circumstances make it inappropriate, mediation should always be used before any other procedure.[4]

Unfortunately, the term "mediator" has been used so loosely that no one who hears it can presume the speaker intends to denote its original meaning—helping people to reach their own settlement. The courts in Michigan, for example, established a "mediation" program with penalties for refusal to accept a recommended decision. (In answer to the question of why the program was called "mediation," court officials confided that they thought arbitration had a bad name.) In addition, the press often uses the phrase inaccurately; a front-page article in the *Washington Post* reported on a "mediator's" binding decision of a local zoning controversy.[5]

Although mediators usually are outsiders to the dispute, the mediator's role may be played by a participant in the dispute who is more interested in securing an agreement than in dictating any particular terms. Thus the mediator may be a real estate agent whose commission depends on having the buyer and seller reach an agreement. Or the mediator may be a supervisor who has the power to resolve a particular disagreement between subordinates but concludes that the best way to reach a solution they both can accept is to help them decide the matter for themselves.

In some situations, "mediators" may not even be purely neutral as to the results of a particular negotiation. Henry Kissinger and later James Baker in their Middle Eastern shuttle diplomacy and Jimmy Carter at Camp David with Meachem Begin and Anwar el-Sadat clearly had an interest in some of the terms of the agreements reached between Israel and its neighbors. Yet they had an even greater interest in having the conflict resolved without bloodshed.

Anyone who is a parent with more than one child has mediated. We seem to know instinctively that it is often better to help people learn to settle their own disputes than to do it for them—or even to advise them of what we would do if we were in their place. To be most effective, a mediator needs infinite reserves of patience, inventiveness, good humor, and persuasion. According to William Simkin, a well-known labor mediator, a mediator should have

1. the patience of Job,
2. the sincerity and bulldog characteristics of the English,
3. the wit of the Irish,
4. the physical endurance of the marathon runner,
5. the broken-field dodging abilities of a halfback,
6. the guile of Machiavelli,
7. the personality-probing skills of a good psychiatrist,
8. the confidence-retaining characteristics of a mute,
9. the hide of a rhinoceros,
10. the wisdom of Solomon.[6]

When mediation is used in technical or legal disputes, some people would add to Simkin's list some substantive knowledge about the subject in controversy.

Regardless of the setting, every mediation that results in agreement has at least six separate (although not always easily identifiable) stages:

- Initial contacts between the mediator (or program employing the mediator) and the parties
- Entry of the mediator into the dispute and setting of ground rules to guide the process
- Gathering information about the dispute, identifying the issues to be resolved, and agreeing on an agenda
- Creating options for settling issues
- Evaluating options for settlement and comparing them to the parties' alternatives to agreement
- Reaching full or partial agreement on the substance of the dispute, together with whatever plan is needed for implementation and monitoring, or concluding that agreement, at least at present, is impossible

As the process moves through these stages, the mediator's role shifts. Once having entered into a dispute and established ground rules for mediation, a good mediator allows the parties to talk about their conflicts and vent their feelings. The mediator listens, asks open-ended questions ("What happened?" "What else?" "What issues are most important?"), and attempts to establish trust by showing interest and evenhandedness.

As the mediation progresses, the mediator assumes a more active role, making a transition from simply gathering information to structuring and guiding the discussion and, if necessary, translating and transmitting information from one party to another. This transmittal is done most obviously when the mediator meets with the parties individually; it also may need to be done when the parties are together but cannot (or will not) comprehend what one another is saying.

The mediator tries to achieve a momentum toward consensus by building on areas of agreement and narrowing areas of disagreement. In a dispute over the price of a piece of land, for example, the mediator may ask, "Can we agree that the price is highly speculative, so we ought to get more than one outside appraisal?" In a conflict between divorcing parents, each demanding sole custody of their children, the mediator might say, "I know that both of you are concerned about providing the most stable lives for Jenny and Joe because you both have mentioned that repeatedly. You also have agreed that the children need regular and frequent contact with both of their parents."

Most (although not all) mediators meet with the parties both jointly and separately. Joint meetings have several purposes:

- To permit each of the disputants to hear directly the other's version of the dispute
- To exchange information
- To allow people to express their anger and hurt feelings to each other in a controlled setting
- To identify quickly the areas of agreement and disagreement
- To help disputants with continuing relationships to learn to communicate in the future

Some mediators, believing that the virtues of controlled confrontation and communication between the parties outweigh any benefits of separating them, never meet individually with each party. Most do meet separately, however, for the following purposes:

- To ensure that the mediator understands the interests and concerns of all parties, who in private can be freed from their reluctance to speak in front of one another
- To explore settlement possibilities without the fear of divulging prematurely a party's "bottom line" to other parties
- To enable people to continue to work toward an agreement in cases where joint hostility, intimidation by one party, or lack of assertiveness by another convinces the mediator that joint sessions are unproductive

Only in separate sessions can a mediator be certain of fully understanding the needs of all parties. It is rare that a party, having been assured of confidentiality, will not add to what already has been said in joint session.

The extent to which a mediator familiar with relevant laws, regulations, or precedents should tell the parties about them is hotly debated. The way in which a court or other decisionmaker, such as a legislature or zoning commission, might decide a particular dispute need not control the outcome of the parties' negotiations. To the extent that it is predictable, however, this information sheds light on the alternatives to agreement. It also may be useful in establishing a standard to guide the negotiations. In a dispute over commercial development in a residential neighborhood, for example, existing zoning laws can be invoked not only to predict how a zoning commission might decide a particular question but also to shed light on the land uses that were intended for the neighborhood and how those uses may be regulated in the future.

Unlike mediation, *conciliation,* or *convening,* usually connotes only pre-liminary involvement by a third party. The outsider may bring the parties together or carry a few messages back and forth. The Norwegians, in bringing together representatives of Israel and the Palestine Liberation Organization, played the role of a convenor. As the secret negotiations that took place under Norway's auspices were later recounted in the *New York Times,* Norway served as a "bridge between Israel and the PLO, not as a mediator but as an expediter, one graced with diplomatic sophistica-tion, familiarity with the key figures and distance from the region and prying cameras."[7] Unfortunately for the clarity of the language, "concilia-tion" has another meaning in labor-management negotiations and has been used interchangeably with "mediation" in several pieces of recent federal legislation.[8]

In earlier usage, "conciliation" was used simply as a synonym for "me-diation." The Federal Mediation and Conciliation Service got its name when one house of Congress wanted a "mediation" and the other a "con-ciliation" service. In statesmanlike tradition, the agency continues to use both names. "Conciliation" fell out of favor in the United States because separating spouses, sometimes forced into court-sponsored efforts to rec-oncile them to staying married, disliked the connotation of "reconcilia-tion." During the civil rights movement, "conciliation" sounded too much like minimizing conflict (as opposed to resolving the issues underlying it) to be an acceptable term. It gradually was replaced by "mediation." In Great Britain, New Zealand, and Australia "conciliation" still is used to mean "mediation."

Facilitators may act as moderators in large meetings, making sure that everyone is able to speak and be heard. Facilitators are not expected to volunteer their own ideas or participate actively in moving parties toward agreement. In effect, conciliation and facilitation are less active forms of mediation. ("Facilitation" also may be used to mean "mediation" when participants do not want to acknowledge that they have a dispute.)

In dealing with large disputes over public policy, mediators have coined a number of new terms to describe their processes: *Regulatory nego-tiation,* or *negotiated rulemaking,* describes the increasingly popular device of inviting as many as twenty or thirty representatives of opposing special interests, such as manufacturers, workers, and consumers, to use media-tion to agree on new government rules covering such topics as safety stan-dards for industrial workplaces and environmental pollution by indus-trial chemicals or garbage dumps. *Negotiated investment strategies* use the same techniques of multiparty mediation to reach consensus about gov-ernment expenditures for social services or public works.

Hybrids: Outcome Prediction

A mediator who predicts how a decisionmaker would decide a dispute ventures at some point into a territory beyond mediation and closer to arbitration. Much of the recent growth in dispute resolution has been in processes that combine some sort of mediation with other techniques designed to prod the parties to settle if mediation fails to produce agreement. These hybrid processes (sometimes confusingly called "mediation") frequently include the mediator's recommendations for settlement, some sort of nonbinding evaluation of competing claims, or even a binding decision if mediation does not settle the dispute.

In order to obtain an objective view of the way in which a court or other adjudicator would decide a case and to assess their respective positions, parties may submit their disputes to *neutral evaluation*. Often called *early neutral evaluation*, this technique, which was created by a federal trial court, involves someone (usually a lawyer) who is knowledgeable in the substantive area of the dispute, such as employment discrimination or personal injury law, who listens to the facts and legal arguments and attempts to predict the probable range of outcomes of a case before the parties have consumed substantial time and money in preparing for trial.

If disputes involve technical questions, *neutral experts* may be hired by the parties or appointed by a court. In a controversy over construction, for example, the expert may be an engineer, an architect, a carpenter, or a mason; in a dispute over school desegregation, the expert may be a statistician or an educator. The expert may mediate, though more often simply provides the parties with an impartial opinion of the facts or applicable standards or a prediction of which party would be found at fault in a trial or administrative proceeding.

Fact-finding uses a third party to give the disputants (or a decisionmaker) neutral findings of fact, often coupled with a recommended solution. Occasionally it is called "advisory" or "nonbinding arbitration."

Government or corporate *ombudsmen* (or the newer, gender-neutral "ombuds" or "ombudspeople") investigate complaints by citizens, employees, or customers and attempt to settle them through mediation. If settlement efforts fail, the ombudsperson recommends an appropriate resolution. These individuals work for corporations, newspapers, universities, and public and private agencies and institutions, such as mayors' offices and nursing homes.

The U.S. version of the ombudsperson borrows from the Scandinavian tradition of a respected, independent public official whose function it is to investigate citizens' complaints and criticize government agencies. In the borrowing, however, a significant difference has occurred: Most U.S.

ombudspeople work for the organizations they monitor. Yet they remain outside of the ordinary chains of command and generally report to the chief executive officer of a company or agency.

Complaint programs operated by newspapers, radio and television stations, or consumer protection agencies first attempt to settle complaints through some sort of conciliation or mediation, frequently by mail or telephone. If informal efforts fail, complaints are investigated. Media programs may publicize the results. Government-run complaint programs may impose penalties for violations of specific consumer protection laws or take away businesses' licenses to operate.

Large corporations are staging increasing numbers of *minitrials* to settle conflicts (most of them with other large corporations or government agencies) that otherwise would be destined for court. In minitrials, lawyers present summaries of their cases to chief executives or other key decision-makers representing both clients; these half-day or one-day sessions are chaired by a "neutral advisor." The managers then try to settle the case. If they fail to reach agreement, the neutral advisor, often a retired judge, may mediate or recommend a particular settlement. A minitrial offers executives a quick, relatively inexpensive look at the realities of their dispute, without the filter of their lawyers' adversarial assessment. It then gives them an opportunity to negotiate directly with opposing executives.

Summary jury trials also involve an attempt to predict the outcome of a full-fledged trial. Designed to discourage protracted trials by providing abbreviated hearings before advisory juries, summary juries have been used by a number of judges to settle complex cases. They are designed to be persuasive by being realistic. The summary jury, consisting of jurors from the regular jury pool, gives a nonbinding verdict, and frequently explains it to the participants and responds to their questions. Whether courts can force recalcitrant parties (or their attorneys) to reveal their cases by participating in summary jury trials has been the subject of recent court battles—with contradictory results.

Non-binding or *court-annexed arbitration* is not really arbitration at all. Used by many states and a number of federal district courts to dispose of civil litigation, court-annexed arbitration bears a faint resemblance to the tradition of private arbitration in labor and contractual disputes. Private arbitration usually is undertaken voluntarily, and its results are binding on the parties. Court-annexed arbitration, on the other hand, typically is mandatory and appealable to a court.

Court arbitrators generally are local lawyers. All civil cases brought for certain amounts of money (sometimes as high as $150,000) must be submitted to arbitrators for prompt, nonbinding "decisions" before the cases can go to trial. Hearings are briefer and less formal than trials. Although people unhappy with the results of court-based arbitration can demand new trials, they may risk paying various costs if they fail to improve their results. For whatever reason, the rate of appeal is quite low. Often adverse decisions in arbitration simply prompt the parties to negotiate further and settle prior to trial—not necessarily for the precise amount of the arbitrator's decision.

Mediation/arbitration ("med/arb") is used by disputants who want a binding decision if they cannot agree. The third party mediates, then if an agreement is not reached, decides the dispute. The same person often is used to mediate and arbitrate so that the parties do not have to start over if they cannot resolve their dispute in mediation. A person performing both functions is not supposed to use any confidential information learned during mediation in reaching the arbitration decision. But no one knows whether such information actually can be excluded from the arbitrator's mind or, conversely, whether the knowledge that the mediator eventually may make a decision prevents the parties from sharing confidential information in the first place. Consequently, some disputants (and many neutrals) prefer to use a different person to arbitrate if they fail to settle in mediation.

Adjudication

Adjudication involves binding decisionmaking by courts, administrative agencies, or private arbitrators. *Arbitration*, or private decisionmaking, has been used in the United States since its early commercial history, when businesses decided they preferred to have their disputes resolved by insiders enforcing the practices of their particular trades rather than to have them decided by outsiders applying legal rules and precedents. Although its popularity has declined somewhat in favor of newer forms of dispute resolution, which permit the parties to retain some control over the outcome, arbitration still is used predominantly in businesses desiring private, binding decisions by third-party neutrals. Many (perhaps most) labor and commercial contracts provide that one or more neutral third parties will decide any dispute that may arise under the contract. The disputants agree in advance to be bound by the arbitrator's decision. Procedures are more like court than like mediation. Short of reversal by a court, possible only where an arbitrator commits fraud or shows excessive zeal in defining the issues that can be arbitrated, the parties must live with the arbitrator's decision.

In the business context, arbitrators generally are insiders, familiar with the subject matter of the dispute and the customs of the parties in dealing with one another. Unlike in court, the disputants can participate in choosing the arbitrator and in drafting the rules that govern the process. Arbitrators need not be bound by precedent; however, the fact that they have decisional authority as well as precedent to guide them may mean that they have an easier task than do mediators. As one professional labor mediator put it, the mediator, unlike the arbitrator, "has no science of navigation, no fund inherited from the experience of others. He is a solitary artist recognizing, at most, a few guiding stars and depending mostly on his personal power of divination."[9] According to Chicago arbitrator John W. Cooley, "It is fair to say that while most mediators can effectively perform the arbitrator's function, the converse is not necessarily true."[10]

Over the years, arbitration has acquired some features of the court process. Between 1927 and 1947, the percentage of cases arbitrated under the auspices of the American Arbitration Association in which lawyers appeared to represent disputants grew from 36 to 91 percent; it has not decreased since then. (In labor arbitrations, 77 percent of employers and 52 percent of unions are represented by attorneys at the hearings.) The lawyers frequently file briefs, which cite precedents from earlier court decisions or arbitrations. As a result, arbitration has developed its own voluminous case law, and prearbitration discovery and prehearing conferences have become common.[11] Yet a 1983 study found arbitration generally faster than the courts, more likely to result in a decision (as opposed to a settlement)—but not necessarily less expensive.[12]

Complaints that arbitration is expensive, unpredictable, and laden with rules abound and have caused increasing numbers of people to switch from arbitration to mediation or various hybrid forms of dispute resolution. According to a recent article in the *Wall Street Journal*, the American Arbitration Association has lost a considerable amount of its business to firms offering mediation. For instance, the number of construction disputes handled by the AAA dropped from 5,189 in 1991 to 4,387 in 1992, the same period in which the construction disputes handled by a for-profit mediation firm increased by between 15 and 20 percent. The increasing shift away from arbitration toward mediation appears to be more than a fad; the AAA has responded to the criticism by enlarging its mediation department and encouraging its clients to try mediation before they resort to arbitration.[13]

This trend does not threaten to eliminate arbitration completely. A growing number of insurance companies and manufacturers use arbitration because it is private, frequently faster, and sometimes less expensive than court. Some businesses are moving towards nonadministered arbitration, in which they craft their own procedures and select an arbitrator without the assistance of the AAA or other neutral organizations.

Even divorcing couples, unable or disinclined to settle their disputes through mediation, occasionally have discovered or rediscovered arbitration as a part of the informal settlement movement.

In localities where courts are particularly crowded or in cases where parties shun publicity, disputants who have no contractual relationship requiring them to arbitrate may hire their own private judges (usually retired judges), who use the form of arbitration seen on television in Judge Wapner's "People's Court" and dubbed "rent-a-judge." The process works like arbitration; in California, however, these private decisions may be appealed through the regular court system. The process has attracted criticism for permitting those who can afford it to opt out of the public trial courts yet retain their rights to a judicial appeal.

3

Settling Disputes
in Families

CONFLICTS WITHIN FAMILIES, WHETHER they occur between parents and teens over adjusting to clashing lifestyles, between adult siblings over caring for elderly parents, or between separating spouses over children or property, spotlight most vividly the advantages and the occasional pitfalls of negotiated or mediated settlements. Families generally operate according to their own rules, either negotiated within the family or imposed by parental fiat. They stubbornly resist the imposition of standards by outsiders. When they are dissatisfied, family members often take the law into their own hands. Unhappy teenagers defy parental authority or run away. Separated parents deny visiting rights to ex-spouses or fail to pay court-ordered child support.

Those disputes that cannot be resolved successfully through negotiation within the family frequently contain a hodgepodge of legal and emotional issues. It may be difficult to discover the real issues in controversy. Is a recently separated wife's anger over her husband's trip to Club Med really based on her concern about the cost? Is a father's anger at his son's failure to clean his room based on the lingering mess or on the son's refusal to follow orders?

Family disputes by definition involve people who will have continuing relationships, even when those relationships are restructured by divorce or by a child's leaving home. When I asked one divorcing couple what had made them choose mediation, the wife confided, "We're going to have to be grandparents together." Even adults arguing fiercely over the meaning of a parent's will, the use of real estate jointly owned by a brother and sister, or the disposition of a family business will have a hard time avoiding one another, if only at weddings and funerals.

Mediation, in which an outsider helps family members to resolve their own disputes, has emerged as a particularly appropriate technique for resolving conflicts family members cannot settle themselves. As we have seen, mediation focuses on the future and on the continuing relationships among the parties. Mediators help participants find mutually satisfactory solutions to problems, thus avoiding the "win-lose" syndrome of court decisions, arbitration, or parental decree. The process is private. Furthermore, some mediators try to teach people to handle their own conflicts in the future, without the need for calling in an outsider.

Anyone involved in the dispute may participate in family mediation. Sessions occasionally include grandparents or older children in disputes about child custody, and teachers or guidance counselors in conflicts concerning a child's truancy. Family members can be given the opportunity to discuss the issues they want to talk about, not those that some outsider might choose to hear. In cases where agreements may need to be modified over time (as children grow older, for example, and their needs change), parents can design their own method of settling any resulting impasse— generally a return to mediation or, perhaps, arbitration by a respected acquaintance or professional.

Finally—and this is of critical importance in an area where compliance with outside rules is so difficult to secure—participants themselves design the solutions. Thus, they generally have a greater commitment to the resulting agreements than to decisions imposed on them by outsiders. This commitment can—and does—ensure greater compliance. When separating parents jointly calculate the cost of raising their children, for example, the resulting child support payments seem to be more acceptable and more often paid than those decreed by a court or negotiated by attorneys acting as intermediaries. In situations where children can avoid court decrees simply by running away from parents or foster homes, and separated or divorced parents evade distasteful orders concerning child custody or support by kidnapping their own children or failing to pay child support, voluntary compliance can be crucial.

It is not surprising, then, that many in the judiciary, such as Judge Susan Strengass of the Wisconsin Circuit Court, stress that "family law is the prime area where alternatives should not only be tried, but insisted on."[1] When divorces involve parties with children, a growing number of courts and state legislatures indeed are insisting that families try mediation before bringing their disputes to court.

Despite the obvious appeal of mediation between family members, this is an area where people may stand to lose irreparably if they negotiate away legal rights out of ignorance or fear. In at least some instances, the benefits of flexibility and active participation may be outweighed by the inability of family members to negotiate for themselves or by psychological problems so severe that they doom any effort to arrive at mutually satisfactory solutions.

Mediation in Ongoing Families

In a few programs, volunteer mediators deal with conflicts within ongoing families. These mediators, part of publicly supported programs that work with families who have been referred by juvenile courts, schools, police, or social workers, attempt to smooth rifts between parents and their adolescent children. Disputes generally involve situations in which teenagers have misbehaved by failing to attend school, running away, or committing minor crimes. Often their parents have given up on dealing with them and attempted to turn them over to juvenile authorities as "beyond parental control."

As an example, the District of Columbia Mediation Service, which runs a program to mediate between parents and teens, received a call from the "hotline" operated by the local Department of Human Services. A mother had complained that her thirteen-year-old daughter was out of control. She explained that for the past several months her daughter had been acting up in school, fighting with her classmates, and failing her classes. She was hostile to her parents.

During their first session at the mediation service, the daughter and her parents talked about what had been happening. Actually, the parents did most of the talking. But in a separate meeting with the two volunteer mediators, the daughter confided that her classes were too difficult for her and that she resented having to stay home every night to care for her younger brother. On learning this, her parents agreed to support a change in their daughter's class schedule, to speak to her teachers about her work, and to allow her to go out on weekend evenings with friends her age "to movies, parties, and recreation areas that we know are safe." The daughter agreed "to obey my teachers, to study my assignments and make every effort to improve my grades," to do a specific list of chores at home, and to abide by a set curfew.

Two months later all family members were abiding by the agreement. Both parents and teen expressed satisfaction and even pleasure with the mediation process. The parents commented that they were able to communicate with their daughter better and that they had started spending more time together as a family.

Researchers studied the results of one parent-child mediation program, called the Children's Hearings Project, which began in Cambridge and Somerville, Massachusetts, in 1980 and then spread throughout that state before succumbing to a state budget shortfall. Although mediation could not—and did not intend to—address the underlying financial and emotional problems of the working-class families that used the program, it clearly eased communication between parents and teens and changed the way they handled conflict. The majority of participating families reached written agreements, generally after two or three mediation sessions. Agreements covered specific details of family life, such as curfews and family chores. Of those who settled their disputes in mediation, two-thirds reported several months later that the agreement was working wholly or partially and that it had helped the overall family situation. The great majority were satisfied with their mediation experience.

About half the family members interviewed after mediation said that the experience had made it easier for them to talk to one another; almost 60 percent stated that the process increased understanding among family members. This improved understanding helped them to deal with subsequent conflicts through negotiation rather than fighting or confronting one another. Seventy percent of the family members reported that arguing and fighting at home had decreased. Over half said that they handled conflict differently from the way they had before mediation, generally by talking things over.[2]

A subsequent study of the Washington, D.C., program reported even more positive results from mediation in low-income minority families. About 90 percent of the families who came to mediation reached agreement; 80 percent of these agreements were being followed two months later. (There may have been some self-selection in this program because no one was forced to mediate.) Over 90 percent of the participants reported that the problems that brought them to mediation were solved at least partially, and most saw a beneficial effect on their relationship and communication with one another.[3]

Divorce Mediation

In view of the advantages of family mediation, it is ironic that by far the greatest growth in its use has been in connection with divorce. Although some family therapists have adapted mediation techniques to their work with intact families, mediation is used most often to work out issues involved in separation. Although the use of mediation to resolve disputes within family businesses has grown rapidly, it is still the rare mediator who has settled conflicts among squabbling siblings or between parents and children.

Why has the use of mediated settlement techniques been concentrated on divorce? Unlike other family problems, the disputes connected with divorce cannot easily be avoided. Except for requiring certain formalities when a couple marries, legislators and courts traditionally have stayed out of family business. (In a well-known case decided by a Nebraska court in 1953, a court declined to consider a wife's complaint that her husband, with whom she continued to live, was refusing to support her adequately.[4]) As long as family members do not commit criminal assaults on one another (and even here enforcement officials have been extremely reluctant to intervene) or grossly neglect their children, families are left alone to solve their own problems in any way they can.

Divorce, on the other hand, is an event that demands decisions about the custody and support of children (and sometimes each other) and division of property and debts. If the parties do not make these decisions for themselves, a judge will do it for them. It is becoming almost a cliché that courts are poorly suited to settling these problems. And the husband and wife, who for whatever reason have decided to separate, generally are ill equipped to thread their way through the legal and emotional consequences of the separation unaided.

According to provisional figures provided by the National Center for Health Statistics, in 1992 there were fewer than 2.5 million marriages in the United States and more than 1 million divorces. In other words, there were almost half as many divorces as marriages. In 1960, by contrast, marriages outnumbered divorces at a rate of almost four to one. Although the late 1980s began to see a slow reversal of this twenty-year trend, the most pessimistic observers predict that three out of five marriages begun in the 1990s will end in divorce.

Although the issues associated with the great majority of divorces are settled by the parties, whose divorces then are considered "uncontested," all divorces must be processed by the courts. Divorces now represent almost half the civil cases filed in state courts. Every state but South Dakota now has "no-fault" divorce laws, under which divorces are granted based on physical separation or "irreconcilable differences." This development is of little solace to children whose parents choose to fight over them. According to psychologist Kenneth Kressel, contested divorces, which require judges to resolve disputes over children, support, or property, involve an estimated 10 percent of childless divorcing couples and 30 percent of divorcing couples with children.[5]

As Kressel points out, however, the percentage of contested cases is a poor guide to the incidence of serious conflict in divorce settlement negotiations: "Many couples who have had a truly miserable time negotiating their settlement agreement have neither the money nor the stomach for a court battle."[6] After divorce, between 20 and 40 percent of all divorced couples return to court to fight over some unresolved problem.[7] The available evidence suggests that from one-third to more than one-half of all divorced people are seriously unhappy with the provisions of their separation agreements or divorce decrees. According to psychologist Judith Wallerstein, who completed a ten-year study of divorced middle-class families in northern California, divorce was "a wrenching experience" for every family.[8]

Almost 4 million single parents in the United States (the great majority of them mothers) theoretically are entitled to receive payments of child support. In fact, many of them do not. According to the data Kressel has assembled:

[Within the] first year after divorce ... approximately 50 percent of non-cus-
todial fathers pay little or nothing of the child support to which they are legally obligated. ... This rate of non-compliance increases slowly but steadily
with time. By the third year the rate of non-compliance is approximately 60
percent; by the fifth year it is up to about 70 percent to 80 percent.[9]

The other side of the coin of the failure to pay child support is the disap-
pearance of noncustodial parents, usually fathers, from their children's
lives. By the second year after divorce, nearly one-third of fathers see their
children less than once in every three weeks; many do not see them at all.
Federal statutes (such as the Parental Kidnapping Act of 1980, a 1975
amendment by Congress to the Social Security Act designed to locate de-
faulting fathers and force them to pay child support, the Child Support
Amendments of 1984, and the Family Support Act of 1988) have failed to
stem the tide of children caught in the middle of postdivorce strife.

Divorce mediation, despite some of the exaggerated claims made by its
most ardent boosters, cannot solve all of these problems. Nor, as we shall
see, is mediation for everyone, although it does hold great promise of reducing the hostilities, the time, and the money required by the ordeal of
divorce. Nevertheless, the great majority of divorcing couples have not
even heard of mediation, notwithstanding the almost religious fervor that
it has generated among many who practice it. Private mediators still are
involved in a small minority of all divorces in the United States—probably no greater than 10 percent. Yet this number is growing rapidly, perhaps by as much as 25 percent a year. The use of court-based mediators to
resolve at least some of the issues connected with divorce is growing even
more rapidly.

Choosing Divorce Mediation

How can someone going through a separation—or the attorney or mental
health professional advising that individual or couple—decide whether
divorce mediation makes sense in a particular situation? Although there is
no way to be certain without actually trying the process, several criteria
can assist in making a sensible choice.

1. First, is the individual eager—or at least willing—to participate actively in negotiations? Is his or her spouse? (Except in those states where
statutes or court rules make mediation mandatory before a court hearing,
or where judges have been given the authority to order divorcing couples
into mediation, both spouses must be convinced to go to a mediator voluntarily.)

2. How important is the ability to maintain some sort of continuing relationship between the spouses? This criterion is particularly significant if
the couple has children or continuing business dealings.

3. Is the couple interested in exploring unconventional arrangements that might not occur to lawyers or courts?

4. How important is obtaining voluntary full compliance with an agreement? Is this consideration at least as important as it is to obtain any specific result?

5. How important are the cost savings that may result from mediation? Although there is mounting evidence that using a mediator is somewhat less expensive than negotiating through separate lawyers and considerably less expensive than litigating, the conclusions about cost savings are based on average figures. A particular mediation, especially if it relies heavily on outside attorneys, may not necessarily turn out to be inexpensive.

6. Is one spouse or the other more motivated by revenge or a need to cling to the other than by a desire to work things out? If so, mediation sessions can be bitter and protracted and even then may not produce a settlement. (On the other hand, many mediators report success even with parties who continue to be furious at each other throughout the process; mediation seems to give them the opportunity to vent and to channel some of the fury.)

7. Is one spouse afraid of the other, whether because of past violence, verbal or emotional abuse, or simply a timid personality? If so, the fearful spouse may not be able to stand up for his or her own interests in mediation.

8. Finally, is there anything about either of the individuals involved that makes them incapable of negotiating for themselves? For example, someone who is under the influence of drugs or alcohol or who is mentally ill is a poor candidate for mediation.

The failures in divorce mediation generally fall into three categories. There are those who seek only vengeance on deserting spouses and who cannot be moved by reminders of their joint interests in being parents together or of getting a fair settlement. Fairness is not what they seek. The second group includes those who use mediation as a way to continue contact with their spouses. Any sign of progress is feared because it may lead to settlement and thus end the relationship. With both of these groups, time (if they are willing and able to wait—temporary agreements can help here) may cause emotions to cool down. Mediation then may make sense. The third group includes relationships in which one spouse, because of violence by the other, emotional abuse, or feelings of inadequacy, simply is not up to negotiating with the other, even with a mediator's help.

The effect of so-called domestic violence on mediation has been hotly debated. Clearly there are cases of serious or repeated violence where mediation is highly inappropriate. Intrafamily crimes demand prosecution. Furthermore, the fear of further violence may prevent the victim from negotiating with the assailant about anything else. In a generally supportive booklet published by the National Organization for Women to educate women about divorce mediation, the authors caution, "If physical, verbal, or psychological battering, or any other kind of intimidation in your marriage, makes you unable to speak without fear of continuing or future harm, mediation is not appropriate, and should not be pursued."[10] Beyond these obvious cases, there is little consensus among mediators and advocates over which situations involving previous violence may be mediated effectively. Nor is there any conclusive evidence about the effect of previous violence on mediation or the effect of mediation on the violence.

Finding a Divorce Mediator

Once people have decided to try mediation, they are faced with the task of choosing a mediator. The degree of difficulty depends on the context in which the mediation is to occur: the private sector, a court, or a community justice center.

Private Divorce Mediation. In the private sector, mediation replaces the conventional model of negotiation through lawyers. In traditional divorce negotiations, lawyers act as intermediaries—the parties talk to their lawyers, their lawyers talk to each other (see Figure 3.1). The couple may or may not speak directly with each other at all during the negotiations; some lawyers in fact advise them against doing so. In mediation, while the parties may well consult with separate lawyers, the negotiations occur directly between husband and wife, with the guidance of the mediator (see Figure 3.2).

One difficulty with the traditional lawyer-centered model is that it sometimes works like the children's game of "telephone": The message changes as it gets passed from one person to the next. Thus a husband tells his lawyer that he wants to play a meaningful role in raising his children. His lawyer, translating the husband's message into the legal notion of "child custody," tells his wife's lawyer that the husband will accept nothing less than joint custody. The wife's lawyer tells the wife (who was perfectly willing to share the job of raising the children) that they are in for a custody battle. The direct communication between husband and wife that occurs in divorce mediation makes it less likely that they will misunderstand each other's motives or intentions.

Mental health professionals, as well as lawyers, have worked with divorcing couples for some time. Until quite recently, however, most psychiatrists, psychologists, and social workers limited their intervention to trying to save failing marriages. During the past ten years or so, some therapists have begun to specialize in working with separating couples, not to patch up their marriages but to deal with the emotional traumas in-

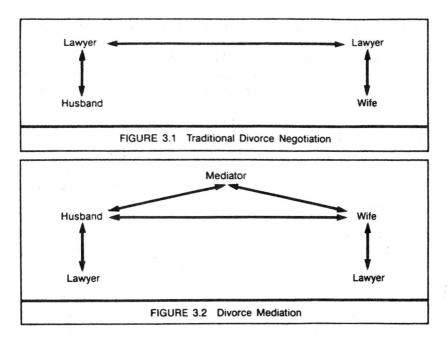

FIGURE 3.1 Traditional Divorce Negotiation

FIGURE 3.2 Divorce Mediation

volved in separation and divorce. Separation therapists may work with husbands and wives individually or together. Occasionally they may try to help couples resolve some of the concrete problems associated with separation.

The basic distinction between mediation and this type of therapy is that mediation's primary purpose is to solve concrete problems. To that end, mediators help participants to focus their efforts on specific tasks. Although mediators generally give the parties the opportunity to vent their emotions, they attempt to manage whatever conflicts erupt so that the process of reaching a settlement can proceed. Therapists, on the other hand, explore conflict in order to help people understand themselves better. If greater self-understanding and some psychological release take place in mediation, all the better. However, neither the venting of emotions nor the understanding of their source is the primary goal of mediation.

Couples come to private mediators voluntarily, typically through word-of-mouth referral by their friends, their therapists, or their lawyers. Private mediators are neither licensed nor organized into a separate profession. One difficulty with this fluid state of affairs is that there is no clearly defined way to locate or evaluate a divorce mediator. Until quite recently, most mediators believed that it was too early, and the field still too experimental, to establish standards. (Organizations that purport to "certify" mediators usually insist only that they take training programs offered by the organization.) Loose standards of practice recently have been promulgated by the Society of Professionals in Dispute Resolution, the American Bar Association, the Academy of Family Mediators, and the Association of Family and Conciliation Courts. They are discussed in the last chapter.

Couples frequently find mediators through personal recommendations, articles or advertisements in the popular press, or even the Yellow Pages. By now any trusted lawyer or therapist should be able to make a recommendation. Some of the court-sponsored or publicly funded mediation programs are willing to suggest private mediators; often they are the best informed about who in a particular community mediates and how well. Some local lawyer referral services (generally sponsored by the organized bar) maintain lists of divorce mediators. If all else fails, the Yellow Pages sometimes serve as the starting point. All good mediators should be willing to supply a list of references on request.

The mediator's professional background, whether in law or therapy (or neither), is less important than two qualifications: First, is the mediator, whether or not an attorney, familiar with the law governing separation and divorce in the jurisdiction? If not, the parties will have to go elsewhere for answers to the many questions that will come up during mediation sessions. Second, does the mediator possess some basic counseling skills, even if they were acquired solely through experience? Is the mediator a good listener? Can the person empathize with the parties' situation?

Although a few states require court-based mediators to have a master's degree in psychology, social work, or family counseling, there is no evidence that ties mediators' educational backgrounds to their performance. Programs in Maine and the District of Columbia, which use trained volunteer mediators with a wide variety of backgrounds, report that attributes such as empathy, creativity, and the ability to communicate are far more important to success than are educational qualifications. (Ironically, the District of Columbia seeks out attorneys who specialize in domestic relations law to train as mediators, while Maine, fearing bias, excludes all divorce lawyers.) Occasionally, a lawyer and a therapist work together as a team. Often this mixture of skills can be useful, but the cost of two mediators may be prohibitive.

Parties should be advised to ask whether the mediator will see them individually. The use of separate sessions can be important if there is anything that either party feels hesitant to discuss in front of the other. Finally, how directive does the mediator seem? Although research on mediation styles is in its infancy, there is some evidence that the more active or controlling mediators achieve higher rates of settlement, but that these agreements are more likely to collapse over time.

Divorce Mediation in Court. Some sort of divorce mediation is sponsored by a rapidly growing number of courts. In-court mediations generally are conducted by court social workers, occasionally by volunteers, or by private mediators on a contract or referral basis. Court programs offer—and sometimes require—people who already have taken their disputes to court the opportunity to try mediation before trial. Thus the programs serve couples who could not afford lawyers or private mediators to help them settle out of court, who were ignorant of the possibilities, or who have tried and failed to reach settlement.

A significant difference between court and private mediation is that court-sponsored mediation frequently is limited to issues of child custody and visitation rights. There are two reasons for the restriction: Court personnel, generally social workers or former probation officers, often are not considered competent to deal with all the issues involved in a divorce. Some courts also fear that permitting them to do so will take business from divorce lawyers and thus antagonize the organized bar. Whatever the reason, some advocates for women are concerned that restricting mediation to child custody and visitation and excluding issues of support and property division unfairly disadvantages women. It encourages (or requires) them to negotiate issues on which their position often is relatively strong (the care of children) and leaves for private settlement or judicial decree the issues on which their position frequently is weak (support and property). In states where the mediation of all child custody disputes has become mandatory, this concern is more acute. Furthermore, the splitting of child custody and visitation from all the other issues may make the give-and-take of ordinary negotiations more difficult to achieve.

In 1981 California became the first state to require the mediation of all disputes over child custody before the parents' appearance in court. Mediation of child custody cases has since been made mandatory in Alaska, Arizona, Delaware, Florida, Kansas, Louisiana, Nevada, New Mexico, North Carolina, Oregon, South Dakota, Washington, and Wisconsin, either by statute or by court rules. Unlike these states, North Dakota places mandatory mediation in judges' hands by explicitly giving them discretion to order it rather than mandating it as standard practice. Michigan simply requires that couples be informed of the availability of mediation. Washington requires its courts to encourage mediation of parent-child disputes only when mediation resources are available. In Iowa and New Mexico, courts may refer parents to mediation when one parent requests joint custody and the other disagrees. Maine and Ohio go furthest by requiring mediation of all contested issues in cases of separation, annulment, and divorce if a couple has minor children.

Mandatory mediation generally involves only the requirement that couples meet with a mediator for one session before appearing in front of a judge. (In Maine, however, courts must determine whether a couple made a "good faith" effort to mediate when no agreement is reached and may send the parties back to mediation before proceeding with a contested trial.) Sessions are confidential and have no effect on what happens in court if no agreement is reached. Maine's mediators report no significant difference in the cooperation between the parties to mandatory and voluntary mediation sessions.[11] For some parties, however, such as those in need of instant relief or those who suffer from serious, ongoing physical or psychological abuse, compulsory participation in mediation could prove not only useless but harmful. In response to these concerns, a number of states have enacted exceptions from mandatory mediation in cases involving domestic violence, threats to health or safety, or "undue hardship."

A few courts, most of them in California, have gone beyond the minimal burden of attendance at one mediation session and require the mediator to recommend to the judge which parent should be awarded custody if the parties do not agree. In such cases, the mediator may be subject to cross-examination by either parent. This procedure is radically different from conventional mediation. It compromises the mediator's neutrality, discards any semblance of confidentiality, and confuses mediation with other procedures of a more investigatory nature. For this reason, the National Standards for Court-Connected Mediation Programs, developed by the Center for Dispute Settlement and the Institute of Judicial Administration, strongly recommends that mediators be prohibited from providing courts with evaluations of or recommendations about the cases they are mediating.[12]

Despite apparent shortcomings in some of the court-sponsored mediation programs, results from Connecticut, California, and Minnesota are encouraging. Couples were required to mediate before a trial or referred to mediation by a judge or court employee (generally with the strong suggestion that they try it). Although all mediators were court employees, no reports went from the mediator to the judge. In contrast with private divorce mediation, mediation generally lasted for only one session.

The California Statewide Office of Family Court Services conducted a "snapshot" study of all family mediation programs in state courts during two weeks in 1991. A significant portion of these mediations involved couples who reported substance abuse, domestic violence, or child abuse. Yet more than 80 percent of the participants considered mediation "positive" or "very positive," reporting that they did not feel rushed, intimidated, or pressured during the mediation session.[13] In contrast to this experience, a 1992 study of the Multi-Door Courthouse domestic relations program in Washington, D.C., revealed that a higher proportion of those who had participated in court-based mediation were unhappy with the outcomes of their cases, and subsequently became involved in further legal action or other disputes, than those who had not participated in mediation.[14]

Researcher Jessica Pearson and her colleagues compared the results of child custody mediation with the results of adjudication or voluntary settlement outside of courts. About half the cases in mediation reached settlement. Participants' satisfaction was high. Among those who did not receive custody of their children, 75 percent of those who reached agreement through mediation expressed satisfaction with the results. Of people whose disputes were decided by the court, only about 30 percent of those not receiving custody expressed satisfaction.

Three months later, when the ex-spouses were asked about the effect of mediation or litigation on their relationship, 40 percent of those whose disputes had been resolved in court reported that the experience had had a detrimental effect. Less than 15 percent of the participants in mediation thought it had a detrimental effect on the relationship, regardless of whether they were able to reach an agreement.

A year later, the proportion of participants who considered some cooperation with their ex-spouses possible was greater than 60 percent among those who mediated to agreement and about 30 percent among those who went to court. Those participants who had returned to court with subsequent disputes numbered 21 percent of those who had reached agreement in mediation, 31 percent of those who participated in mediation and failed to agree, and 36 percent of those who litigated without mediation. Those who had gone back to court at least twice comprised 13 percent of the litigation group and 6 percent of the mediation group.[15]

Joan Kelly conducted a similar study but focused on the differences between northern California couples who voluntarily used mediation at a private mediation service and those who hired attorneys to litigate or negotiate for them in the traditional way. Mediation consistently scored higher marks. Mediation respondents reported that they experienced significantly fewer conflicts with their ex-spouses six months prior to their final divorces and reported significantly fewer conflicts during the divorce process regarding visiting arrangements and child support than did the other respondents. In addition, the study showed that mediation was significantly more effective in fostering cooperation between parents throughout the entire divorce process.[16]

Finally, in both studies mediation produced some financial savings over litigation when it succeeded and did not cost much more when it failed. (Because those in Pearson's study were court-based mediation programs, mediation generally took place later in the process of settlement than it would have with private mediators. Savings through private mediation may turn out to be greater.) Participants in Kelly's study who litigated or negotiated through their attorneys spent an average of 134 percent more in total fees than participants who used private mediation. The mediation sample spent $5,234 per couple compared with $12,226 spent by the other couples.[17]

Despite these apparently impressive results, some critics are concerned that mediation disadvantages women because of their unequal bargaining power, which results from women's frequently inferior financial position and presumed relative inexperience at negotiating. No data support this position. Indeed, a study comparing men's and women's self-reported responses to mediation in both court and private settings showed that the women were more satisfied with the process than the men. Perhaps more significantly, women in both settings were significantly more likely than men to report a greater confidence in their ability to stand up for themselves with their ex-spouses as a result of participating in mediation.[18] Although both mediators and participants should be alert for ways of balancing power in mediation (consultations with attorneys or accountants or individual sessions between each party and the mediator, for example), the distribution of power within an intimate relationship may be far more complex than the critics believe.

Divorce Mediation in Community Justice Centers. The third context in which divorce mediation takes place is in community justice centers, which are discussed in Chapter 6. There, community volunteers mediate disputes over separation, child custody, visitation, support, and division of property. The resulting agreements generally do not have the formality of those reached in connection with divorces, but they perform the same function.

Clients of justice centers, like those of court mediation programs, often are there because they cannot afford the legal representation, the private therapy, or the private mediation that otherwise would deal with these problems. Frequently, couples are referred to the centers by police or prosecutors because of some precipitating crisis between spouses or unmarried partners who have lived together. They end up by agreeing to separate—or to stay together and try again.

A Glimpse of Private Divorce Mediation

As we have seen, the people who come to private divorce mediators form a special group. They not only have chosen the still unconventional process of mediation, they often had to find out about it themselves, learn which mediators were available, and get themselves and their spouses to one of them. Despite their resourcefulness, experience has shown that

these couples are not just those who can get along or who have no significant problems to negotiate.

As an illustration of what goes on in a typical mediation session, the
following dialogue is digested from the notes of my first session with Gail
and Steve Ryder. (I have changed the Ryders' names and enough identifying details to protect their privacy.) The Ryders are in their mid-forties.
Steve teaches management at a local business school; Gail represents a
trade association in its dealings with Congress. They were married for
twenty-three years and have two children, fifteen-year-old Beth and four-
year-old Joshua.

MEDIATOR   *I'm glad to meet you both. I'm curious about how you got here.*

GAIL   *Well, we've already met with another mediator. He kept trying
to tell us what to do. So I told Steve that if I was going to stay in
mediation, it had to be with someone else. Steve agreed, but he
said I would have to do the finding and it would have to be fast.
My therapist suggested you, and I turned out to have a friend
you trained as a mediator. They both said you believe in letting
people make their own decisions.*

MEDIATOR   *I do. Mediators' styles can vary considerably. You were right to
leave someone who didn't make you comfortable.*

*Perhaps it would be useful to have me describe the process I
follow, since there may well be differences from what you have
heard elsewhere. You should feel free to ask questions as we go
along and to share any concerns you may have with what
you're hearing.*

STEVE   *I'd be interested in hearing that. But I'd also be interested in
hearing about the process from someone who has been through
it. Are there any men in my situation that I might talk to?*

MEDIATOR   *Actually, I have several people who have offered to speak confi-
dentially about their own experiences to people who are considering mediation. At the end of the session, when I have learned
a little more about you, I can suggest the people you might find
most useful.*

*I don't want to bore you, but I think it is important to be sure
that we all have the same understanding of what we are going
to do here. I will describe the process I generally follow. Don't
hesitate to interrupt with questions and concerns as they occur
to you—it won't throw me.*

*In mediation my job is to be impartial and to help the two of
you to reach an agreement. I am not a judge. I have no power to
make decisions for you.*

Since you decided to come here, I would guess that the most appropriate comparison is not with what would happen in court but what would happen if each of you hired a lawyer to work out a separation agreement for you. Naturally, your lawyers would talk to you in the process, but they would be responsible for reaching an agreement. In mediation you will be negotiating directly with each other. Although I recommend strongly that you consult with separate lawyers as often as you like, you will be responsible for doing the bulk of the work yourselves, with my help.

GAIL *Don't be so sure we're not going to end up in court. It depends on what Steve is willing to do. I can't afford his stonewalling much longer.*

STEVE *Stonewalling! I practically had to light a torch under you to get you in here! Once you decided you wanted me to move out, you haven't been willing to make a single decision!*

MEDIATOR *What made you choose mediation in the first place?*

STEVE *As you can see, we're both still pretty angry at each other. But we have two children, and we know we're going to have to go on dealing with each other for their sake. We thought that if we could work out things here it would be better for them. Besides, I've never liked the idea of turning my private affairs over to so-called experts.*

GAIL *I agree with all of that but that doesn't mean I'm willing to be walked over either. I'm just willing to try one more time, and then we'll see if you come up with enough money.*

STEVE *I didn't leave you—you left me. And you've been bleeding me ever since.*

MEDIATOR *Perhaps we should finish our discussion of the process before we get into the particulars of your situation.*

STEVE *Yes, Gail is always interrupting people. I'm tired of putting up with it.*

MEDIATOR *You both will have plenty of opportunity to say whatever is on your minds. That probably will work better if we speak one at a time. Perhaps it would help if you had paper and pen to jot down any notes that may occur to you while the other person is talking.*

I will meet with you both together and separately for as many times as it takes us to work things out.

STEVE *What is your estimate of how long it will take?*

MEDIATOR *That depends on how many issues we have to deal with, how complicated they are, and how many things you already agree about. With couples who have both children and property to*

	deal with, I estimate between five and ten sessions, each lasting about two hours. Sometimes things go more quickly.
GAIL	*Why do you meet with us separately? The other mediator didn't do that.*
MEDIATOR	*I know all mediators don't agree on this, but I believe that having at least one separate session with each of you is very important. I want to be sure that I understand what all of your concerns are and whether you are uncomfortable about discussing any of them with each other. If one of you wants to tell me something in a separate session that you don't want me to share with the other, just let me know.*
GAIL	*What if Steve tells you he has money hidden away, but asks you not to tell me?*
MEDIATOR	*If anybody asked me to keep that kind of confidence, I would remind the person that sharing information about all of your property is critical to the process. Without such full disclosure, any agreement you sign could be voided later. If he still refused to share the information, I would have to withdraw from the mediation.*
GAIL	*But you wouldn't tell me?*
MEDIATOR	*No. A critical part of this process is for you to trust me. If I didn't keep your confidences, you wouldn't be able to trust me. Before we discuss your problems in any detail, I will ask you to read and sign an agreement to mediate. It provides that whatever goes on in mediation is confidential. By signing it, you both promise not to attempt to have me testify for or against either one of you if you should ever end up in court. That protects all three of us. The more assurance you have that you can speak freely here, the more likely it is that you will raise all of your concerns and be satisfied that whatever agreement you reach deals with them. In the agreement, you both also promise to disclose fully all of your property. That provided a further answer to your question, Gail.*
STEVE	*Who decides what issues we talk about?*
MEDIATOR	*That is entirely up to you. I will remind you occasionally that certain things need to be worked out in any separation, just to make sure that we don't overlook anything. But the particular topics of our discussion and the order in which we deal with them will be up to the two of you.*
STEVE	*Will the separation agreement we work out in mediation be as good as one we would get from two lawyers?*
MEDIATOR	*Yes, it will be similar—legally binding on both of you and enforceable in court if it ever became necessary. I would hope that*

	you both would agree to return to mediation before doing that, though.

STEVE   *Well, as soon as you're finished telling us about mediation, I want to talk to you about making some permanent decisions. I'm still in a temporary summer sublet because I can't get Gail to sell the house. I need to move soon, and I'm going to need my money for a downpayment on a condominium.*

MEDIATOR   *Does either of you have any more questions about the process before we begin to talk about your situation?*

GAIL   *I still have some questions.*

MEDIATOR   *Let's deal with those first and then see if we can agree on what issues the two of you need to resolve.*

GAIL   *Steve has already taken half my furniture.*

STEVE   *Well, Gail didn't respond to my requests for some furniture for the apartment, even though I asked her for three months, so I just went in and took some while she was at the beach. Our savings are drawn down and I certainly couldn't afford to buy any.*

GAIL   *Steve has been withholding child support payments for the past two months. That's what we have to deal with first. I'm living in a big house with only one income. The other mediator said I might have to sell it, but I'm not ready to move. Steve should be sharing the costs. I'm staying there for the sake of the children.*

MEDIATOR   *Let's be sure there are no more questions. Then we can get to your immediate concerns.*

STEVE   *You know, we've already tried therapy. How is mediation different from that?*

MEDIATOR   *The purpose of mediation is to solve particular problems, such as the ones you've both started to bring up. I am not a therapist, and I won't be asking you about any underlying motives or conflicts. There is a wide range of possible solutions to any problem, and it is up to you to decide what makes sense to you. If you ask me questions for purposes of information, I'll give you the best answers I can. But I have no interest in counseling you and will try not to tell you what I think you ought to do.*

GAIL   *There was an article in* Cosmopolitan *a couple of years ago that said mediation is bad for women. How can I be sure that isn't so in my case? Steve has already taken the furniture and raided our savings to buy a white convertible, of all things. I can't even figure out what we have left, because he has always taken care of our finances. How will I know he isn't trying to pull a fast one on me?*

MEDIATOR   *Well, we are going to focus on what happens from now on and on making sure that you understand everything that is going*

*on. I am going to give you both some forms about your finances
to take home with you today and work on before our next session. Many people find filling out the forms an unfamiliar exer-
cise, but it will help you to understand your own situation. If
you feel uncomfortable doing it without help, I would be happy
to refer you to a sympathetic accountant who can help you sort
things out. Steve, you're smiling?*

STEVE   *I'm smiling because Gail will never fill out that form. She has
always been too busy to pay any attention to our finances.*

MEDIATOR   *It is important that you both understand your finances. That's
the only way you can make an informed decision.*

STEVE   *Well, the assets side isn't going to be very long anyway, at the
rate we're going.*

GAIL   *But the list of debts will make up for it!*

MEDIATOR   *I want to be sure that we have dealt with Gail's concern about
being taken advantage of. You'll have plenty of opportunity to
let me know if you are uncomfortable with the way things are
going. You might want to request a separate session if you
don't think I am understanding all your concerns. Using outside experts such as an accountant can help. I also recommend
that you consult with your own lawyer as we go along. Don't
wait until we have a draft agreement ready to be signed. A lawyer can be far more useful to you if you understand each other
early in the process.*

GAIL   *But you are a lawyer. Why isn't that enough?*

MEDIATOR   *I always recommend that people see separate attorneys. Let me
try to explain why. Since I am a lawyer, I can answer your
questions about what various laws provide or what a court
might decide about a particular issue. No one can tell you what
it will decide. But what I cannot do is to represent the separate
interests of either one of you. You both are amateur negotiators—you may not have done this before. It may be useful for
you to have somebody to talk to who is not as committed as I am
to the notion of reaching an agreement and who is hired to represent your separate interests rather than your interests as a
family.*

GAIL   *You mean you are committed to our interests rather than to my
separate interests?*

MEDIATOR   *That's right. In addition, it is useful to have someone else to
bounce things off as we go along. The last reason is that, at least
for now, if you sign an agreement that has continuing provisions such as child custody and support, there is some possibility that it might not be enforceable in court unless you have sep-*

	arate lawyers. That's another reason why it protects you to see an outside lawyer.
STEVE	*Yes, I have a lawyer already, but I'm not sure that she is sympathetic to the idea of mediation.*
MEDIATOR	*That can be a problem. Even though you consult with lawyers, it is important to make your own decisions. Sometimes lawyers try to tell their clients what to do. I do have a list of local lawyers who have worked with mediators before or who also mediate themselves, if either one of you would like to see it.*
	Does either of you have any other questions?
GAIL	*Just one more. Our daughter is a teenager. I think it is important that she be able to decide which one of us she wants to live with. Will you talk to her and ask her?*
MEDIATOR	*If the two of you agree that your daughter should have a role in deciding where she wants to live, of course you can take her wishes into account. Since she is not yet eighteen, you still are responsible for making the decision. Sometimes I do talk with older children, but I suggest that the two of you talk things over with her first, and then we can decide together if it makes sense to bring her in.*
	Are there any other questions?
STEVE	*No, I think we should get on with it.*
GAIL	*I just have one more. Whose job is it to decide if any agreement we reach is fair? Will the court do that?*
MEDIATOR	*No, generally judges will go along with just about anything two people agree to. In fact, some courts don't even require that separation agreements be submitted for their approval.*
	I will raise questions to be sure you have considered all the angles. And your lawyers certainly can give their opinions about what is fair. But in the last analysis, that will be up to the two of you.
GAIL	*Suppose he agrees and then doesn't do something?*
MEDIATOR	*Mediated agreements are just as enforceable as many other kinds of agreements. But the fact that the two of you have decided to work out your own agreement makes it unlikely that you will have that kind of problem. Since the agreement will be tailored to your own situation, it should be easy for both of you to comply with it. We also can design a structure for dealing with any changed circumstances in the future.*
	You should continue to ask me questions about the process as we go along. For now, suppose each of you talks a little bit about your situation as you see it and tells us what issues you think need to be resolved.

As Steve indicated, his immediate concern was to get the family home sold so that he and Gail could pay off the mortgage and divide the rest of the proceeds to buy or rent something smaller. Gail, who said she had the children living with her (actually, they were with her for slightly less than two-thirds of the time), was reluctant to do so. Issues concerning the children seemed as if they would be less thorny. The Ryders had been sharing responsibility for their care. Although they argued about money, they were able to deal with each other on questions of the children's care, although they disagreed on how much time Beth and Joshua actually had been spending with each of them since the separation.

Questions about dividing property, particularly their pensions (Steve's was much larger than Gail's), and dealing with Gail's claim to a share of Steve's consulting business turned out to be much more difficult. During the previous five years, Steve had developed a small management consulting practice and felt strongly that Gail should have no claim to it. He maintained that the business was earning less than $5,000 a year and that, in any case, it would be unfair to give Gail any share of his business when she had contributed nothing to it. Gail was just as insistent that a share of both Steve's pension and his business belonged to her.

When he met with me alone, Steve related that Gail had left him after a brief affair with a man from her office. Steve said that he was destroyed at the time but that now, four months later, he thought the separation might have been for the best. The couple had gotten married when both were very young. Gail's success, which Steve described as a "meteoric rise," had eclipsed Steve's, and he, as he described it, had "just wallowed along." Steve had refused Gail's suggestion that the couple seek counseling and paid little attention to the marriage until it was too late. Now he did not want to close the door on the possibility of a reconciliation some time in the future, but he termed it unlikely because both of them were so angry.

Steve confided that he had some sympathy for Gail's financial problems. But since he had borne the burden of taking care of the couple's finances while they were together, he thought that it was only right for her to have to struggle now to understand her finances and live within a budget. He was not inclined to help her out. Nor was he inclined at first to pay her child support, even though his income still exceeded hers by more than a third. "She wanted this—she ought to learn to live with it."

Because of their mutual anger, Steve suggested that I meet with him and Gail only in separate sessions. I replied that although I had kept parties separated on rare occasions when they were unable to deal with each other face-to-face, I preferred not to do so. Some of the benefits of mediation would be lost if they did not learn to communicate with each other successfully, at least on matters involving the children. He agreed to try it.

In her separate session with me, Gail repeated her anger at Steve for spending money on a flashy car shortly after the separation. (She acknowledged that he needed some car because she had kept the family station wagon.) She was relieved to be out of a marriage that was not working for her, but terrified of the financial implications and exhausted from caring for the children for much of the time by herself. She needed more money from Steve, she asserted, and help straightening out her finances. I recommended an inexpensive accountant.

In answer to my question about the possibility of a reconciliation, Gail predicted that the marriage would end. She also confessed that she occasionally had mixed feelings on the subject and did not want to close the door to reconciliation. She was confident that Steve wanted to resume the marriage.

Gail repeated her concern about being "walked over" during our negotiations. I reminded her that Steve's possible desire to reconcile (and thus, presumably, to please her) could give him a similar fear.

When the three of us met together, we decided to develop a temporary agreement that would resolve the Ryders' immediate concerns about child care, housing, and support and to defer questions of permanent arrangements and division of property for a few months. I hoped the hiatus would give both of them the breathing space to make some decisions about their future relationship and to get used to living separately, if that was their ultimate decision. Neither of them seemed to be in condition for making permanent decisions if they could be postponed for a while.

Negotiations over child support and housing turned out to be very difficult. In our sessions together, Steve and Gail argued over almost every penny. They started calling me separately to ask me how I thought things were going. I used the telephone calls as an opportunity to explore alternatives with each of them, free from the fear that their willingness to discuss options might show weakness to the other. After several sessions and intervening phone calls, they agreed to have the children spend time with each of them, about three-fifths of the time with Gail and two-fifths with Steve. They had been keeping track of expenses and agreed to share the children's total expenses in proportion to their incomes.

Before we could deal with the question of whether to sell their house, it was important for Gail to understand the couple's finances. It took several sessions with me and two with an accountant before she decided that even with child support payments from Steve, she could not afford to pay the mortgage and maintain the large household. Once she understood the situation she reluctantly agreed that the house must be sold. Both she and

Steve had been spending more than they took in, and it was only a matter of time before they ran out of both funds and credit.

We dealt with schedules and responsibilities for paying off debts and ways of sharing medical expenses and insurance. Gail grew more confident of her ability to manage her finances during the course of our sessions, although she continued to dislike the task.

When they signed their temporary agreement (about two months after they began mediation), both of the Ryders were triumphant. "We never thought we could do this with each other," Steve said.

They came back to see me three months later, as they had agreed, to develop a final agreement. They still had some ambivalence about the permanence of the separation, but divorce now seemed likely to both of them. Their earlier success in working out a temporary agreement made them much more confident that they could deal with the remaining issues.

After some slight tinkering with schedules and formulas for sharing their children's support, the Ryders decided to make their joint responsibility for the children permanent. They agreed to return to mediation in the future if they could not reach consensus on a particular decision.

Disposition of Steve's pension and business was, as predicted, more difficult. Steve turned over his accountant's balance sheets for the business for the last three years, which confirmed his assertions about its income and apparent lack of current value. He resisted the notion that the business should be independently appraised. At this point I suggested that both of them meet with their lawyers to be sure that they understood the range of what a court might do in requiring appraisals and dividing their property. Although I had discussed the possibilities with them in a joint session, I believed it important for them to have their legal questions answered by their own lawyers.

When we reconvened, Gail stated that she insisted on receiving half the difference in the couple's pensions. Steve acquiesced on the condition that he not have to pay any cash immediately. They agreed that Gail would receive her share of the pension when she reached retirement age and that a separate fund would be created immediately to segregate Gail's portion from Steve's. Gail then stated that she had no real desire for a share of Steve's business and did not wish either of them to incur the cost of an independent appraisal. She needed current cash to cover the expenses associated with moving to a new house. She estimated those expenses at $5,000. Steve agreed to pay them in return for her dropping all claims to his business.

The Ryders still sometimes got very angry with each other. Our sessions together were consistently heated, but they were productive. Both Gail and Steve continued to agree that they could deal effectively with each other when the subject was the children. Thus they were comfortable with a final agreement that gave them joint power to make decisions about the children (usually called "joint custody") and flexible living arrangements in which Beth and Joshua would continue to spend significant amounts of time at each parent's house. (Contrary to a prevalent impression of divorce mediation, many couples do not agree to joint custody, but instead decide to give the responsibility for decisionmaking to the parent with whom the children spend the most time. Nevertheless, joint custody arrangements are more commonly reached through mediation than through traditional processes.)

The Ryders have since divorced. They are enthusiastic about their ability to deal with each other concerning the children. Gail has gained increasing confidence about her ability to take care of herself and her children.

Other couples in mediation have different types of problems, which require different approaches. In one case, a husband left his wife after thirty years of marriage just after their youngest child had gone to college. His wife, who had never been employed outside the home, had nothing to do and nothing to live for. Although she agreed to mediation, she did not appear ready to negotiate for herself. I referred her to a therapist who had experience working with women going through separation. Her husband agreed to continue to deposit funds into the couple's joint checking account until his wife was ready to return to mediation to work out an agreement. They came back, but not until a year later.

Couples who jointly own businesses or shares in various limited partnerships or other enterprises need to understand the effects on their business interests or tax liability of separating their property or continuing to operate as business associates. Mediation (with a mediator who understands the financial complications) can be particularly appropriate for helping these people sort things out.

4

Settling
Business Disputes

WHAT BEGAN IN THE 1970S AS A MOVEMENT to settle interpersonal conflicts, racial tensions, and what the legal establishment considered "minor" disputes was quickly seized on by important parts of corporate America as a way of keeping business conflicts out of court. To a large extent, according to law professor Eric Green, corporate interest in ADR constitutes a consumer movement at the upper end of the legal market.[1] "ADR" is the term adopted by corporate managers and their counsel to describe any way of resolving a dispute short of a full courtroom trial.

In the past twenty-five years, managers have felt besieged by the escalating costs of disputing. Their perception is that businesses, both large and small, are facing an avalanche of litigation. In fact, there has been a significant increase in commercial litigation since the early 1970s. The number of contract cases filed each year in federal courts increased from 14,000 during the 1960s to over 47,000 by 1986.[2] A study of these cases in the Southern District of New York (Manhattan), the federal court with the largest commercial caseload, revealed that the average number of pending contract cases increased from 365 during the 1960s to 1,273 (and sometimes exceeding 1,400) from 1973 to 1990.[3] Economist Ronald Gilson suggests that this surge in commercial litigation may have been caused by the end of the previous taboo against large companies suing one another.[4]

The types and complexity of cases going to court also have increased. Claims for injuries to consumers by products manufactured or sold by business, for workers' exposure to occupational hazards, and for damage to the environment, all of which have grown in number, involve complicated causal relationships and scientific uncertainty.

Although reform efforts are proliferating, judicial discovery rules, designed to develop facts and narrow legal issues before trial, permit questioning virtually every officer of a corporation and examining literally thousands of documents in the course of litigating a single dispute—all of which adds to both the cost and the difficulty of steering a business case through the courts. Law firms that represent corporations have expanded dramatically in response to the complexity of corporate litigation. This ex-

pansion, some charge, may have prompted still greater proliferation of
lawsuits. Juries also seem more ready to compensate (some would say
overcompensate) the injured than they once were. For whatever reason,
the business costs devoted to disputing have skyrocketed. With the
growth of legal expenses having greatly outstripped that of the gross national product, managers increasingly find that full adjudication of disputes is a luxury their companies cannot afford and a burden they need
not tolerate.

In an effort to seize control of their companies' runaway legal expenses,
many managers have become actively involved in overseeing the resolution of business disputes. Lawyers employed full-time by corporations,
whose jobs once were limited to dealing with the outside law firms that
handled the companies' legal business, now are taxed with managing litigation in such a way as to keep costs under control. Many of these corporate counsel have become actively involved in seeking alternative, less
costly ways of resolving disputes; a 1992 Harris Executive Poll of 400 senior corporate executives showed that an overwhelming 97 percent favor
such alternative methods over litigation. In 1979, general counsel of several Fortune 500 companies banded together to form the Legal Program to
Reduce the Costs of Business Disputes, under the auspices of the Center
for Public Resources (CPR) in New York. Since then, 600 U.S. corporations, representing nearly one-half of the gross national product, have
signed a pledge with CPR to explore alternatives to litigation whenever
they have disputes with other signatories.

Beyond cutting costs, a significant and growing minority of the more
sophisticated managers and their lawyers is coming to recognize that, for
many disputes, various alternatives offer the possibility of producing better results than do trials. Judges are constrained by the need to respond to
the issues as they are presented by the litigants' attorneys and to follow legal precedents. They often lack the technical or managerial expertise that
may be required to understand technical disputes. These straightjackets
need not confine private mediators, neutral experts, or arbitrators. As
they become more personally involved in the business of resolving disputes, some managers are recognizing that they can apply their own business knowledge and creativity to developing solutions better suited to
their needs than courts and lawyers alone could devise.

In addition to the pressure generated from within, businesses are being
exposed to innovations developed by the courts to settle cases in order to
control their overcrowded dockets. With increasing frequency, courts are
requesting or ordering businesses and their lawyers to participate in a
growing array of in-court settlement devices: minitrials or summary juries; mandatory, nonbinding arbitration by local lawyers; neutral evaluations of cases by panels of lawyers, doctors (for medical malpractice), or

other experts; mediation of complex cases by court-appointed special masters; or even the shutting down of an entire court for a week while volunteer lawyers attempt to settle cases (Settlement Week). The idea behind all these devices is to settle cases before trial, preferably before substantial lawyer and court time is invested in discovery and preparation. Becoming familiar with what these methods can do to resolve disputes in a court setting sometimes acts as an impetus to business litigants to use private dispute settlement services or to craft their own devices outside of court.

This chapter discusses situations in which disputing businesses and their attorneys invented new processes, primarily minitrials, to avoid or (more often) withdraw from the litigation fray or adopted one of the methods already created by other businesses or by courts intent on controlling their dockets: arbitration, summary jury trials, neutral experts, and, most often, mediation.

Arbitration or "Rent-a-Judge": Let Someone Else Decide

When unable to negotiate settlements on their own, through managers or attorneys, businesses traditionally have been faced with going to court or, if they were operating under a contract that required them to arbitrate future disputes, to binding arbitration. In an effort to cut their litigation costs, some insurance companies in the 1970s began to invite those with whom they were disputing to arbitrate, even when no contract required it. Now some automobile insurance carriers offer claimants arbitration through the American Arbitration Association. Others are willing to agree to either mediation or arbitration with a variety of dispute resolution "providers." Twenty-one insurance carriers in Connecticut established their own pilot program, Connecticut Alternative Dispute Resolution, to offer (for a fee) voluntary and either binding or nonbinding decisions in automobile claims valued at $50,000 or less. Of 1,037 cases submitted to the program, more than 70 percent were settled, many by the parties themselves once the program became involved. Claimants in approximately 80 percent of the 351 cases that went to a hearing chose some sort of arbitration; the rest chose mediation. Satisfaction with both arbitration and mediation was high on the part of both accident victims and insurance carriers.[5]

In another variation of arbitration, used particularly in cities and states whose courts have several-year waiting periods for cases to come to trial, parties submit disputes to private trials "by reference," or as the *Wall Street Journal* permanently dubbed the procedure, "rent-a-judge." The parties hire a private referee, frequently a retired judge employed by a growing number of entrepreneurial enterprises. The process is the same as arbitration except that legal precedents are supposed to govern and, in a few localities, decisions may be appealed to appellate courts. Advantages include speed, confidentiality, possibly lower cost (although the parties must pay the referee's fee), and the parties' ability to choose their own judge. Although laws permitting trials by reference have existed in some states such as California for as long as one hundred years, they only recently have been discovered by newly formed companies selling ADR services and by their customers, most of which are businesses anxious to speed up the judicial process.

Despite its acknowledged advantages arbitration has developed a bad name among many business clients and their lawyers, who want their disputes resolved predictably, according to business custom or legal principle. Many arbitrators have the reputation, whether or not it is deserved, for "splitting the baby" in attempting to deliver compromise decisions, even when compromise is inappropriate. If parties believe that the arbitrator will simply split the difference between them, they have an incentive to be unreasonable—to insist on an extreme result in the hope that the final midpoint decision will be close to what they really want.

A few corporations have attempted to modify the arbitration process in order to forestall compromise rulings. For example, Mobil Oil Corporation was sued in federal court by a combination car dealership and service station, which charged that it had been denied its rights under a gasoline supply contract with Mobil. Mobil filed counterclaims, and both parties began the expensive process of discovery. With the help of a private dispute resolution service contacted by Mobil's attorneys, the parties agreed to obtain a stay of the court action so that they could submit the dispute to arbitration. They then selected an arbitrator with extensive experience in the petroleum field and agreed on a comprehensive set of written instructions to the arbitrator. The instructions specified that the parties preferred a "win-lose" decision to a compromise unless the arbitrator in his best judgment believed that a compromise decision was necessary.[6]

Another variation is "final offer arbitration" (often known as "baseball arbitration"), which has been used primarily in labor disputes. It attempts to avoid compromise decisions and to increase the incentives for good faith negotiation or mediation prior to arbitration by having each party submit to the arbitrator its own "bottom-line" proposal for resolving the dispute. After hearing from both sides, the arbitrator is limited to choosing one proposal or the other. The arbitrator may neither issue a compromise award nor modify either party's proposal. The idea behind the process is that each party will attempt to present its most reasonable proposal in an effort to have it chosen. So far the procedure has been used most widely in disputes between public employees and governments, although it is best known for its use in major league baseball salary disputes. It can be added to other processes, such as mediation, when a method of breaking a deadlock is needed.

Minitrials, Summary Juries, and Neutral Experts: When Businesses Need More Information

One of the most spectacular growths of innovations to settle business disputes has occurred in processes such as minitrials, summary juries, and use of neutral experts, all of which attempt to predict for the parties how their cases would appear to a neutral decisionmaker (whether judge, jury, or technical expert), while reserving to the parties the right to make the final decision. In all of these techniques, the representatives of disputing businesses (or, less often, nonprofit organizations, government agencies or individuals) retain control of the outcome. This makes the processes more like mediation than arbitration. On the other hand, the procedures usually are more elaborate—hence more expensive—than mediation. Lawyers generally play a larger role in presenting each company's case. To the extent that they focus more on predicting outcome than on satisfying the parties' interests, these processes may do less to preserve participants' ongoing business relationships than does mediation.

Minitrials: Educating the Business Managers

A "minitrial" is not a trial at all. It is a presentation, almost always by lawyers, of the highlights of each side's case to the chief executives of disputing corporations (or other high-level officials not previously involved in the dispute), who then try to reach agreement. But just as the *Wall Street Journal* replaced "trial by reference" with the more colorful "rent-a-judge," the *Journal* changed the original label of "information exchange" (given to the first such procedure in 1977) to the catchier title of "minitrial." Despite its inaccurate connotations, the name has stuck.

Minitrials are more elaborate than traditional negotiations or mediation. For this reason, they generally are reserved for large, complex disputes involving sharply different views of what each side could prove at trial. Anyone who has listened to a lawyer who is enmeshed in a protracted fight describing the case to the client and then watched the same dispute play out in a courtroom will recognize the frequently stark contrast between the two versions. Recognition of this phenomenon, together with the opportunity to contain costs, their clients' need for speed and privacy, and their own disenchantment with arbitration, impelled lawyers for Telecredit, Inc., and the much larger TRW, Inc., to invent the minitrial in 1977.

In 1974 Telecredit had sued TRW for $6 million in damages and an injunction against what it claimed was TRW's infringement of its patents on the computerized devices that enable stores to verify a customer's credit. An injunction would have put an end to TRW's computerized credit-card and check-authorization machines. TRW not only denied the infringement but pronounced Telecredit's patents legally invalid. If upheld, the claim would have destroyed Telecredit's advantage in the field.

Tempers flared as company lawyers spent more than two years gathering some 100,000 corporate documents and questioning hundreds of employees of both concerns. Still, no trial or even pretrial conference date had been set. The lawyers' sporadic attempts to discuss settlement went nowhere. TRW repeatedly challenged Telecredit to demonstrate how TRW's machines infringed on its patents; Telecredit responded by demanding proof of the patents' invalidity. Telecredit proposed arbitration, but TRW feared a compromise decision, which could have cost it millions in damages.

The "information exchange" was designed to show the parties Telecredit's evidence of infringement and TRW's evidence of the patents' invalidity. Its structure was negotiated between TRW's lawyers and Telecredit's co-founder (not a lawyer). After a brief period for exchanging a few additional documents and position papers, the parties agreed to a two-day meeting, in which each would present its "best case" to senior managers·of each company. After the presentations and rebuttals, the managers would meet privately and attempt to settle the case—out of the presence of their lawyers. The information exchange would be moderated by a "neutral advisor," whose only authority was to preserve order during the proceedings. If the managers failed to reach agreement by themselves, the neutral advisor was directed to give them a written, nonbinding opinion of the strengths and weaknesses of each side's case. After they received the advisor's opinion, the managers would meet and again try to settle.

In the first minitrial, enacted at the Century Plaza Hotel in Los Angeles, Telecredit was represented by its chief executive officer, TRW by a vice-president. Both had authority to settle the case without returning to headquarters for instructions or ratification. The neutral advisor was a retired U.S. Court of Claims trial judge. During the presentations, the executives listened, made notes, and asked questions. Both sides, which up to then had been limited to hearing about the case from their own lawyers, learned of new facts and heard other points of view. The executives got their first picture of how their cases would come across in a real trial.

After the information exchange, the executives retired to another room to discuss a resolution. Despite years of litigation, which had been accompanied by mutual charges of bad faith, they reached a settlement in half an hour. The agreement provided that TRW would pay for a license from Telecredit if Telecredit was able to secure new patents from the Patent Office. It did, and the licensing agreement went into effect.

The total time between agreeing to work out the details of the minitrial and signing a final agreement was ninety days. Executives estimated that they saved a million dollars in lawyers' fees alone, not to mention employees' time preparing documents and testifying at trial. The details of the patent, which would have had to be made public at a trial, remained confidential. Even more significant, the former combatants became joint venturers, to their mutual gain.

The minitrial captured the imagination of corporate executives, at least in part because it put them rather than their lawyers in control of the outcome. The minitrial's use of managers as the primary negotiators has some of the same benefits (though often at a higher cost) as mediation: It turns legal disputes into business decisions, and it gives businesses the opportunity to preserve continuing relationships with valued customers or suppliers, even in the face of disagreement. Where minitrials have prompted executives to negotiate agreements on their own, without the prod of a neutral advisor's prediction, the resulting solutions often have been far more creative and responsive to their business needs than any judgment by a court or award by an arbitrator could be.

In a frequently cited example, the 1982 minitrial between Texaco and the Borden Company, which resulted from Borden's antitrust suit against Texaco, led to the renegotiation of a gas supply contract that had not even been at issue in the original case. The companies' representatives also created a new arrangement for transporting Texaco gas to Borden at prices favorable to Borden. The result was a net gain for both companies, which would have been impossible to predict simply by an examination of the claims each had made in court.

Minitrials can be crafted to fit the parties' situation. Who should be present, at what stage of the dispute the information exchange should take place, which procedural rules should be followed, whether briefs or other documents should be exchanged, the amount of prior discovery, and the apportionment of costs all can be negotiated beforehand. The companies involved may decide to use a neutral person simply as a referee, or they may ask for an opinion about how the case would fare in court. Or the parties may ask the person to become actively involved in mediating a resolution. Finally, the principals may decide to dispense with an outsider completely and preside over the minitrial themselves.

Minitrials have become increasingly attractive to corporations seeking ways of settling disagreements where the parties have different views of critical facts. Among the many reported examples of their use was a dispute between Kaiser Aluminum and Chemical Corporation and American Cyanamid Company, both of which had signed the CPR pledge to try some method of alternative dispute resolution before taking disputes with other signers to court. Yet it took three years for their lawyers to agree to have a minitrial in a $260,000 product liability dispute between the two chemical companies. American Cyanamid had sent sulphuric acid to Kaiser, which Kaiser used in manufacturing fertilizer. Cauliflower farmers on Long Island who had bought the fertilizer charged that it damaged their crops. Kaiser settled with the farmers, then sued American Cyanamid, claiming that its chemicals were defective.

At the minitrial, the managers reached an impasse in their negotiations, but they were less than $20,000 apart. In order to break the deadlocks, the executives decided to permit the neutral advisor, a former justice of the New Jersey Supreme Court, to issue a binding "yes or no" ruling on the difference between them. Each executive wrote his number on a piece of paper, and the advisor was asked to pick the number he thought was most realistic, having been instructed that he was not to split the difference. The case was settled.

When the Sherwin-Williams Company in Cleveland sued a Chicago-based, family-owned corporation for the approximately $4 million due on the sale of charcoal-lighter cans, the buyer counterclaimed for over $2 million, claiming that the cans leaked and that as a result its business had been harmed irreparably. After unsuccessful negotiations, the parties agreed to a modified minitrial. After their lawyers' presentation of case summaries, the parties decided that the executives would remain in separate rooms, while the neutral advisor acted as a mediator, shuttling back and forth in search of a settlement.

The case summaries gave the CEO of the Chicago firm his first knowledge of the details of the transaction, which until then had been handled by his son. Although the company later went bankrupt and the case was resolved in court through summary proceedings, the minitrial cleared the air. Discovery and other extensive pretrial maneuverings ceased, and the parties were able to focus on the one unresolved issue that remained.

In an international contract dispute between Xerox Corporation and a Uruguayan distributor of Xerox products, it took an oral opinion by the neutral advisor, former United States District Court Judge Harold Tyler, to break the logjam between the parties. The executives negotiated for five hours before Tyler's opinion and for ninety minutes after and reached a full settlement. Because the minitrial was agreed to by lawyers in Xerox's in-house counsel's office, the settlement averted the need for hiring an outside law firm. Council for Xerox estimated that the process saved the company four to six weeks' trial time and more than $400,000 in expenses.

A nine-party dispute over the building of a $200 million charitable hospital for children near Wilmington, Delaware, produced a "maxi-minitrial," which lasted a week and featured the daily attendance of 125 to 150 principals, witnesses, lawyers, and observers. Even this mammoth proceeding failed to settle the entire dispute; however, six of the nine parties settled in subsequent negotiations. The lawsuit among the remaining three parties spawned a five-month trial, the longest jury trial in the history of the Delaware federal court. Yet without the minitrial, the trial would have been considerably longer (at least a year, according to some observers) and more complicated. One of the lead attorneys, a specialist in construction law, credited the minitrial with simplifying the case and enabling six of the nine parties to escape the trial. If he had it to do again, he has observed, he would dispense with a written opinion by the neutral advisor and have the advisor become more involved in the settlement negotiations. He also suggested a three-member panel of neutral advisors in order to increase the resources available for assimilating such a large and complex case.

During the Arab oil embargo, American Can Company agreed to furnish the Wisconsin Electric Power Company with garbage from the City of Milwaukee, to be turned into usable energy. Although the scheme was much touted at the time, it failed to work. Wisconsin Power notified American Can that it no longer would need the garbage. American Can sued Wisconsin Electric for $40 million. Wisconsin Electric counterclaimed for $20 million, claiming damage to its power plant from burning the garbage.

For several years both sides took hundreds of depositions, exchanged boxcars of documents, and attempted unsuccessfully to negotiate a settlement. Trial lawyers estimated that it would take seventy-five days to try the case and would generate millions of dollars in legal costs. Then one of the lawyers read an article in the *New York Times* about minitrials. He called a private dispute resolution organization, which helped the parties agree to limit discovery to one more month, with a limit on additional depositions and a focused exchange of documents. A panel was assembled consisting of one representative of each corporation and a neutral advisor. The parties agreed on two days of presentations with live witnesses, after which the principals and their lawyers would negotiate. Although it took the parties two months after the minitrial to reach agreement, they settled all the issues.

Reflecting on this experience, Robert H. Gorske, vice president and general counsel of Wisconsin Electric Power, cites several reasons, in addition to the obvious incentives of cost and speed, why minitrials are attractive to corporate executives and their lawyers:

1. They permit managers to find out what is happening in their lawsuits without having to rely completely on their lawyers to tell them.

2. They give managers the opportunity to interact directly with other managers. Once the relationship is humanized, the principals can see beyond the immediate conflict to develop innovative solutions.
3. Minitrials (or, for that matter, any other structured settlement device) provide an excuse for acceptance of the first settlement offer. In effect, Gorske reflects, something good is expected to come out of the process, so it does.
4. The involvement of a third party enables disputants to see how their positions are evaluated by somebody without a stake in the ultimate outcome. Because there almost always are differences of opinion within each side, the third-party approach may help the voices within an organization urging settlement to be heard above the clamor of those urging war.

Most of the same advantages inhere in simple mediation, without the necessity of the presentations that highlight a minitrial. Gorske hypothesizes, however, that many lawyers favor minitrials because, unlike in mediation, "they still get their chance to go eyeball-to-eyeball with the opposition to convince some third party."[7] In effect, the minitrial retains some of the drama of the courtroom, for which trial lawyers have been trained. They have the opportunity to marshal facts and to present them in a relatively efficient, effective way to corporate decisionmakers, who then make decisions based on their new appreciation of what is involved.

Summary Juries: How Would They Decide?

A few judges have convened minitrials in court. With the litigants' consent, Federal Judge Robert E. Keeton has served as the neutral advisor in his Boston courtroom in an effort to settle cases without a full trial. Other judges have adapted the minitrial format to jury cases in an effort to serve a different purpose: to give parties and their lawyers the chance of a realistic appraisal of how a jury will treat their case.

The use of summary jury trials has helped to settle what Judge Thomas D. Lambros of the U.S. District Court in Cleveland calls the "hard-core durable cases" (those that consume weeks or months of judges' time). Lawyers present summaries of their cases to regular jury panels. (Generally, the jurors are not told that they are participating in a mock trial.) The jurors deliberate, return a verdict, then voluntarily answer lawyers' questions about their presentations and the verdict. Judge Richard Enslen, of Kalamazoo, Michigan, who uses summary juries on an average of once a month, modestly terms them the "settlement device for judges who do not have mediation skills."[8]

Although summary jury trials settle some cases that otherwise might go to trial, the process itself is sufficiently costly and time-consuming that it generally is reserved for disputes in which trials are expected to run into several weeks. Judge Enslen assigns cases to summary jury trials only if he estimates they will take at least two weeks to try and if they involve either a dispute over damages, which a jury's opinion can help to resolve, or emotional overtones that prevent settlement.

Both Judge Enslen and Judge Lambros have orchestrated sample summary jury trials in cases involving multiple claims of injury from hazardous materials in order to show the parties what jurors would be likely to award in typical cases. In claims by twenty-nine families against a chemical company for damages to compensate them for the increased risks of cancer from inadvertently drinking poisoned water, for example, Judge Enslen estimated the trial time at six months per family. With the agreement of the parties, he arranged four summary jury trials, which resulted in settlement of all twenty-nine cases in two weeks.

Like the minitrial, the summary jury is a way for businesses with large-scale litigation to see how their cases would play in court. According to Judge Lambros, "Anything that reduces that gap of perceived probability of winning helps the parties move to settlement." Summary jury trials, along with mediation and minitrials, also succeed, he surmises, because they give people "the opportunity to tell their stories, to get the battle out of their systems."[9]

Not everyone urged by judges to try a summary jury trial has shared the courts' enthusiasm. When a recalcitrant lawyer refused to participate, the judge held him in contempt. The lawyer successfully appealed and obtained a ruling from a federal appeals court to the effect that courts have no authority to require litigants to participate in summary jury trials.[10] Although a different federal appeals court has since agreed with the first, federal trial courts in other parts of the country have disagreed with the decision and required both lawyers and their clients to appear, rejecting arguments that there is no possibility of settlement in the case and that a party desires to avoid the expenditure of time and money that participation in the summary jury trial would require.[11]

Neutral Experts: Helping the Parties to Agree on Technical Facts

When business disagreements result from differing views of critical scientific, technical, business, or even legal information, the parties may be able to negotiate their own settlement, with or without a mediator, if they can resolve their conflicting perceptions. What they often need is an outside expert, whose knowledge and impartiality they all respect, to give an unbiased opinion.

We all use neutral experts when we agree to accept appraisals of property or umpires' calls at baseball games. Courts have begun to employ experts more frequently to educate judges or juries or to provide an antidote to conflicting testimony offered by the phalanx of experts increasingly hired by the parties. In order for businesses to hire experts jointly to help them settle a dispute, one of them must take the initiative to broach the idea. Then they must agree on a particular expert and decide whether they are willing to make the expert's opinion binding.

Job changes are common in high-tech industries. In the heyday of the Silicon Valley, engineers changed employers with amazing regularity—frequently moving every few months or, at most, every year. Inescapably, they took their valuable ideas with them.

As the industry matured, corporations began claiming ideas as proprietary trade secrets as a way to give them legal protection. In order to guard this form of intellectual property, companies began to require engineers to execute confidentiality and noncompete agreements. They also developed exit interviews, which require departing engineers to recite to company officials that they are taking none of the company's trade secrets with them. To the extent that the engineers have such trade secrets in their heads, they must agree not to use them for the benefit of any new employer.

Miles Young, an electrical engineer who specialized in designs for microelectronic devices, became dissatisfied with his employment at Radiotec, a division of a Fortune 500 company outside of Boston. (The names of the people and the companies have been changed to preserve their confidences.) Having signed the usual agreement for nondisclosure of confidential and proprietary information, Young completed his exit interview, signed a statement that he was taking with him no proprietary information, and left. He packed his belongings into his car and drove the few miles to his new job. Young immediately reported for work with his new employer, Micro-Elec, a smaller, recent addition to the high-tech companies that ring Route 128 outside of Boston.

That evening, when he returned to the parking lot to drive home, Young had a rude shock. Someone had broken into his car and taken his clothing, his small stereo, his briefcase, and other personal belongings. He called the police, dutifully filled out the necessary report forms, and went home. The next day he returned to work, found time during his lunch break to talk to his insurance agent, and dismissed the matter as an unfortunate incident.

Several days later, when Young arrived at work, he was greeted with a summons and complaint. The complaint named both Young and his new employer as defendants in a lawsuit alleging theft of trade secrets and violation of his confidentiality agreement with Radiotec.

A resident of a nearby suburb had found a briefcase on her lawn. When she opened it to look for the owner's name, she discovered "funny looking drawings." She immediately called the police, who retrieved the briefcase and, having discovered the name of the engineer and the address and telephone number of his old employer, called Radiotec to report that they had found Young's briefcase containing "plans." After summoning company lawyers, Radiotec officials made a quick trip to the police station, demanding the return of "our plans." When the police learned that Young no longer worked for the company, they refused to turn over either the briefcase or its contents.

When told what had happened, Young readily acknowledged that the briefcase was his, but insisted that the plans, which he had taken from Radiotec and other former employers, were nothing more than a "portable résumé," a way of demonstrating that he knew how to design microelectronic circuits. Radiotec insisted, on the other hand, that the plans were "hard evidence" that he had intended to steal their trade secrets and take them to his new employer.

Disputes over the theft of trade secrets regularly are fought out in court. The claims typically follow a pattern: The old employer asserts that its competitor's new products, produced with the help of its former employee, resulted from the theft of its trade secrets that were disclosed by a breach of the agreement for confidentiality and noncompetition. The engineer and the new employer reply that the noncompete agreement is invalid, that the engineer has a right to work in his chosen profession, and that any new products are the result of new ideas applied to new applications (obviously drawing on all of his prior experience, training, and knowledge)—not the theft of proprietary information. In any event, they argue, such information cannot be protected under the law as a trade secret.

Radiotec and Micro-Elec agreed to test their positions in a different way from the usual skirmishing of complaint, counterclaim, requests for injunctions, protracted discovery, and trial. James McGuire, the Boston lawyer hired by Micro-Elec to defend the lawsuit, had attended a series of training sessions on various settlement techniques that mediator and trainer Michael Lewis and I had conducted at his law firm. McGuire had tried similar cases before and quickly recognized that a trial in Young's case could cause serious difficulties for both sides.

First was the problem of delay. Designs for microelectronic devices can become obsolete in a matter of months. If Micro-Elec was to be prevented from marketing any aspect of the product it currently was building, it needed to know that soon so that it could redesign the device before it had sunk additional time and money into it. Radiotec, on its part, risked losing the lawsuit and losing its market share to Micro-Elec's device—or, hardly more attractive, winning after years of litigation but after both companies' designs had been superseded by newer models.

Delay was only one drawback. Both sides knew that in order to fight the lawsuit, each company would have to see the other's secret designs. The need for swapping the designs engendered the same suspicions that had led to the lawsuit in the first place.

Finally, McGuire was only too aware of the difficulties that face trial lawyers in their attempts to communicate technical details to a judge and jury.

> In this sort of litigation, the usual sequence is engineers talking to lawyers to try to explain engineering concepts, which the lawyers in turn try to translate to a judge and, sometimes, a jury, who then have to decide whether they understand either side and whether they believe one side or the other. From our point of view, any engineer worth his salt would know that the designs were different. The big problem was in figuring out how to convince laypeople of that fact.[12]

Both companies agreed that either their own or any other knowledgeable engineer could tell whether Micro-Elec's design was original or a copy of Radiotec's. The toughest problem lay in finding an engineer that both sides could trust. McGuire proposed to ask an independent engineer, a "neutral expert," to decide whether the two designs were the same or different. If a credible, trustworthy engineer with allegiance to neither company could be found, both companies agreed to be bound by the expert's opinion. Both were reasonably confident that a brief technical presentation by engineers and a comparison of designs by the expert would result in a fair decision.

If the expert determined that the designs were "different," Radiotec would acknowledge that its trade secrets were inviolate and agree not to try to prevent the sale of new products incorporating the design. If the expert determined that the designs were the "same," Micro-Elec would be obliged to redesign, which would be expensive—but not nearly so expensive as defending against claimed theft of trade secrets once its product was on the market.

The solution took a week for the lawyers to create, a month to implement. Engineers from the two companies drew up a joint list of three outside engineers considered knowledgeable about the type of microelectronic design in question. Each company then sent a lawyer and an engineer to interview all three candidates. After asking questions concerning their neutrality, expertise, and other work, each side struck the candidate it found least acceptable. The remaining engineer was chosen.

In the course of designing the procedure for expert review, the parties agreed to drop the lawsuit and wait to schedule the expert's design review until after they had completed their preliminary designs. Engineers from each of the companies then would make a brief, separate presentation of the company's design to the expert, who would compare the designs and decide whether their similarities or their differences were greater. At no time would the expert share one company's design with the other.

The actual denouement was anticlimactic. As it turned out, both sides encountered design problems that convinced them not to make the product after all. Although the review process never actually came into being, the parties recognized that they could not have avoided a trial (with its costs, delays, frustrations, and need for exchanging coveted design information) unless they had adopted their alternative when they did. As for monetary savings, each side estimated about $250,000—a combination of the legal and expert fees that would have been necessary to prepare the case for trial. The actual cost of the dispute to each side up to the time it decided to abandon its design was less than $40,000.

The companies involved had no trouble locating engineers to serve as candidates for the job of neutral expert. Indeed, many of the engineers they approached confessed that their training, which encourages them to approach a problem objectively, fits uneasily in the adversarial process, where they must adopt the role of professional witness for one side or the other.

Disputes like the Radiotec case, which turn on issues that require highly specialized training or experience to make a judgment, are particularly difficult for the adversarial system to handle. Experts deal with concepts that are difficult to understand, they frequently speak in their own language, and they often are coached to select only that testimony that favors the party that hired them. Furthermore, in the most difficult areas, such as environmental disputes and injuries caused by hazardous products, the "truth" may be unknown or in a state of flux.

In complicated disagreements over faulty construction, medical malpractice, personal injuries, patent and securities regulation, and antitrust violations, neutral experts can help disputants to understand what is at issue and to make informed decisions concerning their liability. Even in relatively straightforward disputes, a neutral expert can be useful in breaking the common logjam that results when parties or their attorneys have different perceptions of the size of their claims. The same Boston law firm that used the neutral engineer in the Radiotec dispute later represented a woman who slipped and fell on a staircase owned by a local public transit authority. The lawyers had tried to negotiate a settlement, but were stymied by their wildly disparate views of the monetary value of the woman's injuries. Seeking a way out, they agreed to retain a respected personal injury lawyer to predict how the claim would fare in court. Although they declined to agree in advance to be bound by the neutral opinion, both sides promptly agreed to settle on the terms he suggested.

Despite many successes, a problem with using neutral experts to predict court outcomes lies in the variability of juries' and even judges' decisions, especially in complex cases. One such attempt involved a complicated patent dispute in which the parties agreed to submit evidence to a panel of three distinguished retired federal judges, two with trial court and one with appellate experience, for their evaluation. Having heard both lawyers' summaries of the facts and legal arguments, the first judge predicted a judgment for the plaintiff. The second, just as confidently, announced that he would rule for the defendant. The third, the retired court of appeals judge, shrugged and said that in his opinion the case easily could go either way.

Mediation: The "Sleeping Giant"

A 1985 guide for business executives with legal disputes termed mediation the "sleeping giant" of business dispute resolution, potentially the most powerful means of bringing the parties to terms.[13] Since that time the giant has awakened, and the use of mediation to resolve conflicts among businesses has increased exponentially.

Because of its flexibility, mediation is adaptable to business disputes of all sizes and complexity. Except for the opportunity to observe lawyers' presentation of a case, which may be unnecessary or excessively expensive for most business conflicts, mediation has the advantages of minitrials without some of the complications. Mediation puts business managers in control of resolving their own disputes. Lawyers generally (although not always) participate as advisors and, often, as spokespersons. The process emphasizes solving problems rather than establishing who did what to whom in the past. In the hands of skilled mediators, representatives of sparring businesses can be helped to focus on their future relationships. In the case of suppliers of necessary materials, ongoing construction, or other time sensitive relationships, this focus can be critical. It also may be critical in disputes that involve ongoing business or mixed business and personal relationships. For example, in my experience in dissolving corporations or partnerships or dealing with the withdrawal of key principals, I have found that the mixture of financial and emotional elements is the same as in a divorce, with mediation the most responsive way to deal with the hidden issues behind division of assets and liabilities. Finally, in an effort to prevent a recurrence of the impasse, mediators can help parties to determine in advance how they will resolve any future disputes.

The mediation of business disputes may involve only managers, meeting jointly and separately with a mediator; it may involve only their attorneys; or it may involve both. Most of us who mediate this type of dispute have found the presence of the business principals themselves to be critical, not only in enabling the parties to craft resolutions that might escape the notice of their lawyers but also in revealing their business priorities.

Some corporations and their attorneys had their first experience with the process in cases referred to mediation by the courts. A judge in Washington, D.C., for example, one month away from the scheduled trial of a complicated battle over a multimillion-dollar piece of real estate, asked all the parties and their lawyers to meet with Michael Lewis, an experienced mediator. The parties—a commercial real estate developer, a real estate development partnership, a tenants' association, a trust, and a bank—and their lawyers dealt with Lewis and one another through no formal presentations or hearings, just five meetings and numerous telephone calls.

The dispute arose out of the sharply escalating land values in a section of the city whose potential for commercial development was recognized only recently. The lessee of a portion of the real estate claimed ownership rights based on the provisions of an old lease. The fact that the lessee initially wanted only the land and refused to discuss any amount of money as compensation from the current owners made the conflict appear intractable.

The disputed property involved three buildings: a fifteen-unit apartment building and two two-story, somewhat run-down commercial structures, all owned by the same man. At a time when that part of Washington was considered little more than a wasteland between two bustling neighborhoods, the individual developer, Hassein (the names and identifying details have been changed), leased the commercial buildings from the owner. The terms of the lease provided that it could be extended, with no escalation in cost other than routine cost-of-living adjustments, at Hassein's option for fifteen years. The lease also gave Hassein a right of first refusal if the owner decided to sell the property during the term of the lease.

Five years into the lease the owner of the property was killed during a robbery of the liquor store that he operated on the ground floor of the apartment building. His heirs quickly put all three buildings up for sale, notifying both Hassein and the apartment building tenants of their intention. Notice to the tenants was required by legislation (passed by the D.C. City Council subsequent to the lease) that mandated sellers of residential property to notify existing tenants of their intent to sell and to take a number of other steps, including notice, designed to make it possible for them to purchase any rental property in which they were living at the time of sale.

The tenants exercised their rights under the new law, formed an association, and began to negotiate with the owners to purchase some or all of the property. Hassein and various real estate developers also began negotiating with the tenants' association in an effort to buy whatever rights they had under the new legislation. After about six months of bargaining, the tenants chose two of the developers, formed a partnership with them, and agreed with the owner's heirs on a purchase price for the entire tract. Probably because of the recent tragedy associated with the property, the selling price was far below its appraised value.

The property was sold subject to Hassein's lease of the commercial buildings—a lease that could run another ten years if he chose. Hassein exercised his option to renew the lease then sued the current owners, the heirs of the former owner, and the bank holding the mortgage for "specific performance" of what he claimed was his right to purchase the entire property (in other words, for the property itself rather than for money damages). His theory was that the owners had an obligation to sell the entire tract to him and should have permitted him to bid for it against the tenant-developer partnership. Later he modified his position, asserting that the property was divisible and that the commercial buildings should have been sold to him without the apartments.

The defendants responded by counterclaiming against Hassein for purchase money, carrying charges, and real estate taxes. Each defendant also crossclaimed against the other defendants, claiming that if Hassein had any rights against them, they had a right to be reimbursed by one another. The defendants filed—and lost (two years later)—a motion for summary judgment without a trial, and the case was scheduled for trial three years after it had been brought.

In a pretrial conference with the judge, Hassein stated that he wanted only the land, not money, and that there was no other way he could be compensated for the wrong done to him and his children. The judge, despairing of any settlement on such terms, suggested mediation.

As mediator, Lewis first met jointly with all the parties and their lawyers. Hassein reiterated his belief that he had been wronged, that the properties were divisible, and that the commercial buildings and land belonged to him. Money was not the point, he said; he had attempted to purchase the property to build his family's future and to keep land for his children. He charged that the original sale must have involved shady dealings, because the property had been sold for less than three-quarters of its actual value.

The defendants countered with their assertion that the property was not divisible, that an attempt to separate it would damage the existing structures, and that if the judge awarded any land to Hassein he owed them large amounts of money (though the defendants' various estimates differed greatly). The defendants recited their legal arguments, among them that the property always had been considered as a whole, that Hassein never before the sale had requested less than the total parcel, and that he therefore had waived whatever rights of first refusal had not been preempted by the tenants' intervening rights.

During this session, it became clear to Lewis that there were significant differences among the separate defendants' positions and that there was particular animosity between Hassein and the new owners—either because they had outmaneuvered him in acquiring the property or because Hassein was an Arab and all the other principals were Jewish. A letter written to Hassein by one of the owners during the mediation, demanding some minor fee that Hassein was supposed to have paid, only made the atmosphere worse.

Lewis met separately with each of the parties and their attorneys in order to clarify their concerns and explore settlement possibilities on a confidential basis. Lewis questioned each party about the real estate. In describing the property's great value, Hassein cited the high values of neighboring properties. Rather than arguing with him, Lewis asked him to develop information for all the parties on the selling prices of neighboring properties. Hassein agreed. Lewis then asked the present owners to bring to the group's next joint session a surveyor's plat so that the group could look at a picture of the property as they discussed options for settlement.

The second joint session began with a discussion of numbers. The parties discussed the appraisal that had been conducted just before the sale. Hassein's lawyer asked the current owners to estimate the present value of the property. The parties then agreed that the entire property was worth between $2.5 and $3 million. The group calculated the size of various segments of the property, attempting to pinpoint a value for the portions claimed by Hassein. The defendants offered to pay $400,000. Curiously, Hassein heard only $130,000. Eventually Lewis was able to help him understand that the defendants were talking about much more money than ever had been on the table before. Lewis suggested further homework, designed to determine the value of what Hassein would have received had the property been divided at the time of the sale.

Lewis carefully avoided becoming enmeshed in the arguments about value, believing that his usefulness lay in pushing the parties to document their claims and focusing them on the remaining questions in dispute. Hassein never acknowledged that his focus had shifted from land to money. Nor did the other parties admit that Hassein ever had any rights to buy the commercial buildings in the first place.

By the end of the second joint meeting, the parties had agreed on the structure of a settlement. Within two weeks they had produced a seventeen-point "manifesto." Hassein would be paid $450,000—$400,000 by the current owners and $50,000 by the previous owners. (The bank had been excused, with everyone's consent, after the first session.) Hassein relinquished his lease, thus allowing the owners to proceed with their plans for developing the commercial portions of the property. All claims and crossclaims were dismissed. The parties worked out an intricate arrangement to facilitate favorable tax treatment of the payments.

On the day the parties read the settlement into the record, the judge praised them effusively, pointing out that their agreed-upon arrangements were much richer in maximizing the gains to all concerned than any judgment that would have been within a court's power to issue. In effect, what Lewis had succeeded in doing was to turn an unsettlable issue of principle (which party was entitled to the land by contract or by local legislation) into the tractable one of money damages.[14]

Several courts have begun to discover the potential of mediation for settling complex business disputes. In Chicago, U.S. District Judge Marvin E. Aspen has appointed law professor and mediator Stephen Goldberg to serve as a special master for the purpose of mediating cases involving allegations of fraud, breach of contract, antitrust, and employment discrimination. Claims for damages have ranged from $250,000 to $30 million. According to Goldberg, the judge chose those cases for mediation because each was complex and likely to require a lengthy trial, yet appeared susceptible to settlement. Becoming personally involved in settlement efforts might take more time than the judge himself could afford and involve him more deeply in the substance of the dispute than he considered appropriate.

Before appointing Goldberg, the judge suggested to the parties that they attempt mediation and proposed Goldberg for the task. (Skeptics might question how much of a practical difference there is between a trial judge's suggestion and a court order.) Upon obtaining their agreement, the judge issued an order referring the case to mediation, setting the mediator's compensation, and dividing responsibility for payment among the parties.

Responsibility for payment has not always been apportioned equally. According to Goldberg, "In neither of the cases in which all the mediator's fees were paid by one party was I aware of any lack of trust in the mediator on the part of the non-paying party. It had participated in the selection of the mediator to the same extent as had the paying party, and appeared not to be concerned that the mediator would act prejudicially toward it. Trust, then, rather than payment would appear to be the critical issue."[15]

As with Lewis, Goldberg's only ground rules involve confidentiality: No communications from one party to the mediator outside the presence of the other party will be communicated to the other party without permission, and nothing the parties tell the mediator will be disclosed to the judge. Like most other mediators, Goldberg approaches mediation of cases referred by courts in the same way he deals with private mediation: "My goal is to assist the parties to reach a mutually acceptable settlement that accommodates the vital interests of each, and is viewed by each as preferable to the costs and risks of litigation. I do this by encouraging the parties to focus on their vital interests and to generate options for settlement that accommodate those interests."[16]

Building on positive experiences, some judges now routinely refer business disputes on their dockets to mediation. Others are authorized or required to do so by statutes, such as those in Florida, Texas, Indiana, and experimentally in North Carolina,[17] or court rules, such as the civil rule in Washington, D.C.[18]

The most critical difference among mediators of business disputes, particularly mediators who are lawyers, lies in whether or not they focus only on dollar amounts and attempt to induce settlement based on their view of how a dispute would fare in court. Many professional mediators refrain from doing either. Rather, they focus on solving the business problems that underlie the dispute, believing that it is far more critical to emphasize the parties' stake in settling the dispute and the effect of a trial on their future business relationship than to pressure them into settling by predicting what will happen in court if they do not give in.

Other mediators disagree and readily share their predictions with the parties. These mediators often have greater expertise in the substance of the dispute (construction practices, for example) than in mediation techniques and focus more on producing quick settlements than on strengthening the parties' future relationships. Lawyer Kenneth Feinberg, who helped to settle the class action by Vietnam war veterans against seven chemical manufacturers for injuries claimed to have resulted from exposure to the herbicide Agent Orange, goes farthest in this direction, normally giving parties written recommendations of settlement terms, which include his view of the "settlement value" of each case. The function of the mediator in this role shades into that of a neutral expert (or the neutral advisor in a minitrial), who predicts the probable court or arbitration outcome of a particular conflict. Although the risks to the parties of an adverse recommendation exceed those of more traditional mediation and thus may be less palatable to the businesses involved, participants in both types of mediation to date have been enthusiastic about the results.

Despite courts' growing success with mediation, the greatest potential of mediation for businesses probably lies in the early stages of a conflict, before disagreements have escalated, before disputants have incurred the costs of preparing a case for trial, perhaps even before they have hired lawyers. This potential can be realized only when the businesses themselves, rather than the courts, begin to take their disputes to mediation. A number of businesses have begun to do so. A group of franchisers has formed the National Franchise Mediation Program, an experiment in resolving disputes between franchisers and their franchisees. Designed and managed by the Center for Public Resources in New York, the program offers a multistep dispute settlement process. (In the past, most franchise agreements contained only arbitration clauses.) The idea is to enable franchises, whose success depends on their maintaining positive and productive business relationships with one another, to settle most disputes themselves through mediation. Founding members include Burger King, Dunkin' Donuts, Hardee's, Holiday Inn Worldwide, Jiffy Lube, Kentucky Fried Chicken, McDonald's, Pizza Hut, Southland, Taco Bell, and Wendy's.

Ten major competitors in the food industry, including General Mills, Kellogg, and Ralston Purina, have signed an agreement to mediate their trademark, packaging, and marketing disputes. They cite the safeguarding of corporate image and consumer goodwill, rather than the reduction of escalating litigation costs, as their primary reason for the move. Another motivation is the fostering and preservation of positive business relationships because the companies, though competing for market share, often work together in other areas, such as the negotiation of new labeling regulations with the Food and Drug Administration.

Some insurance companies, already familiar with arbitration, have begun to use mediation fairly routinely. Even where mediation is not provided for in a contract—either because the parties did not think of it or because they had no contract—some carriers are urging their insureds and those who deal with them to try mediation before they proceed with arbitration or court. In the CIGNA Corporation's program to settle disputed claims against its policyholders, for example, the company emphasizes mediation in the belief that mediation gives the parties control over the process while preserving their rights to a court hearing if they are not satisfied with whatever offers are put on the table. Travelers Insurance Company now recommends mediation for 80 percent of the claims filed against its insureds.

The reinsurance industry, which involves insurance companies' doing business with one another in an effort to spread risks among different companies, for most of its history handled its disputes in private, using arbitration when companies could not agree among themselves. Then conflicts began to be litigated, with public allegations of fraud adding embittering elements to the usual claims for breach of contract. Michael Lewis and I recently mediated one such case, with thirteen insurance companies, reinsurers, and several of the brokers who act as intermediaries. Unfortunately, the case was referred to mediation by a federal magistrate-judge after many motions had been filed, depositions taken, press releases issued, and relationships already damaged.

The rapidly changing health care field also offers promise for using mediation at an early stage of a conflict, in an effort to preserve ongoing relationships among, for example, hospitals or extended care facilities, patients, doctors, nurses, staff, and insurance carriers. The potential is just beginning to be tapped, with a few experiments in hospitals and nursing homes. Mediation has particular appeal when professionals are charged with malpractice. According to Barry C. Dorn, associate clinical professor at Tufts New England Medical Center, adjudicatory systems, including arbitration, fail to factor in the human component. Mediation has a better chance of dealing with the frustrations of both doctor and patient when treatments do not turn out as anticipated.[19]

Mediation is now used routinely in the construction industry. When sewer lines failed on a hospital project in Maryland, for example, the owner sued four contractors, the architect, and two engineers for the cost of repairs. The contractors responded that the design professionals were responsible for any error; the architect and engineers were unanimous in blaming construction defects. Observing that the "attorneys were hopelessly mired in that ritual called a 'pleading war,' legal expenses were mounting daily and the suit appeared headed for protracted litigation," claims adjusters from DPIC companies, which insure architects and engineers, suggested mediation.[20]

The case settled at the first mediation session, with all but one defendant contributing to the cost of repairs. (The other parties agreed that one designer owed nothing.) According to the insurance company, "The settlement was fair and expedient, and everyone saved thousands of legal expense dollars, not to mention months of litigation. More significant, perhaps, is the fact that an insured's working relationship with the owner/client was preserved for future projects." One of the defendants recalls:

> In spite of the pain and cost of the affair, several things stand out clearly. ... I was impressed by the work of the mediator. She did a remarkable job of probing, steering, setting limits and structuring the whole process. ... I hope I am never involved in another suit. We are making every effort to avoid it. But should it happen, rest assured I shall look first at mediation.[21]

Participants in DPIC-sponsored mediation efforts have been particularly pleased that settlements did not necessarily "split the difference." This fact is particularly important to professionals sued for malpractice, who fear being pressured to pay something in order to settle a claim and avoid adverse publicity and the policy's requirement that the insured pay the deductible amount if found liable. DPIC cites another construction case in which an architect who had no responsibility for supervising the reconstruction phase of a church renovation project he had designed was threatened by an owner's suit for defects in the reconstruction. Through mediation the parties agreed on a repair scheme. Their agreement completely released the architect from responsibility.

In an effort to get more construction disputes into mediation, the American Institute of Architects, the American Consulting Engineers Council, the American Society of Civil Engineers, and the National Realty Committee jointly sponsored an experimental mediation project with the Center for Dispute Settlement in Washington, D.C. The project's purpose was to experiment with using experienced mediators to settle construction disputes and to preserve ongoing business relationships among the disputants. Reacting to a successful mediation among an architectural firm, an engineering firm, a property owner, and their lawyers, Jay Adam of Soils Engineering Services, Inc., of Whippany, New Jersey, commented: "After five hours CDS mediators guided us to an agreement over a matter that had been litigated for almost three years; and the fee was less than 5% of what we had already spent on legal costs. We would recommend mediation to any group of adversaries wanting an agreement without a protracted lawsuit."[22]

Attempting to move beyond using mediation only on a dispute-by-dispute basis, participants in some large construction projects have instituted a process called "partnering" to settle disputes on an ongoing basis. In what the *Wall Street Journal* termed "group therapy for the construction industry,"[23] the process involves all participants in a project's meeting off-site to air their complaints, aided by a preselected mediator. The dual goal is to prevent disputes and to resolve them before they cause expensive interruptions, delays, and cost overruns. Begun by the U.S. Army Corps of Engineers, partnering is now required on all jobs commissioned by several federal and local government agencies.

When Does a Settlement Process Make Sense?

Disputing businesses and their lawyers now have an array of settlement processes from which to choose. Over 90 percent of all civil cases filed in U.S. courts do settle before the court decides. In most cases, however, settlements continue to take place "on the courthouse steps," whether figuratively or literally, or even mid-trial, when treasuries are depleted and emotions spent. Thus, when to focus on settlement, as well as which process to use, is a critical question. Although there is no litmus test, several considerations may be helpful:

1. What is the relationship of the disputing firms or their principals? The greater the potential of ongoing business relations, the more critical it is to find a settlement option that will preserve them. Disputes between businesses with ongoing relationships are particularly appropriate for mediation. They also cry out for speedy resolution—before any remaining desire for continued dealings is frayed beyond repair.

2. What kind of outcome is desirable? The need for establishing a principle to govern future cases (or, occasionally, for sending a message to future litigants that they cannot sue a particular company without fear of annihilation) may argue against any settlement. The difficulty is that principles often get lost in the fray of litigation and end up being settled anyway—much less effectively than if the business managers were in a position to discuss them from the start. Alternatively, principles sometimes can be established by business experts instead of by courts. Particularly when creative options are imaginable—be they tradeoffs of different property, reciprocal actions, or joint ventures—settlement processes should be considered.

3. How useful would it be to have the business principals themselves involved in developing the outcome? The benefits of active participation argue strongly for negotiation, mediation, or minitrials—all with principals present.

4. How high are emotions running? Although anger and thirst for revenge may propel litigants into the courtroom, face-to-face mediation, with ample opportunity for everyone to vent emotions, often clears the air and permits disputants to focus on future results.

5. Are the costs of battle likely to be high in proportion to the expected returns? Even managers who order their lawyers to pursue a "scorched-earth" strategy sometimes become interested in alternatives once they receive their first litigation-spawned legal bill.

6. Is speed important? Virtually all the settlement options are faster than litigation. Yet many lawyers become stymied by their need for more information about the details of a dispute before they believe they responsibly can advise their clients to pursue settlement. The need for speed (and its effect on litigation-related costs) argues for finding creative ways of obtaining needed information without waiting for the discovery process to run its course.

7. What kinds of information do the parties need before they can focus on settlement? Information on the facts surrounding a particular incident can be obtained in a number of ways. One of the most obvious is to use pretrial discovery tools—but in a limited, carefully crafted way. If the parties are in mediation, they can agree on what information they need and how to go about getting it. Technical information may require the services of one or more experts; early agreement on a neutral expert can

speed resolution. The need for information on the probable outcome of a particular factual dispute—or of an entire case if it were to go to trial—argues for using a minitrial or a summary jury trial. If the outcome in a case may turn on the credibility of particular witnesses with differing versions of an event or transaction, the parties might consider having those witnesses questioned in front of the business principals, who then may be ready to negotiate (or mediate) a settlement based on what they have learned. Finally, information on the interests and priorities of the disputants can be obtained best by involving them directly in negotiations— with a mediator if they are unwilling to confide in one another.

8. How important is it to keep private the details of a particular dispute, such as one involving trade secrets? All of the settlement options discussed offer greater privacy than a public trial. Mediation, which permits confidential discussions between the parties and the mediator, offers the greatest amount of privacy.

Planning for Business Disputes

As businesses and their lawyers become more experienced in using creative ways to settle disputes, the wiser among them are including plans for dispute settlement in their initial arrangements to do business. When entering into a contract, businesses can agree in advance to negotiate, then mediate, then use a neutral expert or an arbitrator to deal with any disagreements that may arise. As a first step, for example, one licensing agreement between the developer and the marketer of computer software specifies:

> Whenever the LIAISON of the two parties are unable to agree on any matter arising in the implementation of this Agreement ... the matter shall be referred to the two REPRESENTATIVES who shall jointly resolve it. In the event that the REPRESENTATIVES are unable to resolve a disagreement within a mutually acceptable period of time, they shall jointly so notify the chief executive officers of the parties. No lawsuit or other proceeding may be filed by one party against the other for 30 days after the date of the REPRESENTATIVES' notice except. ...

Standard contract wording now exists to provide for negotiation and mediation, along with the more usual arbitration clauses. For example, the American Institute of Architects, in support of its pilot mediation project, suggested that members use one of two alternative mediation clauses in all their contracts. The simpler provision reads as follows: "If a dispute arises out of or relates to this contract, or the breach thereof, and if said dispute cannot be settled through direct discussions, the parties agree to first endeavor to settle the dispute in an amicable manner by mediation through the Construction Mediation Service before having recourse to arbitration or a judicial forum." Some contracts even name the outside neutrals who will mediate or arbitrate should dissension arise.

Although agreements to arbitrate have been made enforceable by federal and state laws, agreements to mediate have not been dealt with specifically by legislation. So far, however, federal courts faced with litigation by parties who originally agreed to try mediation (or submission to a nonbinding, advisory opinion) before coming to court have enforced their agreement.[24]

Managers and their attorneys should consider making similar provisions a part of their standard contracting terms and conditions. The processes then become part of the routine of disputing and less reliant on the fortuitous presence of imaginative executives or attorneys to dream them up on the spot. Nor does a party wishing to explore settlement have to consider the real or (more often) perceived strategic consequences of being the first to broach the subject. On the contrary, the party that invokes the dispute resolution provisions of an existing contract can do so as an affirmative step toward enforcing its rights under the contract.

5

Settling Consumer and Employment Disputes

THE GROWING LITERATURE ON NEGOTIATION and mediation in business settings reminds corporate managers and their attorneys that negotiation is a way of life that need not be limited to settling disputes with other businesses. People in business negotiate regularly with their superiors and their subordinates (at least if they care about having them do what they are told). They also negotiate daily with people they cannot command but whose cooperation is necessary if products are to be produced and delivered: production, sales, advertising, and financing divisions; and "task forces" assigned to specific jobs.

Some businesses also have decided that developing innovative ways of handling complaints by consumers or employees can improve their public image, their sales, and their relations with their workers. Innovations such as Citibank's Peer Group Problem Review Procedure and Chrysler's Customer Satisfaction Program were established with employee or customer goodwill as well as avoidance of court in mind. The consumer complaint handler for City Light Company of Seattle, for example, reported that the institution of a company complaint procedure, which responds to consumers' concerns about rate increases, billing, credit, and collection practices, had done more to enhance the utility's public image than any other innovation in the company's history.

When businesses sell to other businesses, they have available all the possibilities for settling disputes that were discussed in the previous chapter. For example, the manufacturer of the fast-selling Toyotas fashioned a specialized arbitration system to resolve disputes with its dealers over allocation of the scarce cars. As a result of the virtual elimination of lawsuits by its dealers, Toyota now includes a clause in all new franchise agreements binding dealers to participate in dispute resolution programs established by the company.

When businesses deal with individual customers, however, it is not clear whether they can require them to participate in company-sponsored dispute resolution programs instead of going to court. Some banks are attempting to institute arbitration of customer complaints on a mandatory basis. Bank of America, the first to do so, adopted a policy to require all of its deposit and bankcard customers to submit complaints against it to binding arbitration. According to the company, customers share in the choice of the arbitrator and stand to benefit from savings in litigation costs and time. Advocates for consumers, in contrast, warn that customers lose various rights incident to a courtroom trial, especially their right to appeal. Customers generally are unaware that they are "agreeing" not to use the courts for future disputes when they open a bank account or purchase a bankcard. Advocates also fear that the arbitration may be biased in favor of the bank because it pays the arbitration fee. Consequently, they assert that arbitration should not be imposed unilaterally on individual customers.

Responding to a different mandatory arbitration scheme devised by ITT, a division of the California Court of Appeals recently refused to enforce a mandatory arbitration clause in a consumer loan agreement, finding that it was "unconscionable" because the transactions involved small amounts of money, consumers were required to pay a fee before their claims could be heard (the opposite of the Bank of America situation), and the arbitration would be conducted in a state where the consumers did not reside.[1] Whether similar agreements involving no prehearing fee requirements and a convenient forum would be enforced remains to be decided.

The Wells Fargo Bank has attempted to avoid these criticisms by instituting a customer dispute resolution program that does not require binding arbitration; instead, its program applies only to claims of over $25,000 and offers mediation. If no agreement results, the customer may choose between a "rent-a-judge" trial, with rights of judicial appeal preserved, and binding arbitration. (Conventional trials still are not an option.)

Investors have lodged complaints similar to those about Bank of America's arbitration scheme against the securities industry, which for some time has required its customers to pursue their disputes through arbitration. In the wake of the 1987 stock market decline around "Black Monday," investors holding margin or option accounts wanted to sue their stockbrokers for fraud in order to recoup some of their damages, but they discovered that their initial agreements contained mandatory arbitration clauses. The agreements limited them to arbitration procedures sponsored by the various stock exchanges as the sole remedy against their brokers. Earlier that year the Supreme Court had ruled that an agreement to arbitrate any future claims was enforceable even if the customer later charged the broker with fraud.[2]

Angry investors complained to the federal Securities and Exchange Commission, its state counterparts, and members of Congress about their inability to sue their brokers in federal or state courts. The New York Stock Exchange produced some evidence from a survey it had commissioned that the average arbitration involving a member firm is faster, less expensive, and provides customers with a greater percentage of their claim than does litigation. Nonetheless, dissatisfied investors and their lawyers leveled several charges: that they were unaware they were agreeing to arbitrate when they signed their initial brokerage agreements; that they received inadequate information about the process or the background of the arbitrators; that arbitration panels were dominated by people with industry ties; that discovery procedures were unavailable; and that it was impossible to learn the results of similar proceedings involving other investors.

These problems have become especially important because of the dramatic growth of the securities industry and the corresponding increase in the number of securities arbitrations. Between 1980 and 1990, the number of arbitrations filed with securities self-regulating organizations multiplied by more than five, from 830 in 1980 to 5,332 in 1990.[3] Attempts by the Massachusetts and Florida legislatures to prohibit brokers from requiring arbitration agreements as a condition of opening an account were struck down by federal courts as contrary to federal law. A bill introduced in Congress that would have prohibited brokers from requiring such agreements failed to pass. The SEC, which had unanimously opposed the federal bill, directed the brokers' own self-regulatory organizations to submit their suggestions for improvement. In response, the New York Stock Exchange proposed to add language to members' agreements to arbitrate warning customers that the agreement waives their right to sue their brokers. The exchange also proposed to clarify which arbitrators had ties to the securities industry; to require disclosure of biographical information about arbitrators; to formalize discovery procedures; and to require the public release of summaries of disputes, with damages requested and awarded in every arbitration. Despite numerous charges that these proposals do not go far enough, the SEC approved them without amendment or the addition of any of its own guidelines. The General Accounting Office, on behalf of the Congress, studied securities arbitration and found no evidence of industry bias; however, it proposed that the SEC require the self-regulating organizations to establish formal standards for selecting arbitrators, verifying information about them, and ensuring that arbitrators are properly trained.

When dealing with both customers and employees, businesses seek finality, some degree of predictability, and reduction of transaction costs. Also critical, at least with customers and current employees, are the maintenance of profitable ongoing relationships and the avoidance of harmful publicity. In the long run, businesses may discover that giving their customers and employees some choice of process, or adopting multitiered procedures in which mediation precedes any attempt at seeking a binding decision by an outsider to the dispute, does more to meet their goals than litigating over their ability to commit their customers (or their employees, as discussed later in the chapter) in advance to binding arbitration.

When Customers Complain

Only a very few dissatisfied consumers use any third-party complaint mechanism, whether through the courts, private associations (such as a stock exchange or Better Business Bureau), government consumer offices, or media action lines. Most customers do not even complain directly to the sellers of goods or services they find unsatisfactory. According to a detailed survey published in 1977 by Ralph Nader's Center for Responsive Law, consumers took no action at all in about a third of the instances in which they were dissatisfied with products or services. In close to another third, they complained directly to sellers or, more often, returned goods for refunds. In slightly more than 6 percent of the cases, they simply changed brands or dealers in the future. Only in 1.2 percent of the instances of consumer dissatisfaction did customers complain to any sort of third party. "Thus," the report concludes, "sellers have a near perfect monopoly on complaint handling."[4]

Even potentially serious injuries prompt only a fraction of consumers to take action. An illustration of this phenomenon has appeared in the litigation involving injuries to women who wore the Dalkon shield as a birth control device. Over a fourteen-year period, approximately 15,000 court cases were filed against the manufacturer. The company then declared bankruptcy. Francis McGovern, the court-appointed special master, was given the initial responsibility for devising a plan to compensate injured consumers out of the remaining funds. McGovern sent out notices urging women to file their claims in the bankruptcy proceeding or be forever barred from collecting. He received over 300,000 responses, between 200,000 and 250,000 of which turned out to be actual claims against the company.

In a 1987 speech, McGovern speculated that these cases, representing approximately 93 percent of the total number of claims, would not have come into the system under ordinary circumstances. Presumably, hundreds of thousands of women, despite their injuries, never would have filed claims had it not been for the company-generated publicity. Together with surveys of consumer dissatisfaction, this example indicates that what appears to have been a flood of product liability litigation over the past several years is in fact dwarfed by the number of unvoiced complaints.

Consumers may feel ignorant about the technical aspects of products or services, particularly cars, appliances, home construction or repairs, and medical care. People may be intimidated by their ignorance or feel power-less in comparison with large, or at least knowledgeable, corporations or professionals. Buying a product, particularly an expensive one, is a rare transaction for the individual consumer. Yet it is a repeat transaction for the seller. As Wisconsin law professor Marc Galanter wrote in the 1970s:

> The contract, grant license, or other transaction—even the accident—is rou-tine for the organization, which designs the transaction. If trouble develops, the occasion is typically one of a kind for the individual—it is an emergency or at least a disruption of routine propelling them into an area of hazard and uncertainty. For the organization (usually a business or government unit), on the other hand, making (or defending against) such claims is typically a routine and recurrent activity.[5]

Businesses must take this phenomenon into account if methods of resolv-ing consumer disputes are to achieve customer loyalty by being, in the words of General Motors' David A. Collins, "good, fair [and] fast."[6]

If a consumer decides to pursue a complaint, several possible avenues exist. Increasingly, neighborhood and citywide mediation centers, such as those in Washington, D.C., Houston, and Atlanta, mediate complaints be-tween individuals and businesses as part of their broader caseload. To date, however, their clientele largely has been limited to small businesses and their customers. Small claims courts, together with the mediation pro-grams that are attached to them in a growing number of cities, attempt to settle the tiny proportion of small money disputes between businesses and their customers that actually reach the courthouse.

In addition to these general dispute settlement possibilities, large num-bers of specialized consumer programs exist solely to resolve disputes be-tween businesses and their customers. The U.S. Office of Consumer Af-fairs lists over 500 such programs, three-quarters of them less than twenty years old, in addition to those run by individual companies for complaints by their own customers. Most of the independent programs are operated by government agencies at the city, county, or state level. Some are spon-sored by approximately 54 trade associations (including the National As-sociation of Home Builders, the National Home Study Council, the Direct-Marketing Association, and the National Food Processors Association) and by more than 160 Better Business Bureaus. Still others are run by newspapers, radio, or television stations, which attempt to deal with busi-nesses on behalf of consumers. Beyond these methods, companies increas-ingly are developing their own programs, such as the nearly 4,000 com-plaint handlers who now work in hospitals throughout the country to respond to patients' concerns.

Fourteen major industries sponsor dispute resolution programs. The oldest, the Major Appliance Consumer Action Plan (MACAP), was created in 1968. It uses a panel of nine experts, none of whom is employed full-time in the appliance industry, to give nonbinding evaluations of consumers' complaints.

AUTOCAP, operated by the National Automobile Dealers Association in 47 states or major metropolitan areas, handles complaints involving several foreign automobile manufacturers and approximately two-thirds of all U.S. auto dealerships. AUTOCAP panels have both dealer and consumer members (consumers must constitute at least half of each panel) and make recommendations that participating dealers are "bound in good faith" (in other words, not legally) to honor.

The most prevalent types of complaints brought to the various consumer programs involve automobile repairs and other issues related to car purchases, landlord-tenant disputes, and problems with mail orders. The methods used include telephone conciliation by government offices or trade associations, investigation and recommendations or public denunciation of uncooperative businesses by media action lines, investigation and possible revocation of licenses by government agencies, and (occasionally) binding arbitration. The attractiveness of most of these methods often lies in their simplicity and, sometimes, their easy accessibility. Their drawbacks are their frequent inability to obtain the cooperation of irresponsible businesses and the usual absence of any face-to-face contact between a representative of the business and the customer. In light of the growing evidence of the importance of personal participation in resolving disputes, this feature has a decided disadvantage.

Programs whose only contact with consumers is by telephone face the difficult task of balancing some sort of "hearing" for the parties involved against the huge numbers of callers that must be dealt with every day. (Even a tiny percentage of all instances of consumers' dissatisfaction can produce a huge number of complaints.) It is difficult to earn disputants' trust when they never see complaint handlers and (except for occasional conference calling) when the disputants never speak directly with each other. Some programs require consumers to put complaints in writing, thus making resolution even less accessible (and presumably less satisfying) to many.

A few programs involving large consumer purchases (primarily automobiles, houses, or major appliances) offer face-to-face mediation or arbitration between businesses and their customers. Many of them are operated by trade associations or industries. The best known of the arbitration panels exist in the automobile industry, where they were developed to reduce lawsuits by dissatisfied purchasers of new cars and to increase customer satisfaction both with specific purchases and with the companies who provide them. Generally the results of arbitration bind the companies but not the consumers. Remedies most commonly include returning to the dealer for repairs; consumers sometimes receive a full refund or replacement of a defective car. Few of the programs award "consequential damages," such as money for lost time from work due to repeated trips for repairs.

The largest program for resolving auto-related disputes out of court is the Better Business Bureau's Auto-Line, which operates under contract with several manufacturers, including General Motors. With approximately ten major car makers precommitted to be bound by the outcome of the BBB's arbitration proceedings, and with some 7,000 volunteer arbitrators around the country, the BBB handles close to 100,000 cases a year. The vast majority of these complaints are resolved by telephone conciliation. In most, the BBB simply gives the consumer the name of the proper person to contact; the consumer then negotiates directly with the manufacturer or dealer. In other cases, BBB staff telephone back and forth between the manufacturer and consumer to bring about a settlement. In some instances no settlement is achieved and the consumer may choose to sell the vehicle, sue, or drop the case altogether.

In the remaining cases (10,500 in 1992), the consumer opts for arbitration. Arbitrators are volunteers who have no connection with the automobile industry; they receive three hours' training. Of the disputes going to arbitration, the BBB reports, 20 percent of consumers are awarded either all or part of their request. According to BBB statistics, two-thirds of the consumers choose to accept the results of the arbitration.

A survey conducted by Consumer Dynamics International indicated that state and local government officials who deal with consumer affairs generally like the idea of arbitration between consumers and automobile manufacturers. However, they believe that the arbitrators, generally volunteers, need additional training and that customers should be given better information about the programs. They rank the effectiveness of trade association-sponsored programs such as the BBB's more highly than that of the programs sponsored directly by Chrysler and Ford. (It is not clear whether the performance of the different programs actually varies or whether those sponsored directly by manufacturers have an insuperable image problem.) Despite the perceived flaws, over 90 percent of the government officials surveyed advised consumers to file their complaints about automobile purchases with an automobile arbitration panel if one is available.[7]

Increasing numbers of state "lemon laws," which entitle consumers to a rebate or a new car if they have recurring complaints during the warranty period, require consumers to go to an arbitration program if it meets certain prescribed standards, before suing the manufacturer. Some states, including Connecticut, Massachusetts, and Maryland, have responded by setting up their own mediation and arbitration programs. In Connecticut, arbitration panels use an independent expert to advise them on technical issues in order to balance the manufacturers' technical advantage.

Since the FTC drafted standards for approval in 1975, several states have imposed their own, more stringent requirements with regard to automobile warranty disputes. The FTC attempted to convene representatives of automobile manufacturers and dealers, state governments, and consumers in a "regulatory negotiation" (of the type discussed in Chapter 7) to revise the agency's standards. Under the federal Magnuson-Moss Warranty Act, manufacturers with informal dispute resolution procedures approved by the Federal Trade Commission may require consumers to use the procedures before suing the manufacturer. The FTC-sponsored negotiations ended in stalemate when the automobile industry representatives insisted on a single national standard and consumer and local government representatives refused to cede the stronger state requirements. Industry representatives continue to be concerned about the resulting lack of uniformity; consumer representatives are interested in strengthening and enforcing existing standards, regardless of whether they may vary from state to state.

Most of the government-sponsored consumer programs and some of those instituted by the trade associations go beyond informal dispute resolution and refer customers to court in unresolvable cases. Sometimes attorney generals or consumer affairs offices use the programs to bring court actions against businesses in what they consider to be egregious cases.

In complaints involving flagrant practices by businesses that bilk consumers, critics have pointed out that informal settlement efforts, unlike courts, cannot contribute to broad solutions. As a former director of the National Consumer Law Center put it:

> The private, settlement-oriented approach of arbitration and mediation will not deter future unfair practices. ... These forums can at best provide only limited relief in individual cases brought before them. They cannot provide the deterrents and broad remedial relief which is often needed when industry-wide practices are exploiting consumers or certain merchants are engaging in exceptionally abusive practices.[8]

In order to connect fast resolution for large numbers of consumers with enforcement efforts in egregious cases, some government-sponsored offices now offer informal settlement as a first step, with referral to investigation and possible litigation if settlement efforts do not succeed. Most independent third-party complaint handlers, associated neither with the businesses complained about nor with their trade associations, agree that they need more effective ways of linking individual settlement efforts with developing evidence of widespread problems. Barbara Gregg, director of the Office of Consumer Affairs for Montgomery County, Maryland, argues that government-run consumer agencies are in a far better position than trade associations or industries themselves to combine individual dispute settlement with prevention of deceptive practices in the marketplace.[9]

Mediating Between Farmers and Lenders

State legislatures in the farm belt, followed by Congress, have turned to mediation in their effort to deal with the crisis in loans to farmers. Nationally, farmers are in debt by an estimated $200 billion to banks, insurance companies, and federal agencies such as the Federal Land Bank and the Farmers Home Administration (FmHA). Newly created programs offer mediation between farmers and lenders in an effort to stave off foreclosure.

In the spring of 1986, Iowa and Minnesota enacted legislation requiring creditors to attempt mediation before beginning proceedings for foreclosure or repossession of farmers' property. Both states previously had experimented with voluntary farm mediation programs. At the same time, Wisconsin chose to retain its voluntary program, which provides simply that a "farmer or creditor wishing to resolve a dispute between them involving the farmer's agricultural property and the creditor's interest ... may participate in mediation."

Once programs were in place in these three states, other farm states quickly followed suit. North Dakota also appropriated $200,000 to establish a legal and tax assistance program to help "financially distressed farmers." The program requires that any person helping a farmer to use legal means to resolve financial difficulties attempt to "use mediation, negotiation, and amicable settlements" to resolve conflicts.

In all the state programs, either farmers or creditors may request mediation. Most farmers seek to mediate only after a creditor has moved to foreclose on mortgaged property. In this situation, a farmer in the states with mandatory programs may demand mediation, as long as the debts secured by agricultural property exceed a specified figure ($20,000 in Iowa, $25,000 in Minnesota). All of the farmer's creditors whose liens exceed the amount set by the legislation must participate. (A mediation in Minnesota involved a farm couple and their twenty-eight creditors.) A creditor may not proceed to enforce its rights against the farmer until mediation has been completed, the farmer has failed to participate, or, in Iowa, the parties have attended one mediation session and failed to reach an agreement.

The Iowa legislation was developed through bargaining between representatives of lenders, farmers' organizations, and farmers' advocates. Minnesota's program was shaped by a legislative committee, which creditors charged shut them out of its final deliberations. Perhaps as a result, there appears to have been far more opposition to the program in Minnesota than in Iowa.

Minnesota's Farmer-Lender Mediation Act goes beyond Iowa's requirement of attendance at one mediation session and contains an unusual provision obliging all parties to mediate in "good faith." Parties must attend and participate in mediation sessions for a sixty-day period, which may be extended if the mediator finds lack of good faith. Creditors must release to the farmer necessary living and farm-operating expenses while mediation is in progress. Mediators are responsible for reporting a lack of good faith participation in mediation to the court responsible for foreclosure proceedings. If the mediator finds a farmer in bad faith, the creditor may proceed to enforce its liens. Creditors' failure to mediate in good faith carries severe penalties, which include suspending all the creditors' remedies against the debtor and taxing creditors with the farmers' costs. An early challenge to the law's constitutionality was rejected by the Minnesota Court of Appeals.

Mediation is confidential in all of the programs. Although it is difficult to determine how severely Minnesota mediators' responsibility for reporting lack of good faith to the court undercuts this protection, Kathy Mangum, director of the Minnesota Farm Credit Mediation Program, has questioned the wisdom of the provision and its effect on participants' perceptions of mediators as fair or unbiased. Contrary to early predictions, approximately three-quarters of the initial affidavits citing lack of good faith were filed against farmers.[10]

So far all mediators have been volunteers, primarily farmers and ministers, who have been trained for approximately thirty-two hours. In an effort to equalize the power between farmers and their creditors, Minnesota provides a credit analyst, who meets with each farmer before mediation to produce a balance sheet, an analysis of cash flow, and a three-year financing plan. Minnesota also furnishes a "farm advocate" to counsel the farmer on legal rights and duties. The majority of farmers entering mediation so far have taken advantage of both of these services. In Iowa, the university extension program and legal services offices are available to work with farmers before mediation.

During the first year of mandatory mediation in Minnesota, about 2,000 agreements resulted from 4,300 mediation sessions—close to a 50-percent settlement rate. Most of these cases involved three to four creditors. Settlements included lowering interest rates, refinancing loans, or rescheduling payments, together with devising agreements to govern the future financial relations between the parties. Mediations lasted from one to eight sessions, or an average of three meetings per case.

In contrast to the large numbers of mediations in states with mandatory programs (Iowa alone has close to 6,000), voluntary programs go begging. Wisconsin and Montana, where programs must persuade lenders to participate once farmers request mediation, between them have mediated only about 100 cases.

A spokesman for the federal Farm Credit System's regional office, which originally opposed the program, now lauds it as fair and its staff as "extremely sensitive to make sure they're not seen as advocates of farmers or financially troubled lenders. They're neutral. They don't force anything on the borrower or the lender."[11] Representatives of Prairiefire, an organization that advocates on behalf of distressed farmers, estimate that at least 30 percent of their clients who participate in mediation are satisfied with the results. They consider this number encouraging in light of the farmers' situation when they enter mediation and the fairly minimal training received by the mediators to date. Prairiefire actively supported the enactment of legislation in Congress to extend mandatory farmer-lender mediation to the entire country.

As a result of the state programs' initial success, the Agricultural Credit Act of 1987 authorized matching grants of up to $50,000 to states to finance their efforts to mediate farm loan disputes. Subsequent congressional legislation increased the matching grant level to 70 percent of the cost of any state program or $500,000, whichever is lower, and extended the authorization of federal funds.[12] In order to receive federal funds, the programs must (1) provide mediation services that result, if decisions are reached, in mutual agreements between producers and creditors; (2) be administered or authorized by a state; (3) provide for training of mediators; (4) provide that sessions are confidential; and (5) ensure that mediation programs are publicized. Under the legislation, the Department of Agriculture's Farmers Home Administration made fiscal 1992 appropriations to nineteen states. The federal law also prohibits lenders from conditioning loans on waiver of mediation rights and requires all federally supported farm credit institutions to participate in "good faith" in any state agricultural loan mediation program and to present proposals for restructuring debts in the course of mediation.

The Administrative Conference of the United States (ACUS), which promotes improvements in the way federal agencies administer their regulatory programs, has recommended some changes in farmer-lender mediation. Spurred by a recent study of the FmHA's administration of the act, ACUS recommends the adoption of a broader approach to mediation and loan restructuring than a number of states have been using. Under such an approach, the mediation addresses the entire circumstances surrounding a dispute, not simply an attempt to restructure the debt. Mediators search for the parties' underlying interests, address other family and personal problems that may have an impact on the situation, and help the parties to develop creative solutions, such as off-farm employment, that answer their needs. In making this recommendation, ACUS explained that the most successful programs have used the broader approach, which has a greater likelihood of resolving farmer-lender disputes.

ACUS also recommends that the FmHA step up its efforts to inform farmers about the program and to encourage other federal agencies, such as the FDIC, RTC, IRS, and the Small Business Administration, to participate in it. The regional IRS office in Wisconsin has responded enthusiastically to such encouragements by participating in all mediation sessions when requested.[13]

Resolving Employment Disputes

Businesses have crucial ongoing relationships not only with their suppliers and customers but with their own employees. As various merit pay and promotion standards are structured in more sophisticated ways in order to induce employees' cooperation, there is a growing recognition that negotiation, even with subordinates, is the most effective way of achieving compliance with company goals. Sophisticated managers also understand that their jobs include the frequent mediation of disputes among individual employees or across company divisions. Even where it is theoretically possible to command whatever outcome a manager may desire, observant bosses perceive that employees will be more cooperative as well as more satisfied if they are involved in developing their own solutions.

From the employees' perspective, the relationship with employers is the most critical one that most people have with any institution. Approximately 15 percent of employees in the United States belong to a union. Unionized employees are covered by collective bargaining contracts, which contain multistep grievance procedures for settling complaints against employers. Access to grievance procedures is channeled through the unions, which decide what complaints to pursue and represent members in the process. The procedures usually culminate in binding arbitration.

Even in this relatively well developed sector, there have been recent strains, many of them caused by the shrinking market for blue-collar labor. In the coal industry in the 1970s, however, a series of often violent wildcat strikes was traced to the inadequacy of the grievance process itself. The strikes took place while contracts were in effect, despite their explicit no-strike provisions. In trying to determine the cause of the strikes, labor arbitrator Steve Goldberg, anthropologist Bill Ury, and researcher Jeanne Brett noted how small a role workers and their supervisors had in solving their own work-related problems. Once a miner raised a grievance, the union and company representatives would take charge and argue about contractual technicalities far removed from the actual cause of the dispute. Although he typically attended the arbitration hearing, the miner was only a passive observer of the process. Decisions, which were long in coming, generally denied the grievance, frequently in language that was incomprehensible to the miner.

In an effort to make the grievance process more responsive to the workers' concerns, the Goldberg-Ury-Brett team devised an experiment, which, interestingly, had much in common with the early experiments with mediation in prisons. Miners and their supervisors met informally with outside mediators, who helped them to discuss the problem and create options for solving it. Some were given the opportunity to choose mediation, others were referred automatically. If the parties were unable to reach an informal resolution in a single meeting, the mediator provided an additional spur to settlement by attempting to predict how an arbitrator would rule on the grievance.

The results were impressive: Of 153 mediation conferences held during the experiment's first year, 136 (89 percent) resulted in settlements. The rates of settlement were the same regardless of whether the parties volunteered to mediate or were sent to mediation automatically as part of the grievance process. The average cost per case was $295, as compared with $1,034 for an arbitration, and the average time fifteen days, as opposed to 109 in arbitration.

A substantial majority of the participants preferred mediation to arbitration: mine operators by a ratio of six to one and union officers by seven to one. According to one mine operator, "You aren't left with a bad taste in your mouth after mediation. Arbitration is a semihostile environment, a win-lose situation. This lets a guy blow off steam right in front of you." The operator noted with pride that even with 739 hourly employees, not one grievance had gone to arbitration in three years. A union representative agreed that dealings between union and management at some of the companies had become more cooperative and less aggressive. "Mediation shows that things can be talked out and settled, even if not always."

Most participants agreed that compliance with mediated settlements was easier to obtain than compliance with arbitration awards. In sum, the experiment succeeded not only in reducing sharply the number of wildcat strikes but in giving individual miners a greater feeling of control over their problems.[14] It has spread slowly to other industries, including telecommunications and retail sales.

Spurred by a variety of motives, growing numbers of nonunion employers have begun to develop internal procedures for settling disputes between employees and management and, sometimes, among individual employees or groups of employees. One incentive for creating such procedures, which grow or shrink in importance depending on the sympathies of the observer, is to make unionizing less attractive to employees. Another is to avoid litigation. A third is to increase productivity by attending to workers' satisfaction.

As federal, state, and local governments have passed legislation designed to protect workers, employees have gone both to courts and to administrative agencies to change their employers' practices or to recover damages for past transgressions. The United States Equal Employment Opportunity Commission (EEOC) projected that it would receive a record 86,000 charges in 1993, a 32 percent increase in its pending caseload since the preceding year. With additional laws enacted and no additional resources to enforce them, the average caseload of each individual EEOC investigator grew from 62.98 in 1992 to 96.3 as of the third quarter of FY 1993. These numbers mean that each investigator faces the task of resolving a case every 3.5 days. At the same time, over 10,000 cases a year alleging employment discrimination are being filed in federal or state courts.

Lawsuits often involve claims of discrimination based on a long list of criteria (generally race, sex, religion, age, nationality, or handicap) or on-the-job exposure to unhealthy or unsafe conditions. Both the Civil Rights Act of 1991 and the Americans With Disabilities Act establish new rights for employees and causes of action to enforce them. Even where no special laws exist, courts in some states have begun to give dismissed employees the right to sue their former employers for wrongful discharge. According to an estimate by the Educational Fund for Individual Rights, approximately 20,000 unjust discharge cases were pending in state courts in 1988; the number now undoubtedly is higher.[15]

Company handbooks or personnel manuals have been construed as employer-worker contracts that prevent employees from being demoted or fired without specified reasons and procedures. Yet reliance on these handbooks by employees may give their employers an opportunity to require them to use internal grievance procedures before they seek help from the courts, even if they have not signed an agreement requiring them to do so. In 1991, a federal court in New Jersey ruled that fired employees who rely on employee handbooks to protect them from termination must exhaust the grievance procedures contained in the handbooks before they can file a lawsuit. The court reasoned that if employees assert that an employee handbook is an implied contract of employment, they must abide by the implied contract in its entirety.[16]

Some forward-looking employers cite two additional reasons for trying to develop responsive employee complaint mechanisms. One is their desire to receive accurate feedback of employees' complaints about management, line supervisors, plant safety, or other internal problems. Sophisticated managers have come to recognize that traditional, even widely broadcast "open door" policies that encourage employees to talk to their supervisors or even top management at any time do not elicit more than a small fraction of employees' complaints. The only reliable way to get this information is by providing employees with safe, sensitive channels of communication and resolution.

Finally, an obvious motive is that anything managers can do within reason to increase their workers' job satisfaction will boost not only morale but productivity and thus, ultimately, their own profits. With various forms of merit pay and group incentive plans being adopted by increasing numbers of private firms, schools, and government agencies, many organizations find complaints on the rise. (Surveys show that approximately 80 percent of U.S. workers believe their performance to be better than the norm. Yet typical merit pay plans reward fewer than half of all employees.)

As a result of these varied incentives, more than one-third of all nonunionized employees in the United States now have at least one company-run dispute resolution procedure open to them for dealing with any type of complaint. Others have access to ways of resolving certain types of complaints, usually those involving discrimination or sexual harassment. Still other employers make complaint processes available only to employees paid by the hour, excluding higher-level, salaried personnel.

Some employers have attempted to formalize their "open door" policies into multi-level grievance procedures, which require responses from each level of management within specified time periods and provide at least theoretical protection from reprisals taken against employees who complain. The four-step procedure adopted by a large hospital is typical. It provides for

1. Formalized response from the employee's supervisor
2. Response from the next level of management
3. Response from the division chairperson
4. Response from the "right of review" committee

The "right of review" committee in this instance consists of a cross-section of managers and supervisors who have been given training about fair procedures, arbitration, and grievance procedures in general.

A few organizations have broadened the membership of this type of committee to include lower-level employees. Others permit an employee with a grievance to name one or two members of the committee that considers the complaint. Whatever the composition, common to this type of procedure is formality, procedural protection for the employee (such as a right to appear at committee hearings, to present evidence, and to require the other side to make a formal presentation), and a formal decision by the committee. The decision may be binding or advisory.

General Electric's "peer review" system places the resolution of disputes in the hands of a complainant's (generally blue-collar) fellow employees and managers. Panels of employees, a majority of whom are nonmanagement, make final and binding decisions, by majority vote. Employee panelists are volunteers who complete an intensive training session. The "peers" review a variety of issues, including discipline and discharge, overtime allocation, promotions, and upgrades. The panels' jurisdiction is limited to questions of whether company policy was followed properly; complaints about pay rates, work rules, and job evaluations are barred.

Other companies have taken notice of GE's apparent success and have established their own peer review programs. Some limit their programs to discharge decisions or performance ratings, whereas others give review panels greater discretion. Common to all peer review programs is that nonmanagement employees constitute a majority of the panel; decisions are final and binding; all proceedings are confidential; and panelists are trained, usually randomly selected, volunteers.

A new trend within the securities industry, whose insistence on mandatory arbitration of claims by investors was discussed earlier in this chapter, is the increasing use of mandatory arbitration of employment disputes. In the 1991 case of *Gilmer v. Inter-state/Johnson Lane Corporation,* the Supreme Court ruled that brokers who sign arbitration agreements for securities disputes have also agreed to arbitrate any future discrimination complaints they may have against the brokerage houses that employ them.[17] The Supreme Court's opinion left open the question of the applicability of its decision outside the securities industry, as well as of the ability of employees covered by mandatory arbitration agreements to file complaints with the EEOC and of subsequent suits by the EEOC against the employers.

So far, at least, the mandatory arbitration schemes in the securities industry are controversial and have not succeeded in avoiding litigation. Nonetheless, some companies outside the securities industry have emulated them and implemented broad arbitration programs. At Rockwell International, for example, high-level current employees are required to sign agreements to arbitrate any future employment disputes as a condition of receiving their annual stock options.

Some employers have elected to forgo formalized procedures, often with multiple steps and hearings, in favor of simpler, more flexible, and often more conciliatory approaches. Growing numbers of corporations are replacing or supplementing their formal procedures with some type of in-house or, occasionally, external "neutrals." One reason, according to the former vice-president for personnel administration at the National Broadcasting Company, is that formal grievance procedures may intimidate nonunionized employees and be seen as competitive by those who belong to unions. The company also wanted to avoid a mechanism that defines employees in adversarial terms, preferring a focus on problem solving and resolution to one on controversy and win-lose decisions. As a result, NBC decided to create an "employee counselor," whose job is to mediate employees' complaints.

Although its creators had expected the vast majority of those using the system to be clerical employees complaining of discrimination, close to half the people talking to the employee counselor turned out to be professional employees concerned with their career mobility or middle managers seeking help in dealing with difficult management problems. Less than one-fifth of the complaints have involved discrimination, even in the minds of the complaining employees.

In a typical case cited by NBC, a white male professional in his late thirties, who had been employed by the corporation for twelve years, complained that he had not been selected for a job for which he considered himself well qualified. On five previous occasions, he had applied for jobs and been turned down. He complained that jobs were awarded on the basis of favoritism and politics rather than merit. He asked the counselor to interview some of the people with whom the employee had worked in order to obtain some anonymous feedback. After the counselor interviewed six people, both supervisors and peers, she reported to the employee that he was widely considered "a pain in the ass." The counselor gave him specific examples of how others saw him, together with suggestions of what he might do to rectify the situation. According to the counselor, the experience made the employee "less openly negative about the company, and a little bit less of a pain in the ass."[18]

In-house neutrals often are called "ombudsmen" or "ombudspeople." Although in the classic Scandinavian model, the ombudsperson never works for the institution he or she is supposed to oversee, in this country the ombudsperson concept has appeared most frequently since the late 1960s as part of the management of a public or private organization. Here, the ombudsperson is considered a neutral member of the corporate structure, located outside the normal managerial chain of command and reporting directly to the president of the organization. The person's job is to help resolve work-related disputes through informal counseling, mediation, or, more rarely, investigation and recommendations to management.

Perhaps because of the difficulty in combining these responsibilities with other duties to the same employer, ombudspeople have been used primarily in large corporations and universities. (However, there is no reason smaller companies could not contract with an outside neutral for more flexible, part-time service.) Approximately 200 large corporations, including McDonald's, Control Data, Federal Express, IBM, American Optical Company, AT&T Information Systems, Rockwell International, and the Bank of America, have in-house neutrals. There are an additional 100 ombuds offices in colleges and universities. The Internal Revenue Service also established an ombudsperson to help resolve taxpayers' problems with the IRS. Organizations with multiple locations frequently establish "800" numbers for easy telephone access to their ombudspeople.

According to Mary Rowe, who has served as ombudsperson at the Massachusetts Institute of Technology for close to twenty years, her functions cover a broad range: simply listening to employees' concerns on a confidential basis (often at night on the telephone or at restaurants or other places outside of work) and giving advice on how difficult situations might be dealt with by the people themselves; acting as a go-between for employees and their supervisors; conducting face-to-face mediation; and performing formal investigation and reporting to the university's president. More than nine out of ten corporate neutrals were chosen from within their organizations, generally because they already were seen as natural mediators. In explaining how they can be neutral when they work for the employer who is part of a dispute, these people say that their job is to assure employees of fair process and that their loyalty to the employer is satisfied when they settle disputes among employees evenhandedly.

Ombudspeople attempt to assure employees not only that they are neutral but that they will keep all communications confidential and help to protect complaining employees from reprisals. In this regard, virtually all in-house neutrals accept anonymous complaints from employees. When dealing with sensitive areas, such as sexual harassment, experienced neutrals have found many employees embarrassed to have their identities revealed. On the other hand, it may not be practical to try to resolve some types of problems (such as complaints of nonpromotion) without determining the identity of the complainant.

The ombudsman at a Fortune 500 company, with several thousand employees in the Washington, D.C., suburbs, cites two examples typical of the complaints his office deals with daily.

Anne had been a secretary with the corporation for ten years. Her office had twelve secretarial bays, with two secretaries occupying each bay. A new coworker was a chainsmoker. Anne asked her neighbor to refrain from smoking at her desk, but she continued to smoke, to Anne's discomfort and annoyance. Anne complained to her boss, who told her that there were too many smokers in the office to ban smoking. Anne considered resigning.

John was one of fifteen mail clerks with the corporation. It was regular practice in the mail room for packages to be stacked so that access to the fire exit was blocked every afternoon. John considered this practice unsafe but was reluctant to mention it to his supervisor, the office manager, because one month earlier another clerk had been fired for "complaining too much."

At the suggestion of her boss, Anne brought her complaint to the ombudsman, who promptly scheduled a meeting to discuss the company's smoking policy in secretarial bays. Invited were all interested smokers and nonsmokers, together with the management representative responsible for assigning secretaries. Although the smokers recognized that many companies recently had implemented no smoking policies in work areas, they vehemently opposed such a ban. The nonsmokers expressed concerns about their health and discomfort from inhaling smoke on the job. The management representative explained that smokers and nonsmokers sometimes are assigned to the same secretarial bay in order to keep the secretary in close proximity to her boss. After hearing suggestions from the employees, the management representative agreed to take smoking preference into consideration when making secretarial assignments and to reassign those secretaries who requested it. Anne was reassigned to another secretarial bay, where her new neighbor did not smoke.

John took his complaint directly to the ombudsman, requesting absolute confidentiality. The ombudsman listened to his concerns and elicited suggestions for resolving the safety hazard. Next, the ombudsman met with John's supervisor and, without divulging John's identity, informed the office manager that there was concern about the stacking of packages in front of the fire exit. The ombudsman asked the supervisor for suggestions to eliminate the safety hazard and conveyed John's suggestions. The ombudsman and the supervisor then together developed a solution to keep the fire exit clear.[19]

Through dealing with such complaints, neutrals can give managers what Mary Rowe calls "upward feedback" and can act as a bellwether of problems that could burgeon into lawsuits: "Ombuds give management early warning of new problems. There was sexual harassment in the early to mid-1970s, for example, and fraud and waste issues in the late 1970s. As counselors to managers and workers, ombuds are in an ideal position to detect major problems as they arise."[20] In this sense, these individuals function differently from most mediators. Some ombudspeople believe that their additional role of undertaking independent investigations and recommending changes to management gives them more visibility and clout than in-house mediators have and helps to compensate for the possible effect on their credibility of the fact that they are insiders.

Despite the growing use of full-time in-house ombudspeople in large corporations, the fastest-growing internal complaint mechanism among both public and private employers currently appears to be the development of a cadre of trained in-house mediators who help to resolve other employees' conflicts with management as but one of their duties. According to one corporate general counsel, "Mediation provides a forum for people to air their perceptions of unfairness, which if not attended to, quickly can be translated into allegations of unlawfulness." Beginning with the U.S. General Accounting Office in the 1980s, federal and private agencies faced with numerous discrimination and other job-related complaints have asked me and other consultants to help them design a system and to train and support selected employees who mediate outside of their own units or regions. The latter feature is important so that the internal mediators are not themselves involved with the parties to the dispute. Also important in some situations is the use of mediators who themselves are at a high enough level in the organization that they do not feel intimidated by management representatives.

Recognizing the limitations of even a carefully crafted in-house mechanism such as these, the U.S. Defense Logistics Agency and the U.S. Post Office recently announced that they would use independent professional mediators to attempt resolution of employment disputes. With disputes occurring at all levels and of various types, many organizations may find room for both of these approaches.

Sometimes employee dispute processes that are created to deal with complaints of discrimination expand naturally to deal with broader areas of disagreement. For example, spurred by rumors of sexual harassment, a national nonprofit organization hired me to teach several of its employees to counsel or mediate complaints of harassment as well as other forms of discrimination. Managers had decided to spread the neutral's role over several employees on a part-time basis in order to give people with problems access to counselors of different races, sexes, and shifts. Shortly thereafter, the general counsel, who had participated in the counselors' training, succeeded in mediating a bitter conflict between workers in two departments over their overlapping jurisdiction to perform different types of work. As a result, employees from the two departments produced a more workable and easily understandable arrangement. Since then, I have been called on to meet with groups of the company's employees (in one case, with men and women separately) in order to mediate disputes that had been festering between them.

Some employees prefer procedures that adjudicate who was right and who was wrong over those that attempt to smooth over differences, particularly in what they consider serious cases of infringement on their rights. Most, however, when given a choice, opt first for private, nonconfrontational avenues, either because they want as much anonymity as possible or because they perceive benefits in preserving their working relationships with their employer or other employees. Especially in such sensitive areas as sexual harassment, complaint handlers report that most complainants prefer counseling, coaching on how to help themselves, or some form of mediation to any sort of adjudication or public exposure of miscreants.

When employees' complaints cannot be resolved internally they still may be settled short of a courtroom through mediation. At this point, when many of the employees involved have been discharged managers who have hired counsel to pursue claims against their former employers, the mediations have been conducted exclusively by outsiders. Some of my own practice has involved settling seven- and eight-figure claims brought by former executives after they already have been filed in court but prior to trial. The widely publicized dispute between athletic tutor Jan Kemp and the University of Georgia was settled with the help of outside mediators after a trial but before the appeal. Sometimes a minitrial or summary jury trial may be useful in showing a complaining employee or responding employer (often by this time a former employer) how each side's case will play to a judge or jury.

This ad hoc use of outside mediators to resolve large claims when both sides are represented by counsel may become part of the official system for processing claims of employment discrimination, many of which are brought by unrepresented complainants. In a pilot program in Houston, New Orleans, Philadelphia, and Washington, D.C., the U.S. Equal Employment Opportunity Commission contracted with the Center for Dispute Settlement to mediate selected categories of claims of employment discrimination shortly after the employee filed a charge. Cases were referred to mediation only where both the employee and the employer (or, in many instances, former employer) agreed to participate. Most of the employees were not represented by counsel. Of the cases in which both parties agreed to mediate, most of which involved challenged discharges from employment, 53 percent resulted in settlements. The average time from charge to agreement was 60 days.[21]

Developing and Choosing
Effective Complaint Procedures

From the business perspective, it is no simple task to create internal complaint mechanisms that are simple enough to be perceived as accessible and nonintimidating by individual customers or employees, that operate quickly, and that are sufficiently free from control of the sponsoring institution to be credible. Similar problems arise when institutions such as schools, hospitals, or prisons design complaint procedures for their students, patients, or prisoners. From the perspective of the individual trying to decide which of the wide array of internal, trade association, government agency, or judicial avenues to use, the choice (and the fear) can be overwhelming.

Based on the experience to date, a few principles should be kept in mind by anyone designing or choosing a procedure:

1. Access should be simple and well advertised. The most accessible procedures permit a choice of people to whom people with complaints may go in the first instance. (The MIT Ombuds Office is staffed by a white female and a black male, for example. Some school- and prison-based procedures use students or prisoners as intake workers or assistants.)

2. The faster the better; unexplained delays frustrate everyone.

3. Mediation should be available at some stage in the process to enable the people involved in the dispute to work it out themselves if at all possible. Ideally both internal and external mediators should be available.

4. Strict confidentiality should be permitted if the complainant or the organization's representative requests it.

5. Someone outside the organization's direct control should make either the final decision or a recommendation that management is pledged to consider seriously.

6. If only for symbolic credibility purposes, the individual's option to go outside the mechanism to an administrative agency or court should be retained, even if it may be impractical for the option to be exercised in a particular instance.

7. Potential users and line staff should be involved in the design and ongoing monitoring of a procedure in order to increase its credibility and practicality.

8. Top management should make a commitment to soliciting and resolving complaints and to using them to improve management. That commitment should be communicated to all employees and potential users of the system. Managers also should guarantee freedom from reprisal for voicing complaints.

Other Disputes Within Businesses

Business firms have other internal relationships that are particularly amenable to informal mediative settlements. Conflicts within partnerships, complaints by minority shareholders of closely held corporations, and quarrels within family-owned businesses all have the combination of legal and emotional overtones to which mediation is particularly well suited.

Besides these naturals, takeovers of smaller businesses by huge corporate acquirers sometimes engender emotional conflicts when the arrangement provides for the continued employment of the smaller concern's former CEO in the new amalgamated venture. In one such instance, the principal shareholder and CEO of the acquired company had taken mediation training. When the acquiring company discharged him and his vice-president and sued them both for fraud, the parties agreed to retain a mediator who could deal with both legal and business issues, as well as handle the considerable emotional baggage of the case.

Even though the parties were located in California and New York, they attended a two-day mediation session, which not only settled the dispute but provided a structure for resolving future differences. Since the settlement, the parties have worked out other problems between themselves and used the same mediator again. As a result, according to a conversation with Marguerite Milhauser, attorney for the acquired company's CEO, the principals "can talk to each other again," and both are avid converts to mediation.

Planning for Internal Disputes

As businesses increasingly have successful experiences with settlement alternatives, it becomes clear that agreeing on the appropriate process need not be left to chance once a dispute has erupted. In fact, many of the processes now in place for responding to complaints from customers and employees represent attempts to plan for future disputes and avoid their escalation.

Organizations can go beyond structuring processes for particular relationships to assess their entire posture with regard to disputes. Akin to undertaking "legal audits," the purpose of which is to identify corporate trouble spots—generally defined as areas in which the concern is vulnerable to being sued—a "dispute resolution audit" has several purposes:

- It can discover whether there are areas of repetitive problems in which dissatisfaction among employees or consumers is rampant (or merely troublesome).
- It can determine whether the organization has any internal processes for handling these problems and whether there are alterna-

tives that might respond better to the organization's particular structure or needs.

- It can consider what provisions the company makes in its contracts with purchasers, suppliers, consultants, or key employees for handling dissension.
- It can list third parties who are acceptable and conveniently available to assist in resolving disputes.
- It can describe whatever processes exist for reporting potentially troublesome disputes to top management or company lawyers before the problems get out of hand.
- It can consider the appropriateness of creating an internal troubleshooter, with a mandate broader than that given the ombudsperson, to be responsible for intervening early in disputes with other organizations as well as with the company's own employees. This sort of arrangement (possible also for smaller organizations through use of outsiders hired on a part-time basis) would permit timely intervention in disputes and perhaps avoid the need to retain outside counsel.

With this sort of information, managers can decide whether to create new settlement processes or to change some of the practices that engender dissatisfaction. Where procedures are modified, both line employees and outsiders can be helpful both in identifying and in remedying trouble spots. Finally, all managers should be asking their lawyers what options exist for early settlement of disputes, what they would recommend for the particular organization involved, whether dispute resolution procedures should be written into supply or employment contracts, and what experience they themselves have in resolving conflicts short of court.

6
Settling Disputes in Communities

As CALIFORNIA COURT OF APPEALS JUDGE Earl Johnson once mused, "It is somewhat ironic that 'small' claims and what many deem 'simple' disputes—rather than large cases or complex controversies—have compelled a rethinking of the prevailing model of dispute resolution."[1]

Ironic it may be, but a large proportion of the innovations had their beginnings in the community dispute centers. Probably the majority of the emerging professional cadre of dispute settlers got their start there as well. These centers, which range from the truly grassroots to adjuncts of local court systems, now dot the urban landscape. There is at least one such place in each of 48 states, the District of Columbia, Puerto Rico, Guam, and Canada. Called neighborhood (or community) justice (or dispute) centers, these are the places to take arguments not only between neighbors or family members, but also between landlords and tenants, employers and employees, buyers and sellers, offenders and their victims. Some centers handle relatively complex cases involving separating couples or citizens' groups and businesses or government. They rely heavily, sometimes exclusively on volunteer mediators, and they are committed to listening to people and helping them solve their own problems. Their products: the settlement of disputes among individuals, and, perhaps equally significant, as many as 20,000 trained, experienced, and committed advocates for mediated settlements.

A Look at a Community Dispute Center

It is 6:15 on a hot, sticky summer evening. At the District of Columbia Mediation Service, housed in an old court building in downtown Washington, the waiting room is crowded. Several women fan themselves. A baby is crying. Two men pace back and forth in opposite directions, their hands in their pockets.

A tall, thin, slightly stooped man with white hair and dressed in a sweater and slacks, white shirt and tie walks into the room and calls out:

"Mr. and Mrs. Quander? Mr. Taylor?" An elderly woman rises, as does a young man of about eighteen who is attired in blue jeans and a metallic blue shirt. They come forward from opposite sides of the room. The older man puts out his hand, smiles, and shakes hands with both of them.

"Good evening. My name is Robert Lester. I will be one of your mediators this evening. Please come with me to the back."

Neither of the two says anything. They follow Lester through the waiting room and down a hall to a row of offices and enter a small room containing a round table and five chairs. Sitting on one of the chairs is a young black woman, dressed in office clothes.

"This is Kathy Harris," Lester says to the newcomers. "She and I will be working together with you this evening. Ms. Harris, this is Ms. Quander and Mr. Taylor. Please sit down." Lester turns to the older woman. "Ms. Quander, is your husband here?"

"He was too sick to come. All of the carrying on by this young hoodlum and his friends has sent him to his bed. It's got to stop. Can you do something to have him arrested?"

"Wait a minute! Her husband threw a trowel at me! All I did was go into their yard to get my frisbee! And they won't give me a moment's peace in my house. You've got to do something about these crazy old people!"

Kathy Harris breaks in. "Just a minute please. Mr. Lester and I can't do anything to either one of you. That's not what we're here for. We're here to help you work out your *own* solutions to the problems that brought you down here. We have no power to make any decisions for you.

"You've been told about the Mediation Service by the staff, but let's take a few moments to explain what we are all about and how we work. What we say may be helpful to you as we go along. Often in our community, situations end up in the hands of police and courts when they shouldn't. The Mediation Service has been set up so that you can decide on the solutions to your own problems rather than having someone else decide them for you.

"After Mr. Lester and I listen to both of you, after you each have a chance to tell us all you want to tell us, we are going to try to help you arrive at an agreement. We think that it is important for people to decide as much as possible for themselves. There is a lot more confidence in an agreement on everyone's part if that happens."

Harris looks at Lester, who takes over. "Before we begin, Ms. Harris and I want you to know that nothing either one of you says will be repeated outside of this room. Our discussions are confidential. Only your agreements, if you do agree, will be recorded.

"Throughout this meeting you will notice that Ms. Harris and I take notes. The notes are merely to help us remember the things that you say to us. They will be destroyed at the end of the session. You are welcome to take your own notes if something comes up that you want to remember.

"Later we probably will meet with you individually—to find out more about your concerns and any alternative solutions that you can think of. It may be that you will be able to talk more freely meeting alone. We will respect your confidence in those sessions. Just let us know if there is anything that you don't want us to repeat to the other person.

"We may also want time to talk between ourselves, or you may want a break. Just ask us.

"The way we will work things now is to hear from both of you, one at a time. Each of you may hear things this evening that you disagree with. We guess you would not be here otherwise. But we are going to ask you to hear the other person out—without interrupting. That way we can all hear everything. We are not going to hurry you. Both of you will have the chance to tell us everything—that's what we are all about.

"Have you any questions?"

Quander: "Not about what you said—just about what this all can do for us. Can you make him turn the music down?"

Lester: "No, but we can try to help the two of you agree on what is reasonable. Our experience is that people generally comply with agreements they've worked out themselves. But perhaps the only real way to answer your question may be to get on with it. Mr. Taylor, do you have any questions?"

"No," Taylor replies glumly.

"Well, then, Ms. Quander, I believe that you started our process. Let's begin with you. Will you tell us about the situation that brought you here?"

As Quander begins to speak, Taylor pushes his chair back from the table and turns away so that his shoulder is toward the others. He folds his arms against his chest. Harris and Lester occasionally glance at him but give most of their attention to the woman.

Quander: "Well, Ted and I have lived at 3117 Fairmont Street for thirty-one years. It's a nice, quiet neighborhood, with small row houses and picket fences—that is, it was until a few months ago, when he (she points at Taylor) moved in. Since then all it's been is loud parties, drugs, and blasting music."

Taylor quickly turns and faces Quander. "There have never been drugs in my house! How dare you say that when you don't know what you're talking about?"

Harris: "Mr. Taylor, you will have all the opportunity you want to talk about the situation as you see it. Please let's let Ms. Quander finish speaking first."

Quander continues. "The parties are the worst thing. We can't make him understand that most people go to bed at a decent hour in order to get some sleep. We keep calling the landlord and the police, but they won't do anything. After the last time, the police just told us to come down here.

"Last Saturday was the end! He must have had thirty people over there at a wild party. We called three times asking for quiet. The last call was after midnight and he had the nerve to claim that there was no noise!

"The next day Ted went outside and found that most of the sculpture ornaments in our garden were broken. We want him to pay at least a hundred dollars for them. They can never be replaced! Then we started getting telephone calls, and when we answered there was no one there. We're getting frightened, and all this commotion has made Ted sicker."

Lester: "Ms. Quander, what would you like to see happen as a result of coming down here this evening?"

"Actually, what we really want is for him to move out and leave us in peace. At the very least, we want all the noise and wild parties to stop, and we want him to pay for the sculptures he broke."

"Mr. Taylor," Lester says, turning to look more closely at the younger man, who is still shifting around in his seat. "Now perhaps you will tell us about the situation from your point of view."

Taylor: "Look, I just want all this harassment to stop. I want some peace. Good housing is almost impossible to find in this city, and she and her husband keep calling my landlord and the police. Last Saturday they embarrassed me in front of all my friends. I've got to be able to have a party every now and then. Otherwise I might as well move back in with my parents!"

Harris: "Is this the first time you've lived away from home?"

Taylor: "Yes, I'm a college freshman and my parents are letting me live in my own apartment instead of in a dorm. It's much nicer, but these people are driving me crazy. Do you know that her husband threw a trowel at me?"

Harris: "Mr. Taylor, what would you like to see happen as a result of coming down here this evening?"

Taylor: "I want all this carrying on to stop. I just want them to leave me alone."

Lester: "Is there anything else?"

Taylor: "No. I don't think so."

Harris: "It sounds as if all three of you want to be left alone to enjoy your homes. Is that right?"

Both parties nod silently. Harris looks at Lester, who nods.

Harris: "If you will give Mr. Lester and me just a couple of minutes to look over our notes, we will speak to each of you individually, as we said earlier. Thank you for your patience. We hope that we can help you work things out this evening."

The mediators met separately with each party, first with Sylvia Quander. Quander confided that her husband had been in poor health lately and that their frustration at their inability to control the noise from next door had frayed both of their nerves. Ted Quander was embarrassed that he had thrown the trowel, but he had told his wife he might do it again if they could not deal with the noise. Quander accused the young people of being high on drugs, but acknowledged that she really did not know whether it was drugs or just good times. The police, she acknowledged in response to the mediators' questions, had found no evidence of drugs when they checked the parties.

Further questions by the mediators revealed that the Quanders were in the habit of going to bed early and that the late-night noise from parties was particularly debilitating to them. They occasionally spent weekends with Ms. Quander's sister, and had done so more often since Taylor had moved in next door. Their other serious complaint was the noise from Taylor's stereo playing in the early afternoon when Mr. Quander tried to take his nap.

The sculptures were homemade. Their value was simply a guess. Sylvia Quander estimated that the cost of the materials, if she decided to make new ones, would come to about $25.00.

Quander said that she and her husband would do almost anything to stop the noise and that peace was much more important to them than replacing the sculptures. Although she did not want the mediators to repeat this to Taylor, she confided that she and her husband were becoming frightened of Taylor and his friends. Lester reminded her that she already had said as much when they all were meeting together.

When the mediators met with Taylor, he expressed anger and frustration at the Quanders' repeated calls to him during parties and to his landlord and the police. "Apartments are hard to find. I want to keep this one, and I want them to stop bugging me."

Taylor acknowledged that he felt foolish about the calls to the Quanders after the trowel incident, but in a way thought that they deserved whatever annoyance he had caused them. He did not know that Ted Quander had been ill and said that the Quanders should have told him so. He agreed that lately it would have been difficult for them to do that, given the way their conversations had been going.

Taylor stated emphatically that he had had nothing to do with the damage to the Quanders' sculptures. After the third call from Sylvia Quander during last Saturday's party, he had told his friends about the "nagging old bags next door." His friends might have destroyed the ornaments in a misguided effort to help him. He did not know that his friends had done the damage, but felt somewhat responsible because of the things he had said to them about the Quanders at a time when they were all having a good time.

Taylor said that the police had come in and checked his party in response to the Quanders' call. Although they had left without doing anything other than to suggest that Taylor's friends keep the noise down, Taylor was embarrassed by the entire incident. In answer to a question from Harris, he agreed that he did not want anything like it to happen again.

Taylor said that his stereo was located near the wall that abutted the Quanders' house and that his windows had been open lately because of the heat. He offered to move the stereo to the other side of the house, but doubted that a few feet of difference would satisfy the Quanders. Except for his parties, which occurred roughly once a month, most of Taylor's listening was done when he was alone, either studying or fixing and eating his meals. The mediators asked if he ever had tried listening to his stereo with earphones. He said that he had, but owned none. He acknowledged that earphones would present no problem for him when he was studying or eating, but was unenthusiastic about wearing them when he was cooking or washing dishes.

The mediators reminded Taylor of his earlier statement that apartments were difficult to find, that he cared about keeping this one, and that he wanted the trouble with the Quanders to stop. Taylor said that perhaps wearing earphones when he was alone would not be such a hassle as long as he could still have occasional parties. He said that the parties were planned about a week in advance and that he would have no problem with notifying the Quanders about them if they would treat him civilly and stop accusing him of being a drug addict and a hoodlum.

After a brief huddle to discuss strategy, the mediators met once more with Ms. Quander. They told her that Taylor too wanted the problems to stop and that he was willing to do his part. They said he had denied there were any drugs at his parties, and they reminded her that the police had left the party without taking any action. Quander acknowledged that the police check did give her some comfort on that score. The mediators also reported that Taylor had not known Mr. Quander was sick and that he regretted the damage to the sculptures, although he insisted that he had had nothing to do with it.

The mediators explored with Ms. Quander the various options open to her and her husband if they had prior notice of Taylor's parties. They told her that Taylor was thinking about the possibility of buying earphones so that only he could hear his music most of the time, and that there should be no problem with stopping all the noise during Mr. Quander's early afternoon naps. Ms. Quander perked up.

The mediators then brought both parties together to discuss the elements of a possible agreement. Taylor stated that he was willing to move his stereo to the opposite side of his house, to purchase earphones, and to wear them most of the time, including early afternoons. If his music bothered the Quanders when he was not wearing the earphones, they could call him and say so. He would then turn it down or try to wear the earphones more often.

Ms. Quander said that she and her husband had no problems with Taylor's coming into their yard if he needed to retrieve a frisbee or anything else. It was the trouble with the noise that had so upset her husband. She said that if Taylor called them a week or so before he was planning a party, they might decide to spend that night at her sister's house in order to avoid the loud music. If not, at least they could take longer naps the afternoon before the party and plan to be up later that night. Taylor thanked her for that idea.

Taylor said that he was sorry about the sculptures, although he had nothing to do with the damage. He offered to drive Ms. Quander to wherever she had purchased the original materials to help her replace them and to pay something toward replacing them (although not $100). Ms. Quander responded that she appreciated the offer of a ride, but she did not want to take any money from him if he had not broken the sculptures. Besides, she said she thought it was much more important for him to spend his money buying the earphones than the plaster and hoped that he would do so immediately.

The mediators stressed the importance of direct communications between the Quanders and Taylor in the future and pointed out the difficulties that had been caused when they did not talk to each other. The mediators then drafted an agreement that reflected the parties' promises. Sylvia Quander called her husband and read the draft agreement to him. He said that he had no objection to it. The parties then signed the agreement and thanked the mediators for their time. Lester and Harris both thanked Quander and Taylor for all their hard work. The session had lasted for a total of two and one-half hours.

The agreement was less than a perfect solution because neither the parties nor the mediators had been able to discover any objective standard to govern the amount of noise reasonable under various circumstances. Yet the mediators took comfort from the fact that both Quander and Taylor seemed satisfied and that, according to follow-up studies by the Mediation Service since 1980, between 75 and 80 percent of the participants who reach agreements through mediation report that both parties are fully living up to them. The mediators told Quander and Taylor not to hesitate to return to the Mediation Service if they had any problems in the future.

Lester, a retired foreign service officer, had been mediating close to once a week for eight years. Harris, a government computer operator, had served for less than a year. In return for forty hours' free mediation training, followed by an apprenticeship in which more experienced mediators such as Lester serve as mentors to less experienced mediators such as Harris for at least five cases, mediators agree to handle a case each week for at least one year. Many of them, like Lester, serve longer.

Shortly after she completed her mediation training, Kathy Harris was asked by her supervisor to mediate a persistent dispute between the secretaries and professionals in her office. She succeeded in doing so and was increasingly called upon to resolve internal problems on the job. In effect, she has become the office ombudsperson.

The Quander-Taylor case is typical of the thousand or so disputes actually mediated each year at the Mediation Service. Five times that many are screened; less than half of them are considered appropriate for mediation. Serious crimes are rejected. In fewer than half the cases scheduled do all the parties actually appear for mediation; a substantial minority of the "no shows" resolve the dispute themselves after a call from a Mediation Service staff member has alerted them to the organization's involvement.

Other disputes occur between family members, employers and employees, or businesses and their customers. Many of them, such as disputes over home improvements, money owed, or car accidents or repairs, could have been filed in small claims or even regular civil courts. A few cases have nowhere else to go but mediation, since they could not have been taken to court. Some of the neighborhood disputes involve many parties; up to eighteen people have crowded into the small mediation rooms at the service's office. It may take hours for their shouting to recede into normal conversation and, usually, agreement. Written agreements are reached in close to 80 percent of all cases mediated.

The District of Columbia Mediation Service, one of the larger of such programs throughout the country, is operated by the nonprofit Center for Dispute Settlement under contract with the city government. Like many of the other centers, it also receives financial support from the local bar association and private donors.

Most people who have experienced mediation prefer it to the experience of going to court. "The mediators really listened to me," said one homeowner interviewed after she and her husband had a mediation session with a contractor who had not completed work he had agreed to do on the couple's kitchen. "They also helped us come up with ideas for getting the materials we wanted and getting on with the job." The contractor was equally enthusiastic: "I've been in business for twenty years, and I can't afford to be dragged into court and wait around all day for a judge. But neither can I afford to make twenty changes in the work I'm supposed to do and not get paid for them. The mediator let all of us hear the other's point of view and helped me explain to the customers how I work. We're getting along better now, and the job should be easier to finish."

The mediators are quick to see the benefits also. And the director of a Phoenix program that furnishes legal services to the indigent confessed at a meeting of poverty lawyers convened by the National Institute for Dispute Resolution: "I'm trained to go to court, and I've won a lot of legal victories. But nothing I do can give my clients as much control as when they're sitting in that chair."

The Growth of Community Dispute Centers

Criminal courts and prosecutors launched the first experiments with community dispute settlement in an effort to deal with minor crimes. Programs in Philadelphia (Arbitration As An Alternative), in Columbus (the Night Prosecutor Program), and in New York City, Rochester, and the Dorchester section of Boston all were closely associated with criminal courts. They attempted to treat minor crimes between people with continuing relationships as matters for negotiation and restitution between the people themselves rather than as matters for prosecution by the state. In 1978, when then Attorney General Griffin Bell announced that the U.S. Department of Justice would sponsor three experimental neighborhood justice centers in Atlanta, Kansas City, and Los Angeles, about a dozen such programs already existed in other cities.

The neighborhood justice centers were misnamed from the start. Of the three Justice Department-funded models (and the three additional programs in Washington, D.C., Houston, and Honolulu that soon followed), only Los Angeles served a single neighborhood. That program failed to outlast its federal funding. But the basic idea—training volunteers to settle disputes between individuals—survived.

Estimates of the number of community justice centers in the United States range from 250 (by the National Institute for Dispute Resolution) to 440 (by the American Bar Association's Section on Dispute Resolution). This figure does not include the growing number of programs that handle only specialized complaints, such as housing or consumer disputes. Although some centers have closed down each year for lack of stable funding, more have opened. There were widespread predictions that the programs would be out of business when the Justice Department's Law Enforcement Assistance Administration folded and all federal support ended in 1980, but these fears were not realized. According to Albie Davis, director of community mediation for the Massachusetts District Court system, "the principal success" of the programs "has been survival," their "tenacity ... to hang in there through the tough times."[2]

Canada and Australia have developed their own neighborhood justice centers based on the U.S. model. Within the United States, the growth has been uneven geographically, with most of the centers clustered in the Northeast, South, Midwest, and West Coast states with large urban populations. Massachusetts alone has thirty-two centers; California has sixty-four.

The developers of community justice centers built on three foundations: the successful experiences of the Community Relations Service, which was created as part of the U.S. Department of Justice in the 1960s to settle community-wide racial disputes; the work done by a few pioneer private dispute resolvers to deal with conflicts in prisons and in northern and midwestern cities; and reformers' efforts in the 1960s and early 1970s to divert minor criminal and juvenile offenders from prosecution and imprisonment. Some of the movement's intellectual underpinnings came from a 1974 article written by Richard Danzig, then a Stanford University law school professor, who advocated the creation of "community moots" for family, minor criminal, and other disputes among community members:

> The present system does not, after all, perform the job of adjudication in most of these cases. Civil proceedings are generally avoided. ... Many matters which may technically be criminal violations will not be prosecuted because they are viewed by the prosecuting authorities as private and trivial matters. ... [D]ue to institutional overcrowding and established patterns of sentencing the vast majority of misdemeanors and some felons are not likely to be imprisoned. For these defendants, the judicial process is not a screen filtering those who are innocent from those who will be directed to the corrective parts of the process. Rather, it is the corrective process; as such it fails to be more than a "Bleak House," profoundly alienating, rather than integrating.[3]

The growth of community justice centers has been fueled by many of the same divergent motivations that are evident throughout the dispute settlement movement. The programs created by courts and prosecutors generally had as their primary goal the diversion of minor cases, mostly criminal, from the courts. Some of them sought simply to reduce costs and delays. Others focused more on creating a better way than assembly-line judicial procedures for dealing with the everyday disputes between family members, friends, or neighbors that so often appeared as criminal charges.

Court processing seemed not to work well for these cases, which included assaults, minor theft, and various forms of harassment. According to Daniel McGillis, chronicler of the neighborhood justice movement for the U.S. Department of Justice, "Complainants very often withdrew their complaints as trial neared because their opponent was a neighbor, relative, or acquaintance. The complainants were not seeking incarceration for the adversary or a fine (paid to the state); they wanted changed behavior, an apology, or money paid to them as restitution for the harm done."[4] Trials, when they occurred at all, were very brief affairs and focused on the behavior complained about rather than on the long series of events that often had taken place between the parties. The real issues in dispute often were never aired. Diverting these cases to a more personal forum was a way to deal more effectively with the underlying disputes, as well as to unclog the courts.

Other reformers, while also intrigued with the idea of providing more humane ways of dealing with criminal disputes, focused on increasing people's access to some sort of forum for a wide variety of disputes, however categorized. They noted that many of the disputes for which community justice centers were designed formerly had no means of resolution. In some cases, such as the dispute between the Quanders and Tyrone Taylor, there would be no institution for settling the dispute if the centers did not exist.

Realistically, a large portion of the conflicts brought to dispute centers never would have appeared in court. Either prosecutors would not have bothered to bring charges in many of the less serious cases between family members or neighbors, or there would have been no effective judicial remedy. For what could Tyrone Taylor be prosecuted? Creating a nuisance? And what of the assault charge by Taylor against Ted Quander? Would Sylvia Quander have sued for $100 in damages for destruction of her sculptures?

Even the most court-connected of the community dispute centers, which place primary emphasis on settling cases diverted from the courts, acknowledge that disputes that have no remedy form a significant portion of their caseloads. McGillis cites the work of researchers in Florida, where community justice centers were created by the courts. They estimate that approximately 22 percent of the centers' caseloads could not have been brought to any court. People managing the centers estimate that in fact far fewer than the remaining 78 percent of their caseloads would have gone to court had the centers not existed.

In some cities, community dispute settlement programs are operated by public agencies—the courts, prosecutors, police, or human services agencies. For example, the Miami Citizen Dispute Center and similar centers throughout Florida are sponsored by the courts. In other cities, various private, nonprofit organizations run the centers but receive the bulk of their referrals from police and courts. Examples include the Justice Cen-

ter of Atlanta, Inc., three centers in New York City, the Honolulu Neighborhood Justice Center, and the District of Columbia Mediation Service.

Finally, there are the truly neighborhood-oriented centers, which are
privately sponsored and attempt to search out conflicts directly from the
community. The best-known example is Community Boards of San Francisco, which was started fifteen years ago with volunteers who literally
traveled from door to door seeking their neighbors' conflicts. Although
the volunteers no longer go through the neighborhoods seeking disputes
to resolve, Community Boards maintains a direct connection to its community by attending street fairs to pass out information on alternative
methods of resolving disputes and by attempting to recruit most of its
cases from community members. Based on a similar model, "Block-By-
Block," a recently inaugurated program in Los Angeles, is planning to recruit and train mediators from every block of two inner-city neighborhoods. These programs naturally handle far fewer disputes than do those
that receive the bulk of their cases from the official system. And even the
San Francisco program succumbed to funding pressures and began to accept both money and cases from public agencies.

Regardless of emphasis, dispute centers are staffed primarily by volunteers. Sponsors save money by using few (often poorly paid) salaried staff.
They also have tried to prevent the bureaucratic burnout that so often af-
flicts court staff, who are forced to deal with large volumes of cases day after day, by augmenting full-time staff with part-time volunteers.

Justice centers may be housed in a courthouse, an office building, a
church, or a storefront. The centers hold sessions in convenient locations,
at hours convenient to working people. These features alone represent a
significant effort to give citizens access to a new way of resolving their disputes, many of which might have festered with no available means of resolution.   ·

Justice centers almost always use the same process—mediation. Mediation encourages all parties, regardless of their often arbitrary designations
as "plaintiff" or "complainant," defendant" or "respondent," to recognize a common interest in resolving their problems. The process attempts
to place triggering incidents (such as Ted Quander's throwing the trowel
at Tyrone Taylor) in the context of the parties' ongoing relationship. And
it stresses the active participation of all parties in settling their own disputes.

Although a few of the programs that are closely associated with the
courts still use arbitration if efforts to settle through mediation fail (thus
leaving no unsettled cases to be returned to the system), most of the programs have discarded the "med-arb" model as being too coercive. The
more grassroots programs use panels of as many as five mediators per

case; programs associated with public agencies, on the other hand, use one or two.

Despite the centers' differences in sponsorship, location, and emphasis, the clientele of community justice programs is similar throughout the country. Most clients are poor or lower-middle class; many are members of minority groups. There are exceptions: Even wealthy neighbors have used the centers to settle disputes over noise from barking dogs, air conditioners, or music or to resolve complaints against local merchants or home improvement contractors. And the few centers that have been located in middle-income neighborhoods have attracted substantial numbers of neighborhood residents.

Mediators, on the other hand, come from all social classes, although because they are almost always volunteers, they tend to be wealthier and better educated than the disputants. They often are white, whereas many of the parties are from various minority backgrounds. An exception to this phenomenon occurs in the few programs that are attached to existing ethnically identified organizations, such as the Asian Pacific American and the Martin Luther King Dispute Centers in Los Angeles. Many programs have attracted more female than male mediators; they report different degrees of success in keeping a truly heterogeneous group. Some of the mediators are professionals eager to learn a new skill.

From the start, the programs set no requirements for their mediators of particular education or prior experience. According to George Nicolau, one of the pioneers:

> We didn't really care whether this person had a college degree or a high school diploma or was a drop-out because we didn't believe that education was a relevant measure of what we were looking for. We were looking for people who could postpone judgment, who did not try to impose their values on participants in the process, who were not upset by, but sensitive to and able to deal with cultural differences, people who could listen with understanding. We knew that if we could find such individuals, we could give them the skills to bring people together.[5]

Most of the volunteers are enthusiastic about their experiences and are avid supporters of the process. A typical comment comes from one of the longtime community mediators in Washington, D.C.: "This is the most valuable thing I've ever done. It lets me see how people, no matter what their formal education and resources, can come up with their own ideas—ideas I never would have thought of myself."

What does seem to make a difference in the success of community mediations is the amount of training a mediator has had, coupled with the person's experience in actually mediating disputes. Data collected by

Jessica Pearson and her colleagues in Denver suggest that training and experience (not their race, age, sex, or professional background) are the only characteristics that consistently influence participants' satisfaction with the process.[6] Thus, it is worth noting that while some programs give their volunteers forty to fifty hours of free training spaced over several weeks, followed by apprenticeships to experienced volunteers and close supervision by professional staff, others train only for a weekend. The training requirements under state statutes include a minimum of twenty-five hours in New York and thirty in Massachusetts. Many veteran mediators question whether this is enough.

Although many of the centers got their start with funds from federal grants, no federal money has been available for a number of years. Community mediation centers are supported increasingly by local and state governments, although a few rely on a combination of private funding and foundation grants. Some of the centers have suffered severe cutbacks as a result of shrinking state and local budgets. In Texas, Oklahoma, and Florida, community justice centers are supported by a small addition to court filing fees (in Oklahoma, $2 for each case and $5 for each party participating in a mediation); state legislation in New York, California, and Illinois appropriates funds to local justice centers. Except for a small (but growing) number of programs (many in New York State) that are required by state law to raise private matching funds in order to get government money, services almost always are free. A few programs charge user fees on a sliding scale.

Both the budget crunch of the late 1980s and early 1990s and the funding schemes created in an attempt to provide ongoing support to community justice centers have kept some programs from realizing their full potential. Perhaps the starkest example can be found in Los Angeles.

The events of April 29, 1992, shocked the country as it watched Los Angeles erupt into violence and burn out of control for several days. Southern California's employment base has shrunk drastically. In the early 1990s, jobs lost in Los Angeles accounted for 27 percent of the jobs lost in the United States.

At the same time, with waves of immigrants arriving from Mexico, Central and South America, and Asia, Los Angeles has become the new melting pot of the United States. At last count, 40 percent of the city's population were born outside the United States; 49 percent speak a language other than English at home. Schisms exist not only between the immigrants and the native population (the African-American population is shrinking, for example, making up only about 10 percent of the city) but among various immigrant groups and between immigrants and earlier arrivals (for example, recent arrivals from Central America versus established Mexican Americans).

The substantial increase in Los Angeles's Latino population has caused leaders of the varied communities that make up that population to call for greater power sharing. The call is viewed by many African-Americans as an attempt to take from them hard-won gains in access to the levers of power. The battle has been fought over issues ranging from how many Latino seats there will be on the City Council to who will lead the labor union at Martin Luther King Hospital in Watts, whose patient population has been transformed from being overwhelmingly African-American to being predominantly Latino. As the demographics of Los Angeles's population have changed, questions related to the relative distribution of power among its various ethnic groups have produced new conflicts far more complex than the bipolar divisions between African-Americans and Anglos that spawned the violence in Watts a generation ago.

Mediation could be used far more widely to assist disputants with cultural and linguistic differences by bringing people of different backgrounds together in a forum conducive to the airing and sharing of perspectives, frustrations, and fears. For example, a furniture manufacturer moved into a solidly Latino Los Angeles neighborhood without any prior consultation with community members. The factory quickly generated traffic, noise, and pollution and hence concern among its neighbors. Language proved to be a substantial barrier, and the dispute mushroomed. Ultimately, it was resolved with the help of a bilingual mediator from the Buena Fe Dispute Resolution Center, who met with all the parties individually, determined their respective interests, and helped bring about a settlement in which the factory altered its hours of operation and the traffic patterns of its delivery trucks and the neighbors and factory owner began to communicate with one another.

Resolving neighborhood disputes between groups or complex, multi-party disputes involving people of different races or ethnicities requires substantial resources. It is not unusual for mediators in a dispute of this type to spend weeks identifying the interested parties and months getting them to the point that they are willing to negotiate. This commitment of resources cannot be made unless a program's funding sources are willing to accept the notion of devoting that level of effort to a single conflict. That situation currently is not the case for any of the existing dispute resolution services in Los Angeles.

Despite the acknowledged need, state and local budgets for community dispute resolution, as for other social services in California, have been shrinking, with a resulting loss of staff positions. Even more significant structurally, Los Angeles County's scheme for dispersing state funds discourages centers from attempting to resolve all but the simplest disputes. Although state law makes money available to local programs from court filing fees, dispersing it by local regulations involves reimbursing programs for each case that is *resolved;* all cases are valued equally for purposes of compensation. Thus, a dispute between two neighbors, requiring perhaps two hours of a mediator's time, is reimbursed at the same rate as a complicated, multiparty case, which may require a team of mediators and take weeks or months to resolve. In addition, restricting reimbursement to cases actually settled has an inhibiting effect on a program's even beginning to tackle different or complex cases.

The Los Angeles demographics, coupled with a struggle for access to jobs and social services, have parallels throughout the country and the world. In many countries, the breakdown of authoritarian structures has permitted sectarian violence to flourish. In addition to the latest versions of religious warfare, a particularly persistent problem has involved the resentments of local residents toward prosperous ethnically identifiable merchants, such as Koreans in Los Angeles, New York, and Washington, D.C.; Azerbaijanis in Russia; Chinese in Southeast Asia; and Coptic Christians in Egypt. If community dispute resolution is to realize its full potential for substituting self-determination and peaceful collaboration for violence, both imaginative adaptations and adequate funding are necessary, along with formulas for financial support of community mediation that acknowledge needs far beyond those of diverting cases from the court system.

Increasing the Demand
for Community Dispute Resolution

Despite their limitations, the survival and proliferation of community dispute settlement programs, especially in light of the routine demise of many other social programs developed in the 1970s, suggest that they must be doing something right. What is it?

It is not the reduction of court caseload or substantial savings of public money. Although the cost of mediating a case in a justice center is less than the cost of taking the same case to trial, many of the disputes handled by community justice centers would be dismissed in court—if they ever got there in the first place. Furthermore, the comparatively low caseloads of all but the largest centers have made them not particularly economical to operate, even with volunteer mediators.

The dispute centers do seem to be doing two things right. First, they are giving access to ways of resolving conflict to many people who do not find the traditional system comfortable, affordable, or suited to their needs. Second, they are providing a more complete and satisfactory process for many of the types of cases they handle. The parties themselves remain in control of what problems they discuss and how they resolve them.

One study of a Brooklyn, New York, program that randomly assigned serious criminal cases between acquaintances to mediation or to court processing revealed only slight differences—which favored mediation—between the two groups' future criminal behavior. However, there was a clear difference in both the participants' satisfaction with the process—mediation was greatly preferred to court—and the effect of the experience on the parties' relationship. Mediation strengthened it; court further alienated the parties.[7] As Daniel McGillis's report to the Justice Department recognized:

> Research studies support the casual impression that people like to have their cases mediated. They typically view the process as more fair and more understandable, and they like the agreements that are achieved. Agreements are reached in approximately 80 percent of mediation sessions. Disputants consistently report that they are satisfied with the mediation process and view outcomes as fair. ...[8]

With these types of results, it seems odd that community justice centers, despite their newness, are not used by more people with disputes. Except in places where courts require (or at least urge) people to mediate, caseloads have not been high. This is so notwithstanding efforts of the centers to publicize their activities (billboards in Springfield, Massachusetts, announce, "We're Looking for Trouble!"), convenient hours and locations, and sympathetic intake workers.

The most obvious explanation for the failure of people with problems to rush to their local community justice centers is the American fixation with courts as the only institutions for settling disputes. Anthropologists Sally Merry and Susan Silbey have suggested a slightly different, more subtle reason:

> Citizens do not use alternatives [to courts] voluntarily to the extent hoped for by proponents ... because by the time the conflict is serious enough to warrant an outsider's intervention, the grievant wants vindication, protection of his or her rights (as he or she sees them), an advocate to help in the battle, or a third party who will uncover the "truth" and declare the other party wrong. Although courts rarely provide this, particularly to plaintiffs in interpersonal cases, inexperienced plaintiffs do not know this. They go to court for an advocate and to get justice; they do not respond eagerly to the opportunity to take the problem back into their own hands.[9]

Even when plaintiffs (or "complainants" in criminal cases) choose mediation, defendants often simply fail to show up. The question of how much coercion should be used to increase defendants' attendance at justice centers has sparked controversy. In general, the appearance of the noninitiating parties at mediation sessions increases as the level of coercion (or the unpleasantness of the alternatives to mediation) increases. In programs in which participation in mediation is truly voluntary, an average of only slightly more than one-third of all disputes scheduled for mediation actually are mediated because at least one party (generally the defendant) fails to appear. Programs that inform people of the potential for criminal charges being brought against them if they fail to appear have about half the defendants show up. In district attorneys' programs, which require attendance at mediation sessions as a condition of dropping criminal charges, up to 90 percent of the parties attend.

This problem presents a dilemma for program organizers, whose ideas of voluntary participation clash with the realities of operating programs that must justify their budgets to state or local governments in terms of the number of cases handled. As a result, some programs downplay the fact that in most places participation in mediation remains voluntary. For example, in New York City, parties to disputes in which someone else is seeking mediation receive a document entitled "OFFICE OF THE MAYOR, CRIMINAL JUSTICE, SUMMONS PART—CRIMINAL COURT." The "Request to Appear" is printed in much smaller letters, and the document ends with the admonition "IF YOU FAIL TO APPEAR, A CRIMINAL ACTION AGAINST YOU MAY BE COMMENCED."

It may be appropriate to require parties to attend a brief educational session to learn about mediation. Yet is is quite another thing, as a founder and former supporter of the program that now uses the "summons" just quoted remarked in frustration, "to dragoon or bludgeon an individual into accepting mediation without a full understanding of all that entails and what he or she might be giving up."[10]

City and state agencies and courts increasingly have begun to require mediation for special groups of problems. In cities and heavily urbanized states such as Maryland and Massachusetts, the most common of these programs handle consumer disputes. Consumers and businesses are directed to try mediation before a local or state agency investigates consumers' complaints. In these instances, which involve businesses that often have more power than the consumers who complain, consumers report satisfaction with the required participation of businesses (sometimes by telephone) and with the mediators' identification with a government agency that has the power to discipline private firms. In some farm states, as discussed in the preceding chapter, mediation is now required between farmers and their creditors before the creditors may foreclose on loans that have been taken out against farm property. And some court or agency programs that handle landlord-tenant problems, such as the Philadelphia Housing Court, offer or require mediation between landlords and tenants as a first step in resolving disagreements over housing. Courts in several states now require litigants in all "small claims" cases (upper dollar limits range from $500 to $5,000) to attempt mediation before trial. Mediators are volunteers, many of them retired. Few are lawyers. About two-thirds of all cases mediated in small claims courts are settled. Somewhat surprisingly, almost as many disputes among strangers are settled as disputes among people with ongoing relations.

A comparison of the outcomes of small claims mediated in Maine with outcomes of cases heard in courts where mediation was unavailable revealed several advantages of the mediated settlements. Not only did participants greatly prefer mediation to trial, but mediation was much more likely to produce compliance with the resulting agreement. Of the mediated agreements with monetary settlements, 71 percent were paid in full. In contrast, only 34 percent of the court orders were fully paid.

Perhaps some of the explanation for the difference in rates of compliance is that far more of the mediated agreements than court orders provided specific plans for payment. Much of the difference, however, appears to be that people who participate in working out their own agreements are more likely to comply with them than people who are ordered to do so. In interviews, 73 percent of the defendants who mediated said they felt a legal obligation to pay, compared with only 12 percent of the defendants who went to court. In addition, those whose cases were mediated understood more of what was going on, believed that they had a greater opportunity to explain their side of the case, and in general were more satisfied with their overall experience than were those whose cases were decided by a judge.[11]

In still another adaptation of community mediation by the courts, both juvenile delinquents and convicted adults are participating in mediation with their victims to work out mutually acceptable sentences to be recommended jointly to the judge. Approximately 100 victim-offender mediation programs operate in the United States, with other programs in Europe and Canada. In the first half of 1993, the U.S. programs are reported to have resolved 16,500 cases, involving 12,931 victims and 14,059 offenders.[12] In most of these programs both the defendant and the victim, who may be a representative of a store or other business, must volunteer for mediation. (In Oklahoma, half the defendants and approximately 72 percent of the victims do; more victims volunteer in rural areas, fewer in urban.) Mediators are community volunteers or, occasionally, probation or parole officers.[13]

Agreements generally include some sort of restitution to the victim, in the form of money or services, or service to the community instead of or in addition to imprisonment. One offshoot of victim-offender mediation, the religiously inspired Victim-Offender Reconciliation Program, considers reconciliation between the parties, rather than punishment or compensation, to be the primary goal of mediation. Offenses for which sentences have been mediated range from burglary and drunk driving to armed assault and manslaughter. Both victims and offenders report satisfaction with the process, with victims saying they appreciated the opportunity to describe directly to the offender how the crime changed their lives and to suggest their own remedies.

Courts and local governments increasingly are adopting community dispute settlement centers. At least one-third of all centers are now connected to the court. This development has caused the centers to worry that they may be turned into another cog of the bureaucratic machinery and lose the human qualities that have made them distinctive. According to a recent review of community justice centers:

> Closer relations with the courts produce tensions about how to meet the needs of disputants as distinct from the needs of the courts. Community-based programs focus on the needs of disputing parties and define cases in terms of the relationships between the parties. Mediators are trained to ask: "Do these people know one another? Are there underlying issues ... ? Are the parties willing to work out a voluntary agreement?"
>
> In contrast, courts tend to define cases by the category and nature of the offense or dispute. Court personnel ask: "Is the matter civil or criminal? Is it a misdemeanor or a felony? How can we dispose of this case?"[14]

Unfortunately, some of the larger metropolitan mediation centers today leave little sense of the notion of neighborhood justice. The eventual character of the centers is unclear. Yet the frequent enlistment of new volunteer mediators, with their enthusiasm and their flexible, humanistic approach to settling disputes, may succeed in preserving the notion of community and caring in the free-standing centers and infusing those attached to the justice system with at least some of these virtues. What does seem clear is that the growing numbers of trained volunteer mediators, many of them lawyers, social workers, and public officials who transfer their new skills into their existing jobs, are fueling the increasing momentum of the movement to find new ways of settling conflict.

7

Settling Public Disputes

IN THE EARLY 1970S NEW YORK CITY's Housing Authority announced its intention to build seven large low-income apartment buildings in the middle-class Forest Hills section of Queens. The Housing Authority paid little attention to growing opposition by local residents, apparently assuming that passions would cool over time and that the buildings eventually would be accepted in the neighborhood as another unavoidable fact of urban life. Only when pickets appeared and violence was threatened in 1972 did Mayor John Lindsay take action to appoint Mario Cuomo, then a respected lawyer in Queens, as a "fact-finder." Cuomo was assigned to recommend a solution to the mayor, the Board of Estimate, and other city officials.

The full story appears in Cuomo's 1974 *Forest Hills Diary*, a shorter version in *Roundtable Justice* (a series of published reports to the Ford Foundation). As Cuomo recalls, his only instruction was "to do as I saw fit and to report precisely what I felt." Although he recognized that the mayor's motive for appointing him was to deflect hostility from the mayor himself, Cuomo nevertheless believed that a dispassionate review of the facts, "without foggy rhetoric," would help. He declined the title of mediator for what he then considered the more neutral one of fact-finder. He refused money because he believed that it might compromise his credibility, and he rejected a staff as "too cumbersome."

Despite his chosen title, Cuomo played the role of mediator. At the outset he saw his most important task as giving people an opportunity to ventilate their feelings, not only so that they would believe they were being heard, but so that they could hear themselves. "If you let them talk long enough, it becomes apparent even to them that they are being emotional," Cuomo recollects. But Cuomo did more than listen. Pressured by the fact that the buildings were being constructed while the disputants talked, Cuomo recommended his own compromise solution of smaller buildings and cooperative ownership by the low-income residents. Both the Housing Authority and the residents eventually accepted this solution.

In the midst of the turmoil, one of the most vocal residents opposing the project challenged the area's state senator in a primary election. He lost by a 4-to-3 margin. Thus, Cuomo could assure whoever would listen that the "silent majority" did not support the extreme opposition to any public housing in Forest Hills.

Reflecting on the experience, Cuomo later disavowed any interest in becoming a full-time mediator or fact-finder:

> It's a strain. You can't afford a whole lot of ego in these things either, and you can't want to come out a winner, you will get hurt because that will distort you. You'll start measuring by different criteria—that is, how will this be received by the world out there? That is the worst, trying to make yourself popular. In Forest Hills ... the one way to gain points was to decide which of the two sides was the stronger politically, or whatever, and then go with them. If you want to make points, you make the wrong decision in Forest Hills. To make the right decision, you had to chance being hurt by both sides and not worry about winning. If, by some misadventure, people say, "Gee, he was objective," that's wonderful, but it's unlikely to happen. What normally would happen is someone saying, "Ah, the bum."[1]

Seventeen years after Cuomo's successful intervention in Forest Hills, the New York City Board of Education joined with four legal services organizations to ask me to mediate their differences on an ongoing basis. The organizations had been suing the city for twelve years over the right of handicapped children to an appropriate education at public expense. At about the same time the city's Office of Administrative Trials and Hearings began to assemble a roster of professional neutrals from whom city agencies could choose whenever they wished to use an outside dispute resolver. During the years between Cuomo's mediation in New York and my own, the use of mediators to resolve community-wide conflicts had begun to be accepted as a worthwhile alternative to violence, stalemate, or litigation.

When Disputes Involve Entire Communities

Before World War II, the most visible and violent community-wide conflicts in the United States frequently sprang from labor disputes. In many industries, the development of widely accepted, legalized systems of mediation and arbitration has made resolving these disputes almost routine. This is not so for racial and ethnic conflicts, which culminated in the often violent opposition to the integration of schools and other public facilities in the 1960s. Since then, disputes between groups of blacks and whites have been joined by conflicts over changing neighborhoods and tensions caused by the influx of refugees from Southeast Asia and newer arrivals from Cuba, Haiti, and Central America.

Conflicts between minority groups and the police often have fueled already tense situations. In one of the most horrifying examples, a series of ad hoc mediators (all of them untrained and inexperienced) attempted unsuccessfully to settle seven years of confrontation in Philadelphia between the radical, back-to-nature "MOVE" group, its neighbors, and the local police. Clashes arose over MOVE's habits, which included recycling garbage in their yard, welcoming rats and stray dogs, mounting loudspeakers in front of their houses, and haranguing neighbors with abusive language. For their part, MOVE members believed that some of their members had been arrested and imprisoned unfairly. After one serious incident, one of the group was severely beaten in front of television cameras while resisting arrest.

The intervenors included an active minister, a young lawyer who had represented a MOVE leader, and an established businessman and civil rights proponent. Later, in an effort to understand the reasons for the series of failed negotiations as part of their own ongoing training, mediators from Pittsburgh's Conflict Resolution Center pointed to the mediators' failure to involve either MOVE's neighbors or the police in their efforts to cool tensions and criticized their exclusive focus on representatives of MOVE and the city. They also cited the difficulty of understanding MOVE's decisionmaking structure (the group appears to have operated by consensus rather than majority rule) and the omnipresence of the media, which made it difficult for the city to meet MOVE's demands without losing face.[2]

The standoff ended in May 1985 with an armed assault by police on MOVE's headquarters. Remembering that one policeman had been killed and other police and firefighters injured in an earlier attempt to evict the group in 1978, police shot 10,000 rounds of ammunition in 90 minutes. They finally dropped a bomb from a helicopter, killing 5 MOVE members and 6 children, and destroying 61 homes.

Since that time, interracial violence in Los Angeles (discussed in Chapter 6) and in the Crown Heights section of Brooklyn has underlined the need for constructive ways of responding to conflicts among racial and ethnic communities. This is not a problem that is confined to the United States, as the events in Bosnia, Eastern Europe, and the former Soviet Union starkly attest.

The federal government's first—and so far only—step toward providing a way of resolving racial conflict was to create the Community Relations Service. As part of the Civil Rights Act of 1964, Congress established CRS in the Justice Department "as an impartial catalyst in settling racial disputes, helping people to resolve their differences through cooperation rather than as adversaries on the streets or in the courts." Beginning in the Deep South with the most intractable school desegregation and public accommodations cases, CRS's work as peacemaker among racial and ethnic disputants continues today.

Although smaller and less visible than it was in the 1960s (a series of budget cuts has shrunk its staff by half), CRS reports that it resolves close to 1,000 racial crises each year. Some of these, such as the Liberty City riots in Miami in 1980 and the clashes between Hispanics and Italian-Americans in Lawrence, Massachusetts, in 1984, retain the characteristics of riots or serious street violence. In these conflicts, the former social workers, journalists, and civil rights workers who make up CRS see their role as to reduce or contain the violence and get the conflict from the streets to the table. CRS is experienced in negotiating race-related hostage and barricade situations, controlling rumors, and generally dealing with large-scale racial disorders.

CRS has been criticized for dealing with racial problems only when they are at or near the point of violence. Responding in a speech to the Society of Professionals in Dispute Resolution, former CRS mediator Wallace Warfield replied: "Some dispute resolution theorists suggest that it is borderline unethical for interventionists to 'cool a situation out' and not deal with the underlying issues, as though to do so would be to lend oneself to co-option. As an ultimate progression of dispute resolution, I agree. However, you will never get to those underlying issues unless you deal with the crisis at hand."

Curiously, CRS's thirty-year history of low-profile intervention in community disputes, sometimes at the request or order of a federal court, very rarely has led to the creation of similar state or local teams. And its skeletal staff, and lack of ability to augment it with private, professional mediators hired on a contractual basis, have severely limited its effectiveness. During the aftermath of the violence in Los Angeles in 1992, for example, CRS was forced to respond from its office in San Francisco. It could deploy only one, and occasionally two, of its staff to Los Angeles. At the federal level CRS's mandate has been confined to racial disputes. The ironic result is that the agency is restricted to dealing with violent conflicts in schools, prisons, or jails only when the violence is racially motivated.

Although still far from developing the routinized, widely accepted system of dispute settlement that has evolved in the labor field, individual mediators have intervened successfully in growing numbers of community-wide disputes. Because of the highly visible and political nature of these conflicts—and because disputants sometimes will settle for no less—some of the intervenors have been well-known, respected public figures, many of them enlisted by local politicians.

In an early mediation of a rent strike in Saint Louis in 1969, for example, when residents of public housing refused to pay rent in protest of a new policy that pegged rents to the size of each apartment instead of to family income, the mediator was Harold Gibbons, a leader of the local Teamsters' Union. The Teamsters had supported the strikers and opposed the refusal of the local housing authority to negotiate directly with them. Gibbons was an unusual labor leader, who had earned the respect of both the corporate executives with whom he negotiated and the blacks who lived in public housing. His intervention brought about a settlement: Strikers agreed to repay all rent they had withheld, in return for a reorganization of decisionmaking authority over public housing in Saint Louis.

The larger and more incendiary the conflict, the more likely it is that the parties will demand intervention by a public figure, frequently an elected official. Some politicians, sensing the danger to themselves as well as to participants if mediation is highly visible but unsuccessful, refuse to get involved. Thus, in the 1972 riots at Attica State Prison, prisoners' calls for Nelson Rockefeller, who then was governor of New York, went unheeded. Many critics of the decision believed that the governor's appearance on the scene, especially if he had been assisted by experienced mediators, might have saved lives of prisoners and hostages alike.

Other politicians get involved in local disturbances with varying degrees of success. Former mayor Marion Barry of Washington, D.C., attempted to mediate a dispute between residents of a poor neighborhood and the owner of a Chinese carryout restaurant who had pulled a gun on an obstreperous customer. Residents, led by a local minister, threatened a citywide boycott of all Asian-owned businesses. Barry failed to quell the conflict and was publicly embarrassed for his efforts. The ensuing controversy became a local symbol of the increasing strife between longtime residents and Asian immigrants (most of them Korean), who own a growing share of inner-city convenience stores, carryout restaurants, liquor stores, and dry cleaners. On a more positive note, the controversy led to the creation of a privately funded program, operated by the local mediation service, to focus on these difficult disputes.

Some public officials, including former Massachusetts governor and presidential candidate Michael Dukakis, consider their ability to mediate among constituents one of the most important ingredients of their political stock in trade. According to a talk by one of the governor's aides in 1986, "If these large disputes [over, for example, the siting of prisons] don't get mediated, they don't get solved. They are the sorts of problems that defeat many governors."

A guide to using consensual approaches to resolving public disputes begins by pointing out the social costs of stalemate in the siting of any badly needed but frequently unwanted public facility—sometimes referred to as a "Locally Unwanted Land Use" ("LULU"), which is defeated by a "NIMBY" ("Not In My Backyard") response:

In the United States we are at an impasse. Public officials are unable to take action, even when everyone agrees that something needs to be done. ... Almost every effort to build prisons, highways, power plants, mental health facilities, or housing for low-income families is stymied by nearby residents. There has not been a single hazardous waste treatment facility built in this country since 1975, even though everyone agrees that such plants are needed to avoid "midnight dumping" of dangerous chemicals. Public officials find that even substantial electoral victories do not translate into the power needed to build such facilities.[3]

The personal involvement of public figures as mediators may exacerbate the ever-present problem of how to deal with publicity when they attempt to settle a community-wide dispute. The public interest in the outcome of a widespread conflict is at war with mediators' usual emphasis on keeping negotiations private and urging participants to refrain from playing to the press. (Parties cannot take risks in divulging their interests or inventing creative options if their every word has the potential of coming back to haunt them in the daily news.) Consequently, professional mediators involved with disputes of interest to the general public generally attempt to convince the parties' representatives to agree in advance to a news blackout as long as negotiations are in progress. Sometimes their success or failure at obtaining this early agreement predicts the eventual outcome of the entire effort.

Which people should be at the table and who should represent whom (the loudest voice may have no constituency) are even trickier questions. Many of the mediators who have dealt with community-wide disputes worry about how to determine the interests of those who do not come forward. Do they, in fact, constitute a silent majority? In Forest Hills, Cuomo was concerned about the fact that only the opponents of public housing were vocal. Where were the supporters?

The quick impression is that there may be no strong feeling in the black community for the project, but that's probably not the fact. One of the difficulties is that the black side of the question is hard to identify. On the Forest Hills side, geography is enough to isolate and mark the adversary—we know who and where they are and that makes communication relatively easy. But unless the Housing Authority is regarded as the other party in interest it's difficult to say who is. ...

The answer—that the potential residents of public housing were diffuse and hard to identify—is what makes settling such large-scale disputes particularly challenging. Mediators debate vigorously among themselves about the extent of their responsibility to bring such unrepresented constituencies to the bargaining table. There is consensus, however, that if groups believe they have been excluded unfairly, their lack of participation will undercut any agreements reached in their absence.

Despite the limitations on funding that were described in Chapter 6 in the context of Los Angeles, a few of the larger, longer-established community justice centers are branching out from dealing solely with individuals' disputes and are applying their experience to settlement of highly emotional conflicts among groups of citizens or between citizens' organizations and businesses or government agencies. In Hawaii, for example, the staff of the Honolulu Neighborhood Justice Center assisted in a series of meetings, culminating in a nine-hour marathon session, that produced agreement between backers and opponents of opening a "Ronald McDonald House" (for temporary stays by the parents of hospitalized children) in a wealthy Honolulu neighborhood. (Opponents had charged that the residence would "change the character" of the neighborhood.) In New York City, a community mediator helped various factions on the Board of Education to resolve some of their differences by training them in negotiation techniques and having them role-play actual disputes.

In Washington, D.C., the Center for Dispute Settlement, which operates the local mediation service, became involved in a dispute among three commercial real estate developers and four citizens' groups over issues of commercial development. A volunteer mediator and CDS Deputy Director Brenda Irons-LeCesne succeeded in bringing about one of the first mediated agreements in the growing number of disputes of this type. The conflict pitted economic growth against the preservation of urban neighborhoods—the "classic conflict of interests that is faced, in one way or another, by all urban centers," as former city council chairman David Clarke later told the *Washington Post*.[4]

Residents were angry and frustrated over the encroachment of a planned regional center, the Chevy Chase Pavilion, on their middle-class neighborhood. The issue of commercial development near residential areas had emerged as a primary sore point in the mayoral campaign. Zoning permits already had been granted to allow three large office buildings and a hotel to be erected on Wisconsin Avenue, a four-lane commercial strip located one block away from a residential neighborhood. Residents were sophisticated, vocal, and divided among themselves over the appropriate mix of traffic, noise, and conveniences along the thoroughfare that abutted their homes.

Two years of arguments with the developers had produced nothing more than a stack of paper four feet high for the residents, who had lost a series of court and zoning battles. As William Vose, negotiator for the largest developer, later confessed: "We'd been through the mechanics of trying to communicate, but we thought we had nothing to gain from them."[5]

Then the city council decided to postpone until after the election its vote on authorizing the closing of a city-owned alley, which cut through the middle of the proposed development. As chairman of the council, Clarke suggested that the parties use the nine-week delay to negotiate. As CDS's director, I discussed with him the possibility of our furnishing mediators. As a result, representatives of the developers, the citizens' groups (which included two elected "advisory neighborhood commissions," a voluntary citizens' organization, and one group from nearby Maryland), and attorneys for both sides were told that Clarke would like them to meet with two mediators from the city's mediation service.

Not having been consulted about whether they wanted the mediators' help, most of the parties resented the overture. Nevertheless, they all showed up for the first meeting. As Vose later recalled: "When the chairman of the City Council asks if you'll cooperate, certainly you'll cooperate. At that time I didn't know what mediation meant, but I thought it meant no good for us. ... No odds makers could be found to accept bets on a successful conclusion."[6]

The group's first gathering was conducted in a large city council hearing room teeming with public officials (the mayor and the city's zoning, planning, and traffic agencies all sent observers) and the press. It was relatively easy for the mediators to help representatives of the seven primary disputants and three of their attorneys agree that meetings with greater privacy would be desirable; these would be held alternately in developers' offices and local community centers. Officials would be invited only if their input became necessary. (It did not.)

For the next eight weeks, nothing about the conflict, which up to that time had engendered widespread media coverage, appeared in the local press. Mindful of the numerous constituencies that were interested in the outcome, the group decided that it would be unwise to agree to keep everything said in mediation sessions confidential. The parties did agree not to seek publicity during the mediation or to use anything said in their sessions as a weapon in future legal proceedings. Their agreement stuck.

None of the participants had been in a mediation before. Although all of them were skeptical, most later acknowledged that the novelty of the process had intrigued them. Initial doubts about the intervenors' lack of credentials as urban planners (they had none, although one of the mediators, a longtime employee of IBM, knew something about traffic engineering) soon evaporated. The parties were impressed by the mediators' willingness to put in long hours in order to learn the necessary terminology. As Maureen Dwyer, attorney for two of the developers, later wrote to them: "Your dedication and commitment set an example for all of us. In fact, it may be fair to say that the only thing we all agreed on at the beginning was your belief that an agreement could be reached."

The group met twenty-three times over the next ten weeks. As one of the self-described "strong-willed" participants depicted the meetings:

> In the early stages, we participated in structured meetings where we had the opportunity to say what was important to our interests and what we hoped to achieve. More than once, we heard the familiar phrase "tell us more about that." It reduced tension. It got the participants in a task oriented mode. Under the deft and subtle influence of the mediators, we pursued the challenge of finding a solution.[7]

Only halfway through the process did the parties agree to break down into smaller working groups, which worked separately with each developer and enabled the residents to focus on their specific concerns with each of the projects. All of the participants later identified their agreement to try a more workable process as the critical one in helping them to reach the series of agreements that settled the dispute.

The resulting agreements changed the mix of commercial and residential space and provided for community involvement in the form of an "oversight committee" in the future planning and construction of the developments. All three developers agreed to some reduction in the density of their projects. One project was moved farther from a residential street; several stories were lopped off an apartment building; an atrium was extended to change the view from residents' homes. The developers agreed to widen nearby streets and modify intersections in order to reduce the impact of the anticipated traffic on the neighborhood.

As is frequently the case in any settlement, no one was completely satisfied with the agreement. While the *Washington Post* congratulated participants in a laudatory editorial, the *City Paper*, a small "alternative" newspaper, castigated residents for what it saw as their lack of courage in agreeing to settle. Donald Weightman, attorney for the residents, commented, "It was not a victory but it was certainly not a defeat. Ultimately, it is a small masterpiece in damage control for the residents."[8]

Having lost a number of court and zoning battles, the citizens' groups reluctantly had come to accept the inevitability of development. They were anxious to have whatever influence they could on the size and scope of the projects. Developers were motivated by their need to put their stalled plans into action, their desire to put a stop to the unfavorable publicity, and their impatience with what they saw as years of fruitless negotiations. Chairman Clarke's refusal to extend the tight deadline, which irritated several of the participants at the time, turned out to be a blessing. Although final negotiations were hurried, the deadline served to keep up the momentum toward agreement and to cut off tendencies toward endless debate.

Since the Wisconsin Avenue settlement, Center for Dispute Settlement staff have worked with neighborhood organizations, local governments, and commercial developers to agree on plans to redevelop downtown Silver Spring, Maryland, and to reconcile the needs for low-income housing, historic preservation, and residential development in Arlington, Virginia. Clearly the same process can be applied to many other disputes over development, to conflicts between neighbors and governments wishing to locate unpopular facilities (such as halfway houses or waste treatment plants), and to neighborhood complaints about existing businesses (noisy bars or restaurants, for example).

In Connecticut, the state legislature passed a law that brought thirty-five municipalities together, with the help of mediators, to negotiate a regional consensus on how and where to increase affordable housing in the Hartford and Bridgeport areas. Although most of the municipalities shared concern over the lack of such housing, none was willing to begin building. They feared that their towns would draw the majority of the demand, thereby allowing the other towns to ignore the problem. By creating an opportunity for community leaders to work on the problem simultaneously, this collaborative decisionmaking process enabled them to reach consensus on a plan, which ultimately was adopted by the majority of the local governments involved. It takes time and effort—and some financial resources if the parties must pay for the mediators' services. (The state paid for the mediators in Connecticut, the county planning board in Arlington; the parties shared the cost in Silver Spring. In light of the large investment of time and high level of skill required of the mediators in these complex, multiparty disputes, the use of volunteer mediators generally is inappropriate.) Yet there was broad agreement in all of these situations that the alternatives to agreement would have been far more expensive for all concerned.

The Growth of Environmental Mediation

The history of mediating disputes over land use and other environmental issues is usually traced to 1973. Daniel J. Evans, then governor of the state of Washington, invited Gerald W. Cormick and Jane McCarthy to mediate a fifteen-year-old dispute over an Army Corps of Engineers' proposal to build a flood-control dam on the Snoqualmie River, thirty miles from Seattle. The dispute was so divisive—and potentially so threatening politically—that Evans decided to take a chance on what was then a new procedure. At the very least, mediation would allow him to buy time and to postpone making the controversial decision over whether to permit construction of the dam. Cormick, then a community mediator, and McCarthy, a former investment counselor, had been searching for an appropriate dispute to mediate since they had convinced the Ford Foundation to support their efforts to apply the evolving techniques for resolving community-wide racial and ethnic conflicts to disagreements over the environment.

The battle over whether to construct a dam pitted farmers and residents, who periodically had suffered from serious flooding by the Snoqualmie River, against politically powerful environmentalists, hikers, sports fishermen, and kayakers, who feared development and suburbanization if the river was dammed. According to one of the key environmentalists, "We had gone through this ... experience in [the nearby] Green River Valley in which ... a dam provided 100-year flood protection in the lower valley and it went to instant development and cement."[9] Cormick and McCarthy cautiously spent six months meeting with the various parties, considering whether they really wanted to resolve the controversy and whether they were ready to give mediation a fair chance. The issues appeared intractable, but the parties were willing to try a new way of resolving them.

In the course of meeting with the mediators, the parties discovered that farmers had the same interest as environmentalists and sports enthusiasts in preventing development of the river basin. The farmers came to understand that development would bring greater land values and hence higher taxes on their land—taxes that eventually could force them to sell. Over time they concluded they would have to tolerate a certain amount of flooding in order to keep land values within reason, withstand the pressures of development and taxation, and keep their farms. In December 1974, the parties signed an agreement in which they agreed that the site for the dam should be moved to one giving less flood protection but causing less environmental disruption. They also recommended that additional flood control measures be taken and a basinwide coordinating council established.

The agreed-upon dam never was constructed, probably because the various agencies of government responsible for implementing the joint recommendations that resulted from the mediation were not at the bargaining table. (The mediators made the choice, which since has been criticized, not to invite government decisionmakers in an effort to keep the parties on an equal footing; both the mediators and Governor Evans continue to defend the decision.) But many of the groups' recommendations were implemented and, more important, the widely publicized agreement inspired others to try mediating large-scale public disputes.

Since the mid-1970s, the parties to growing numbers of disputes over the development and use of land and other natural resources have tried mediation. Recently the subject matter has become more complex, ranging from the protection of groundwater to the cleanup of abandoned haz-

138

Settling Public Disputes

ardous waste sites. According to Gail Bingham of the Conservation Foundation, which monitored such efforts until the mid-1980s, 82 percent of the first 200 conflicts to be mediated involved federal or state agencies and units of local government. Local citizens' groups were at the table in about half the attempts.

Close to 80 percent of the early disputes reached agreement through mediation. When the parties at the table had the authority to make decisions agreement was reached more frequently than when they had to defer to someone else for the ultimate decision. Furthermore, when the public officials with the authority to implement agreements participated directly in the negotiations, resulting agreements were fully implemented 85 percent of the time; agreements were implemented only 67 percent of the time if officials did not participate.[10]

The only absolute condition for the successful mediation of public disputes seems to be that all parties must have some incentive to reach agreement. Even unwieldy numbers of parties, the lack of a deadline, or the failure of those who have the power to implement the agreement to participate directly in the settlement process have been overcome by skillful mediators. In 1980, for example, Russell Train succeeded in bringing about an end to the controversy over whether Consolidated Edison Company of New York should build a hydroelectric and pumped storage plant at the foot of Storm King Mountain in the Hudson River highlands. Eleven private companies, government agencies, and environmental groups reached agreement after fifteen years of litigation and administrative hearings and twenty months of mediation. More recently, twenty-five environmentalists, state officials, and private industry representatives in Maryland reached a landmark accord on solid waste management. Working with an out-of-state facilitator, the diverse participants not only arrived at over fifty recommendations by unanimous consent, but did so in less than their two-month deadline for presenting the accord to the Maryland General Assembly.

What cannot be settled are fundamental divisions based on clashing values: for example, the question of whether nuclear power ever should be used. What is a fundamental division will vary with the people involved and may require some probing to discover. If the sides are divided over a matter of principle, the most creative of solutions will not be able to satisfy their divergent interests.

Recent environmental conflicts settled with the help of mediators have ranged from allocating responsibility for removing asbestos from local schools, to finding mutually acceptable uses for closed schools, industrial sites, or old railroad rights-of-way, to reducing odors from sludge-composting or other facilities. As a condition of licensing, state laws in Wisconsin, Massachusetts, and Rhode Island now require the builders of hazardous waste treatment plants to negotiate with representatives of local communities over reducing environmental hazards and compensating local individuals or businesses expected to be affected adversely by the choice of location.

The U.S. Environmental Protection Agency (EPA), which has been applying ADR methods since the late 1980s, has institutionalized its use of ADR in environmental enforcement actions. EPA's Office of Enforcement adopted an agencywide "ADR Implementation Plan" in 1990 to establish standard operating procedures for obtaining the services of outside mediators, arbitrators, and other ADR practitioners in disputes to which EPA is a party. The agency provides its regional enforcement staff with training, assistance in the review of potential cases and the preparation of required procurement documents to retain mediators, the identification of qualified ADR practitioners, and the publication of periodic status reports on agencywide ADR activities. Although EPA supported the establishment of a computerized nationwide list of dispute resolution specialists by the Administrative Conference of the United States, EPA also maintains a separate list of neutrals who have experience with environmental enforcement cases.

These proactive efforts have paid off. EPA has tripled its use of ADR since 1991 and, consequently, has resolved cases that otherwise most likely would still be languishing in court. The Department of Justice, which represents the Agency in Court, also is participating in growing numbers of mediations, involving hundreds of millions of dollars. Other mediators and I have worked with the EPA, private companies and state and local governments under the auspices of an umbrella dispute resolution organization to help parties agree on allocating the costs of clean-up—or to perform the clean-up themselves. The city of Youngstown, Ohio, the EPA, and a private manufacturer in 1989 announced the first such case involving significant amounts of money (the settlement was for about $300,000) to settle through mediation. According to a lawyer for the city, the settlement "sailed right through" approval by the city council, perhaps because my co-mediator and I were able to involve some of its members in the settlement process.[11] Since then, I have worked with the EPA, the Department of Justice, two state agencies, the Minnesota legislature, three private companies, and the northern Minnesota town of Bemidji to settle the issues involved in the multi-million dollar clean-up of a local landfill. Pollutants from the landfill had threatened both the local water supply and the Mississippi River. Binding arbitration also is available in EPA disputes involving less than $500,000. EPA is planning a pilot program in nonbinding aribtration of any Superfund case.

Although EPA is resolving increasing numbers of cost recovery cases, in which the agency cleans up hazardous waste sites using federal funds and then pursues "potentially responsible parties" for reimbursement, through mediation it has only begun to experiment with using a consensual process, with an outside mediator, to address the elements of the clean-ups themselves. At the state level, I am working with the City of Toledo and a number of private companies to assist them in agreeing on the design of a remedy, to be followed by the allocation of financial responsibility for funding whatever clean-up actions are selected by the State of Ohio.

Increasing the Use of Environmental and Other Community-Wide Mediation

Even with the recent growth of environmental mediation, with fees paid by governmental and private parties, questions remain about how to finance mediators' services on an ongoing basis and how to make them affordable to citizens' groups and public interest organizations. These are particularly difficult issues because of some concern that mediators' neutrality might be compromised if their fees are paid solely by the government agencies or corporations involved in particular disputes. The problem is exacerbated if mediators must spend substantial time investigating the matter even before they are retained.

The provision of government support for private mediators, the creation of federal or local agencies to mediate broad categories of conflicts, or the establishment of some sort of revolving fund into which disputants who could afford it would contribute for the general support of mediation all are ideas that remain to be explored. In an effort to test one of these options, the privately supported National Institute for Dispute Resolution underwrote a portion of the costs of experimental state offices of mediation in New Jersey, Massachusetts, Hawaii, and Minnesota. The purpose of the state offices is to convene disputing parties—to get them to the table, as it were—by discussing with them various dispute resolution processes, helping them to agree on a process, and helping them select an appropriate mediator or other neutral. There are now twelve state mediation offices, including those recently created in New Hampshire and Texas.

As with any other public processes, such as influencing legislation or going to court, citizens who wish to participate effectively in negotiating disputes over public issues must be organized. They must be able to attract public attention. They may need technical advice. It is virtually impossible to oppose the building or expansion of a commercial development, for example, without access to traffic experts. Participants may decide to negotiate directly for themselves or through attorneys. Whichever route they choose, they generally will find it advisable to discuss their alternatives to settling (filing suit, taking zoning appeals, or using other administrative avenues) with lawyers.

If they choose to negotiate, with or without a mediator, participants will need to invest large amounts of their own time. Indeed, settling may take even more time in the short run than fighting. Negotiation, mediation, and other processes designed to build consensus generally require substantial direct participation by the parties themselves, not just by their attorneys. In the long run, however, as settlements devised by those directly affected prove to be more satisfactory and thus more permanent than solutions imposed by outside decisionmakers, the time spent in negotiating or preparing to negotiate frequently pays off.

When Disputes Involve Government Policy

In addition to savings in cost and time, one fundamental reason for the growing acceptance of methods to build community consensus is the growing recognition of limitations on the way in which governments handle public disputes. Governments often pass laws or promulgate regulations that do not reflect the needs of diverse constituencies. Decisionmaking processes, which often include negotiations behind closed doors in the proverbial back room, leave out many interested parties, who then attempt to block the resulting decisions. Mediation, or "collaborative decisionmaking," attempts to bring all interested parties, or constituencies, whether government agencies, corporations, advocacy organizations, or private citizens, together to discuss their concerns and to work together to craft solutions acceptable to all.

Using ADR in Administrative Proceedings

Adjudication does not occur only in courts. Federal, state, and local agencies have well-developed systems for deciding cases that arise under the jurisdictions of each agency. Each agency has its own corps of administrative law judges and attorneys, precedents, case documents, and, not surprisingly, backlogs in the resolution of disputes. Established as part of an earlier effort to reduce the heavy volume of litigation in the court system, these administrative proceedings sometimes have become as cumbersome as those in the court system itself.

To help streamline this bureaucratic disappointment, Congress enacted the Administrative Dispute Resolution Act of 1990 (ADRA), which authorizes and encourages federal agencies to use mediation, arbitration, negotiated rulemaking, and other forms of consensual ADR in a variety of administrative procedures. Under the ADRA, each agency must adopt a policy for implementing ADR, designate a senior official to be the agency's dispute resolution specialist, and provide training on a regular basis to employees involved in implementing the agency's ADR policy. Subsequent to the enactment of the ADRA, a presidential executive order required agencies to consider appropriate alternatives whenever a government agency is a party to litigation.

As a result of these developments, a number of federal agencies have begun pilot programs to determine which ADR methods are most suitable for their particular agencies. One such program was a six-month regional pilot program in the Department of Labor, which mediated civil enforcement disputes involving alleged violations of federal wage and hour laws and workplace health and safety requirements. At the completion of the pilot, DOL reported great success: More than 76 percent of the cases that went to mediation were resolved and some of them resulted in "particularly creative settlements unlikely to have been reached in litigation."[12] Questionnaires and interviews of participants revealed considerable satisfaction with mediation on the part of both government representatives and private parties.

Other agencies increasing their use of ADR under the ADRA include the Federal Deposit Insurance Corporation (FDIC) and the Resolution Trust Corporation (RTC). The federal agencies, responsible for cleaning up, bailing out, and restructuring banking and savings and loan institutions after the debacle of the 1980s, have spent millions of taxpayers' dollars in fees to outside law firms in order to resolve the affairs of the hundreds of financial institutions taken over by the government and to pursue individuals (including outside lawyers and accountants) considered responsible for bilking depositors, lenders, and taxpayers. Much of this money, oddly enough, has gone to support litigation among various institutions (often over the participation by various banks or savings and loans in the same transaction), all of which are controlled by the U.S. government.

Recognizing the folly of litigating against themselves, the FDIC and the RTC have directed that all institutions controlled by either agency must use an ADR process to resolve disputes with one another. The process used most often is mediation, followed by arbitration by a high-level agency official in the rare event that mediation does not produce a settlement. In order to implement this directive, Michael Lewis and I trained cadres of FDIC and RTC lawyers and managers to mediate disputes among agency-controlled financial institutions. As a result, according to director of ADR Cathy Costantino, the FDIC saved $14 million and, according to director of ADR Martha McClellan, the RTC saved $2.3 million in legal fees from 1991 through the first three quarters of 1993, not to mention the management time of their own employees that otherwise would have been spent in litigation.

Disputes between the federal watchdog agencies and private parties who have done business with failed banks or savings and loans have gone to mediation at a much slower pace than internal disputes, despite the agencies' establishment of a roster of private neutrals experienced in mediating complex, multiparty cases. The FDIC did report great success with a small ADR Creditor Claims Pilot Project, in which it used independent, non-FDIC mediators in twelve court cases involving claims against failed banks in New England that the agency had taken over. The nature of the cases ranged from complex commercial matters to consumer and automobile loans; the amount in controversy from $12,000,000 to $6,753. Nine cases were settled through mediation, one was settled before mediation began, and only two cases were returned to court. The FDIC estimated savings in legal fees and expenses of $410,475 from the pilot alone.[13]

In my own experience with a dispute between a federal receiver and a company that owed money to a closed, government-controlled savings and loan association, I experienced again the power of mediation to assist parties in settling their affairs and getting on with their businesses and their lives.

Two longtime successful commercial developers, both graduates of a prestigious business school, prided themselves on never having missed a payment on a loan. Then they had the bad fortune to borrow several million dollars from a Texas savings and loan association to finance a commercial office development, at the height of the 1980s real estate boom. When it came time for the construction financing to be replaced by a permanent mortgage at a lower rate of interest, as had been agreed in the original loan documents, the lender stalled. One year and countless excuses later, the savings and loan had been taken over by a series of federal agencies and two of its officers indicted and imprisoned for fraud.

Although the various government agencies with whom the partners dealt over the next few years, and the six different representatives who were put in charge of the account at various times, all acknowledged the loan commitment, new federal requirements intervened. The developers' lack of funds for tenant improvements or leasing commissions stalemated their efforts to lease the space. They made a series of new proposals, all of which were rejected by the various government officials who were put in charge of the matter at different times; sometimes, agency employees were too overwhelmed by their workload to respond at all. Ultimately, the real estate market turned bad, the developers ran out of money for the project, and they defaulted on several million dollars in loans. At the time of the default, the property was worth significantly less than the money that was owed on it and far less than it had cost to build. A federal lawsuit resulted, and a receiver was appointed to manage the property. The developers' attorneys suggested mediation.

Both developers attended the mediation, in the hope of getting the matter resolved and rescuing their business, which by then was extremely short of cash. Also present were their attorneys, an attorney from an outside law firm representing the agency, and the agency's internal business representative, whose job it was to recoup as much as possible for the agency and, ultimately, the taxpayers. She and the developers had never met. A representative of the agency's internal legal staff attended by speakerphone in order to minimize costs.

The session began with the developers describing their business and attempting to communicate some of their background as reputable businesspeople and their frustration at what they perceived as seven years of being lost in a bureaucratic morass. The agency representatives explained the process of obtaining the approval of a committee for any settlement that was reached (often the situation for a government agency in any complex negotiation) and the legal and economic criteria that the committee would apply.

I then separated the parties and spoke to the people on each side about their interests, their negotiating constraints, and their thoughts about possible avenues for settlement. The developers made a proposal, which the government rejected as inadequate. The agency representatives did express a willingness to consider any alternative structures that met their requirement of regular infusions of cash and a realistic deadline for refinancing, sale of the property, and repayment of the loan, or, alternatively, foreclosure by the government. We went back and forth, alternating between joint and separate sessions. The joint meetings gave the parties the opportunity to work on alternative scenarios for restructuring the loan. The separate meetings permitted me to spend time with each, assessing and developing responses to what became a long series of offers and counteroffers.

By working with the parties individually, I was able to develop with each of them a different standard by which to measure each of the options as they were being developed. For the agency, each possibility was measured against the estimated cost of winning the pending litigation (their winning never really being in doubt, since the money was owed and federal law relieved the agency of the equitable arguments that could have been used against the original lender), the loss of the use of the funds in the meantime, the risk of the developers' becoming bankrupt, and the agency's desire to reduce its inventory of repossessed property. For the developers, each proposal was measured against their ongoing needs for living and operating expenses, their desire to ride out a bad real estate market with their property intact, their interest in limiting legal fees, and the value of their reputation as businesspeople who paid their debts.

By the end of the long day, we had worked out a structure that made sense to all of the parties, including the agency staff in the regional office. The eventual agreement left both sides better off financially than they would have been if the agency had to foreclose on the property and force its sale. The loan was restructured, with some immediate infusions of cash from the developers. The developers' exposure to personal liability, while not eliminated, was reduced. Enough money from tenants' rents was left in an operating account that the partners were able to improve the condition of the building, service the debt, and maximize the value of the property over time. And, critical to the partnership, the management of the property was taken out of the hands of the court-appointed receiver and returned to the business.

The resulting agreement was written up in a day and approved by the agency on schedule. The letters I received from the developers recognized the potential of mediation for turning legal disputes back into business problems, even when large government bureaucracies are involved. One developer wrote:

> You cannot imagine how surprised and pleased we are to have, at long last, settled this dispute. Although we have always felt that the matter could have been resolved by each side sitting down and facing the issues, there never seemed to be an adequate opportunity.
>
> I appreciated your thoughtful listening, forceful guidance in the preparation of counterproposals, dogged representation of each side's point of view, and the meaningful inputs to each step of the negotiation process. I know how persuasive you were in arguing to us on behalf of the agency's proposals and the final result satisfies me that you were every bit the advocate on our behalf.

And the other:

> As one who has experienced the tremendous costs in terms of money, time, and emotion that result from litigation, I am convinced, based upon our experience with you, that it is imperative for the combined viability of our judicial system that mediation continue to play an ever increasing role in the process. The combination of your thorough presentation, the thoughtful framework and process which you provided and your extraordinary mediation skills clearly served as the catalysts which brought about the settlement of this case within a time frame which, I believe, astounded all parties involved.

Negotiating Government Regulations

Government agencies at the federal, state, and local levels issue huge numbers of rules that establish standards for everything from industrial safety to air pollution. Federal agencies alone issue thousands of regulations each year. In order to give those who will be affected by the rules some input into their development, drafts of federal rules are published in the *Federal Register* to notify citizens of impending regulation and elicit their comments. Once a final rule is promulgated, dissatisfied groups may take to court their complaints that the agency has not done its job properly.

This process often satisfies no one. People who care about the rules are frustrated by their inability to affect their content; agencies have broad discretion, as long as they satisfy the technical requirements of creating a "formal record" and allowing public comment. The agencies, on their part, are engulfed in paper and plagued by seemingly endless court challenges to their rules. Philip Harter, one of the pioneers in attempts to change the way federal agencies issue rules, has decried "the malaise of administrative law, which has marched steadily toward reliance on the judiciary to settle disputes and away from direct participation of affected parties."[14] Former EPA official John McGlennon puts it more bluntly:

> In the traditional rulemaking process, a few individuals in a back room at EPA come up with a draft rule that is circulated around EPA for comment, then published in the *Federal Register*. That process ignores the collective thinking of the impacted parties who then take shots at the published rule and are immediately positioned in adversarial relationships. Litigation usually follows.[15]

The EPA, which alone issues 300 regulations each year, most of them detailed and technical, has seen 80 percent of its rules challenged in court. The agency devotes the equivalent of 125 staff positions each year to defending its rules from legal attack. Consequently, the EPA has become active in the search for a way to settle disputes over regulations. According to former EPA Administrator Lee Thomas, the best solution is to promote consultation and negotiation with those parties most directly affected by the agency's regulations: "These are also the parties most likely to sue us. By communicating with potential litigants, and involving them more directly in the rulemaking process, I am hopeful we can establish a broader base of support for our decisions. By giving potential adversaries some ownership in our rules, I am confident we can reduce litigation and increase the speed with which our programs can be implemented."[16]

Who are these adversaries? They include the few hundred small companies that manufacture wood stoves in one case, all the companies that manufacture truck engines in another, and every oil and chemical company in the country in a third. They may include state governments, which have their own interests in the environment and its regulation, and almost always include groups of private citizens who band together to promote clean air and water.

In an effort to involve these diverse parties in negotiating the content of rules, EPA and five other federal agencies have formed ad hoc committees representing the interests affected most directly by a new rule and have charged each committee with drafting the rule. If the committees can reach a consensus, the resulting rule is published for comment in the same manner as rules issued through traditional methods. (Some of the agencies have agreed in advance to publish the committees' rules as their own drafts; others have agreed only to consider them seriously.) The results: Many of the committees have agreed, and so far no regulation produced through the new process has been challenged in court.

The first agency to try the process—given the pet name of "reg-neg" by those who have used it—was not the EPA but the Federal Aviation Administration in the early 1980s. Since shortly after World War II, the FAA had had a rule governing the maximum periods of time pilots could fly and their minimum rest time between assignments. With changes in technology, the regulation long since had grown obsolete, but although the agency had issued more than 1,000 pages of "clarifying" interpretations, revision of the rule had been blocked repeatedly by one group or another. Challenges to the rule twice had reached the Supreme Court.

The FAA decided to try to involve representatives of the warring groups in writing a new rule, both to show them the difficulty of doing so and to blunt their opposition by involving them in the process. It asked a mediator to convene representatives of large and small airlines, unions representing pilots and cabin attendants, public interest groups, aircraft operators, and agency representatives to attempt to draft a joint rule. The committee agreed (as all committees have since) that its decisions must be unanimous or it would produce no new rule.

Although the group failed to agree on all the details of a new rule, the participants asked the FAA to develop a proposed rule within the bounds of its discussion and bring it back to the committee for consideration. The committee then decided that the rule should be published. None of its members submitted opposing comments, the new rule went into effect, and it was not challenged in court.

Since that time, the EPA has used private mediators and reg-negs (the mediators invite the appropriate groups to participate and preside over the negotiations) to develop rules for a variety of situations: granting emergency exemptions from pesticide controls; devising penalties for manufacturing diesel engines that fail to comply with the Clean Air Act; developing emission control standards for wood stoves; cleaning asbestos from schools; and regulating the underground injection of hazardous wastes. In the last instance, environmental groups withdrew from the process before any agreement was reached.

In response to such successful experiments, Congress passed the Negotiated Rulemaking Act of 1990 (NRA), which approved the agencies' prior experiments and established a framework for negotiated rulemaking in the future. Congress defined negotiated rulemaking as the development of agency rules and regulations by the consensus of interested parties. Under the NRA, federal agencies' discretion to convene negotiated rulemaking committees requires only an agency head's determination that the negotiated rulemaking is in the public interest. In making the determination, agency heads are directed to consider whether the following considerations exist: there is a need for the rule; a limited number of identifiable interests will be significantly affected by it; a balanced representation of these interests can be convened and has a reasonable likelihood of reaching consensus in a fixed period of time; the negotiated rulemaking will not delay unreasonably notice of a proposed rule and issuance of a final one; the agency has adequate resources and is willing to commit them to the process; and the extent to which the agency will base its proposed rule on the version reached by the negotiated rulemaking committee. If an agency decides to use negotiated rulemaking, it must publish a notice in the Federal Register announcing its decision, describing the issues and rules to be developed, and explaining how interested participants can become members of the committee. Once convened, the committee also approves the selection of facilitators by consensus.

Since enactment of the NRA, the Federal Communications Commission resolved a seemingly intractable rulemaking proceeding when six parties vied for authorization to mount a new satellite service. In addition to reaching consensus on the parties' sharing of the satellite frequency bands and instituting a framework for the future resolution of many other issues, the FCC obtained objective technical information and analysis that would have been difficult to obtain otherwise. According to an attorney for a participant, "What the committee accomplished in the way of information gathering and analysis in a mere three months could not have been achieved in many more months by the FCC due to its lack of monetary and personnel resources."[17]

The Department of Labor recently experienced similar success with negotiated rulemaking when, as part of its regional pilot program, it developed OSHA standards for the use of the chemical Methylenedianiline through a "reg-neg." Although the process was often controversial and adversarial, not one lawsuit was filed challenging the final rule, with which corporate participants complied even before it was published.

Not all attempts to reach consensus (defined by every committee to date as unanimous agreement), however, have succeeded: The Federal

Trade Commission used a reg-neg unsuccessfully to develop a new rule governing the informal settlement of complaints about products under warranty; the Department of Transportation was unable to deal with handicapped travelers' access to airlines; the Occupational Safety and Health Administration failed to develop a standard governing workers' exposure to the chemical benzene. A participant in the DOT negotiations, which collapsed over the issue of the applicability of airline exit row seating restrictions to blind passengers, described the issue as one viewed by the National Federation of the Blind "as a pure and simple matter of discrimination" and by the carriers "as a clear cut safety issue."[18] In the OSHA attempt, the group was unable to agree on a joint regulation, although the industry and union representatives came much closer than many skeptics had predicted. Undaunted, OSHA began another reg-neg to propose a standard for workers' exposure to MDA, a carcinogenic chemical used in the manufacture of plasters.

One difference between the process for negotiating regulations and other settlement attempts is that issues in reg-negs frequently have not yet crystallized into "disputes." Consequently, the ever-present question of who should be at the table is made even more complicated. At first, reg-negs involved no more than fifteen people; now, under the act, the number is usually limited to twenty-five, unless the agency head determines that more are needed. Some of the participants avoid the strict limitations on numbers by bringing with them a seemingly endless supply of "alternates." This practice creates difficulties for groups with comparatively fewer resources, particularly when "alternates" have been permitted to serve on subcommittees to consider specific issues.

Agencies often ask mediators to recommend which people must be invited to participate if the result is to be credible to the necessary constituencies. In this situation the mediators contact literally dozens of individuals, asking each one to suggest others who should be included in order to give the resulting rule broad public acceptance. An announcement of the negotiations is published in the *Federal Register*. When someone who wants to attend is not invited (a disgruntled inventor of woodstoves, for example, in an industry where there are 200–300 manufacturers, all of them small), the person may request admission—or simply show up anyway.

Federal and state "sunshine" laws have been interpreted to require that reg-neg committee meetings be open to the public. Unlike in most mediations, which are premised on confidentiality, an official notetaker keeps public minutes of meetings, and anything revealed can be used in litigation. As a result, much of the negotiation takes place in sidebar caucuses or small working groups.

As in other face-to-face negotiations, participants find that the process dissipates some of their stereotypes and forces them to work together. Coalitions form quickly. For example, Kelly Brown, manager of emission control planning for the Ford Motor Company, commented: "[F]or the first time, my competitors and I were part of a team. Rather than trying to outsmart each other, we had to consider each other's needs as part of an industry group."[19] Frequently, representatives of similar interests start the meetings by clustering together. Over time, these patterns loosen, with people sitting all over the room and chatting during breaks. Mediators run the meetings, often using humor to get through the tense spots. At a recent EPA reg-neg, for example, the parties resolved unanimously to pass the hat for cookies when the agency failed to provide them. Many of the participants see the greatest benefit as the opportunity to deal directly with one another, rather than being relegated to submitting reams of paper to an invisible agency.

Nevertheless, participation in frequent all-day meetings in Washington is expensive. When asked what special problems reg-neg posed, Ford's Kelly Brown replied, "Time and money. My travel budget got destroyed."[20] For representatives of environmental and other public interest groups, the handicaps are more serious. David Doniger, an attorney with the National Resources Defense Council, noted that participating in a reg-neg takes about ten times as much of the group's resources as commenting on a rule.[21]

EPA attempted to meet this problem by establishing a "resource pool" to enable interests that otherwise could not afford to participate to be represented. The resource pool, administered by a private, neutral organization, has reimbursed some representatives for travel expenses and technical studies. But there are strings attached: Reimbursement for technical consultants requires the consent of the whole committee, and the information produced by consultants is accessible to the entire group. The FTC's failure to set up a similar fund evoked bitter complaints at its single reg-neg. So far, no agency has been willing to pay participants for their time, and the act does not require or encourage them to do so.

Significant imbalances of power among participants remain. For example, when the environmental manager of Du Pont attended the negotiation over regulating the underground injection of chemicals he was accompanied by a phalanx of attorneys, engineers, chemists, geologists, and drilling experts. Representatives of environmental interests felt outnumbered and outgunned. When the issues are as technically complex and scientifically uncertain as those concerning burying hazardous chemicals, environmental and other citizens' groups naturally become distrustful of agreeing with industry-generated proposals.

At an early point in the FTC meetings over procedures to be followed in resolving warranty disputes, a representative of the Massachusetts attorney general's office noted that removing conflict from the process of writing rules may not be desirable if it leaves consumers vulnerable to industry interests. Barbara Gregg, director of the Montgomery County (Maryland) Office of Consumer Affairs, and a participant in the FTC regneg, expressed her fear of "giving away the store" by becoming too caught up in the process and too eager to be agreeable. After more experience with the process, the Massachusetts representative concluded that the reg-neg experience was useful even if it failed to produce a new rule. At a minimum, she thought, the intense interaction among participants helped the manufacturers to understand how existing policies actually affected consumers in practice and to focus on the practical realities of resolving complaints about their products.

Some mediators have managed to neutralize differences among the parties in numbers and resources. These individuals see their role as one of clarifying issues and helping participants to understand and communicate their interests. Other mediators have been criticized by participants for being too passive. The more complex and controversial the issue, the more likely it is that the mediators will become actively involved.

The process of rulemaking by consensus has its critics. In 1986, for example, a Congress frustrated with the inadequacy of a volunteer program to handle asbestos in schools passed the Asbestos Hazard Emergency Response Act, which required the EPA to issue regulations with specific instructions for local education agencies. Forced to deal with complex issues in a short time, the EPA decided to handle the task through a reg-neg process. Participants included the National Parent-Teacher Association, the Service Employees International Union, school officials, former asbestos product manufacturers, members of the environmental community, engineers, representatives from the states, and EPA officials.

The group had only eight weeks to reach agreement on a wide range of highly difficult and technical areas. At the end of that time, twenty of the twenty-four participants ultimately signed a document, but they made clear it was only to be a proposal that they reserved the right to (and in fact did) criticize after its publication. Although most involved were pleased with the discussions and the "good faith and good will" different groups showed in addressing the issues, many participants, especially those from nonprofit organizations, felt overwhelmed by the brief time they had to absorb difficult materials.

A more fundamental criticism of the consensus-oriented process was voiced by Brian Christopher of the Alice Hamilton Occupational Health Center. He later had misgivings about having signed the document. "The presumption of compromise may not serve the purpose of protecting public health and environment under law," he said. "The goal of getting a good regulation that protects the health and safety of workers and students is almost submerged by the desire to produce a regulation by consensus."[22] Similarly, Margaret Zaleski, of the Public Protection Unit of the Massachusetts Department of the Attorney General, expressed her concern that the "process became more important than the substance."[23] Although others saw substantial problems with the negotiation experience, they emphasized that the end result looked far better when compared with the typical notice-and-comment rulemaking process. According to reg-neg mediator Philip Harter, the EPA rules that have resulted from reg-negs have been both more environmentally protective and more practical to implement than rules developed through the traditional process.[24]

It is too soon to tell whether the environmental and consumer groups' reservations can (or should) be overcome. Environmentalists walked out of the EPA's reg-neg sessions on the underground injection of hazardous waste, citing their mistrust of the industry participants and the large number of interrelated, technically complex issues that would have to be resolved before a rule could be written.

In the meantime, the process of developing regulations or other policies by consensus has spread to state public utility commissions in Colorado and New Mexico, to the Coastal Zone Agency in Massachusetts, to the state environmental protection agency in Vermont, and to Departments of Sanitation in New York City and Philadelphia. The Maryland Office of Environmental Programs used a mediator to involve scientists, fishermen, and representatives of businesses and state and local government agencies in drafting a "nutrient control strategy" for the Patuxent River. In Virginia, the state legislature asked a mediator to convene a roundtable of farmers, foresters, businesses, and state legislators to develop joint recommendations concerning the hotly contested question of land use around the Chesapeake Bay.

Finally, former congressman Morris Udall used a variant of regulatory negotiation—yet to be called "leg-neg"—to develop federal legislation. Landowners, businesses, and the Papago Indians jointly developed a bill, which eventually became the Southern Arizona Water Rights Settlement Act of 1982, to define access to water in the region surrounding Tucson. At the state level, many observers credit the success of the legislation establishing Iowa's farm credit mediation program to the fact that it was negotiated by representatives of the farmers and bankers who would use it.

Negotiating Budgets

In addition to drafting regulations and recommendations to legislators, mediators occasionally have succeeded in bringing together parties with diverse interests to agree on priorities for spending public money. In the late 1970s and early 1980s, the Kettering Foundation recruited three midwestern cities to experiment with a process it called "negotiated investment strategies." Faced with declining federal and state aid and industrial flight from the Rust Belt, the cities of Gary, Indiana, Columbus, Ohio, and Saint Paul, Minnesota, volunteered. Negotiating "teams" were formed in each city to represent various levels of government—city, state, and federal. The teams met regularly with a mediator and, in between, among themselves to agree on priorities.

The process produced a set of joint recommendations for allocating funds in all three cities. In Saint Paul, for example, William J. Usery, former secretary of labor and director of the Federal Mediation and Conciliation Service, guided mediation sessions over a five-month period toward detailed agreements to pursue four projects requiring both governmental and private funding. Participation in the negotiations convinced members of the business community that local government was serious about contributing tax funds to rebuilding the city and attracted private resources to the city's redevelopment.

After the three initial experiments, a mediation in Connecticut distributed cutbacks in the federal money available for state social welfare services. The director of Social Services agreed to forward to the legislature the joint recommendations of a group representing private organizations and local governments if the group could reach a consensus on distributing the remaining funds. It did, and the legislature adopted its recommendations.

In Malden, Massachusetts, the mayor convened a similar group, this one composed of three teams—citizens, businesses, and city government. The group was charged with coming up with a plan to handle the burgeoning budget deficits that resulted when Massachusetts voters in 1980 approved Proposition 2½, a law limiting state and local taxes. The mayor, who had been elected only recently by a narrow margin, anticipated substantial controversy over any reductions in city services that a reduced budget would force him to make. Each team met with a mediator in order to develop its own consensus on the city's most pressing needs. The entire group then convened and produced a draft final agreement, which it published in the local newspaper. Taking citizens' comments into account, the group then produced a final series of recommendations, most of which were implemented by the city. The label of "negotiated investment strategies" also has been applied to the process employed in New Jersey by state and local governments to coordinate growth management plans, in Washington and Florida to resolve disputes among local governments, and in Connecticut to reach agreements among municipalities on plans for disbursing affordable housing.

Convening and working with teams of citizens and government officials require so much time on the part of both participants and mediators (as well as money to pay the mediators) that only a budgetary crisis or the support of a foundation has as yet provided enough incentive to bring all the necessary parties together. Participants in the mediations that have taken place generally report satisfaction with the process. Because they occur on a state or local level, the problem of long-distance travel is not nearly as acute as in federal-level mediations. Furthermore, the issues generally are less technical than in the reg-negs, and participation consequently is more accessible to all who are interested.

Disputes in Public Institutions

High school students Mike and Gary were at a Christmas party at a friend's home when Gary heard a rumor that Mike had been calling him names behind his back. Gary confronted Mike, and the two began to argue. The other guests crowded around them, and one of Gary's friends took out a gun and pointed it at Mike. The party broke up short of violence, and everyone left.

The first day back at school after Christmas vacation, Mike found Gary and said he wanted to fight it out once and for all. Gary replied that he did not want to be suspended and thus did not want to fight. He went to the office of SHARP (Students Helping with Alternative Resolutions Program) and requested mediation.

The mediation was held in a small room at the Calvin Coolidge High School in Washington, D.C., where both Gary and Mike were sophomores. A sophomore girl and a freshman boy mediated. No teacher was present, but the SHARP coordinator, employed by the Center for Dispute Settlement, watched from the back of the room.

The mediators began by explaining to Mike and Gary that SHARP offered an alternative to suspension and a way for them to solve their own problem. In the course of the next hour, both Mike and Gary agreed that their fight had been caused by an unfounded rumor and that it would not continue. Mike acknowledged that he had been more angry at Gary's friend than at Gary, but that when he could not fight the friend, he sought revenge on Gary. Gary confessed that he had no taste for fighting, especially since he was much smaller than Mike. Both boys asked the mediators about SHARP and expressed interest in becoming mediators themselves. They promised to return to the program if they had problems in the future.

After the mediation session ended, Mike told the coordinator that he had come in wanting to fight. "I figured I could just cool it through the meeting, then leave and punch Gary out. I expected the mediators to tell me what to do. I thought I'd just let it roll off my back. But they didn't. They asked what I thought about what had happened—and what I wanted to happen in the future. It felt really good to let it all come out. I'd like to be able to do that myself." The coordinator immediately enrolled Mike in the next training course for student mediators.

SHARP, a program modeled after a similar project dubbed SMART (School Mediators' Alternative Resolution Team) in New York City, trains students and teachers to resolve in-school conflict. Its aims: to reduce school violence, to provide an alternative to suspension, and, perhaps most importantly, to help students learn ways of responding to conflict other than by fighting or dropping out. In the 1987–1988 school year, a time of increasing violence among teens in Washington, three-fourths of the students subject to suspension for fighting and misconduct in Mike's and Gary's school resolved their disputes with student mediators and stayed in class. Two years later, following a shooting incident between students at a local high school, the District of Columbia Board of Education took over fiscal responsibility for SHARP and expanded the program to seven schools. The school system now has adopted a policy of training teachers and other school personnel in mediation, with the goal of expanding SHARP to every elementary and junior and senior high school in the system.

Mediation programs in New York City junior high and high schools are supported by the Board of Education's school dropout prevention program. As one principal told the *New York Times,* "Mediation has cut our suspension rate in half."

In San Francisco and a few other cities students mediate in elementary schools. In Anchorage, Alaska, more than half of the city's fifty-five elementary schools offer "conflict resolution training." According to the *Anchorage Daily News,* 8 percent fewer children were suspended from school in 1992 than in 1991 as a result—even though elementary schools experienced a 2 to 3 percent increase in attendance. Pupils in grades four through six have broken up scuffles on the playground and lunch money extortion rings. One sixth grader—who wears a jersey emblazoned with the words "Conflict Resolver"—confides: "We learn what our gestures, such as crossing our arms in anger, mean to other people. We make sure we don't tell anybody what to do so they can figure it out themselves and so they don't get angry."

According to the National Association for Mediation in Education, over 5,000 schools, many of them in New York, Massachusetts, and California but a few scattered across the Midwest in Cleveland, Chicago, Kansas City, and Minneapolis–Saint Paul, now have school-based mediation programs. In other cities, mediators from local dispute centers train students to help other students handle their own conflicts; the centers also train student-teacher teams to mediate disputes between students and teachers. One sign of the programs' success is the number of students who go through mediation as disputants and then ask to be trained as mediators. Another is that some students, after taking part in mediation as disputants or as mediators, take problems to the programs on their own initiative, without waiting for fights or school-imposed discipline.

Participating in mediation gives students a chance to cool off, to express their anger in a nonthreatening atmosphere, and to discuss the causes of their scuffles, preferably before they escalate. Preliminary observations of the New York program suggest that the student mediation efforts, in addition to keeping students in school, have reduced school violence to some extent and have improved teachers' attitudes toward student discipline. The program's most dramatic effect, however, has been to improve the self-image of the students who serve as mediators—often themselves former disciplinary problems. As one New York high schooler described his experience, first as a fighter who was sent to mediation, then as a trained mediator:

> Within minutes, the mediator had me and the person I fought with laughing together. I knew that if I could talk and act calmly instead of getting upset, I may never have to fight again! ... As I went through the training I realized that 9 out of 10 times the most unlikely words could cause people to get very upset. I learned that the best way to avoid a fight is to talk out the problem. ... I began getting better grades in my classes. I do not react in a violent way to people who are only out to bring everyone else down with them. At home I found that I did not argue with my family as much as before.[25]

The successful initial experiments, although far from the total answer to school violence, have begun to pique educators' interest. As a result, the first teaching materials on ways of resolving conflicts other than through violence or formal courtlike hearing procedures have been produced. The Aetna Insurance Company has launched a program to distribute conflict resolution curricula and teaching materials at its own expense to any school that requests them. With conflict resolution making its first appearance in social studies curricula, the next generation may be more likely than its predecessors to know the difference between mediation and meditation (with which it often is confused).

It was not always so. In the 1970s some of us who had developed programs for resolving conflicts in prisons and trained prisoners and line staff to help settle grievances began trying to apply the same techniques to public high schools. A short-lived era of prison reform in the 1970s, brought about by shrinking prison populations and increasing court interest in prisoners' rights, provided an environment conducive to developing grievance procedures, some of which involved both outside mediators or arbitrators and prisoners themselves in resolving other prisoners' complaints. Only some of those programs, primarily in states such as California and New York, which passed legislation mandating the procedures, remain today. The reform movement has abated, prisons are bulging with excess populations, and administrators' fears of ceding any measure of control to prisoners or outsiders have returned.

Efforts to establish students' rights made even less headway than prison reform. Students' challenges to authority and attempts to develop lists of rights that could not be infringed by school officials never made much progress in the courts. Perhaps because of the continued imbalance of power between students and school administrators, few processes to resolve disagreements between students (or their parents) and teachers or school administrators developed until the 1980s, when a few community dispute centers began to extend their use of mediation into the schools and to focus less on developing rights than on settling disputes. It is too early to tell whether their efforts can encompass conflicts between students and their parents and teachers or administrators as well as disagreements with other students.

In a somewhat different context, one governed by a federal law, parents and school administrators are using mediation to deal with disagreements over educating handicapped children. Massachusetts was first to use the process (in 1976); now over half the states provide for mediation between local school officials and the parents of handicapped children. The purpose: to avoid the costly, time-consuming, and emotionally draining administrative hearings that are permitted annually under the Education for All Handicapped Children Act.

The purpose of the legislation, passed by Congress in 1975, is to ensure that handicapped children receive an appropriate education at public expense. To meet this goal, the act provides federal funds to state and local school systems. In order to qualify for federal aid, a state must provide parents of handicapped children with an annual "impartial due process hearing" if the parents disagree with the school's plan for educating their child. The parents may file suit in federal court if they dispute the state agency's final decision.

Although no form of dispute settlement other than court or formal administrative hearings is mentioned in the statute, a growing number of states are devoting significant resources to mediating disputes over special education. In most of the programs, mediators are full- or part-time employees of the state educational agencies, which hear parents' appeals from local plans. They offer parents the option of mediating before convening formal hearings. (In the larger states, the mediators' sole function is to resolve disputes over special education.) Although the quality of individual states' programs and the number of disputes actually resolved through mediation vary considerably, most of the programs appear to settle about three-quarters of all the cases they mediate.

A colleague and I observed an example of this type of mediation in a small industrial city in Massachusetts. The mother of a three-year-old girl with a mild case of cerebral palsy had requested that the public schools assume responsibility for the various therapies her daughter would need in order to benefit from education. The school acceded to some of her demands, agreeing to provide occupational therapy and consultation with the private day-care program that the little girl would continue to attend. But the school resisted the mother's request for one hour of physical therapy each week. The student's "individualized educational program," required by federal law, was believed to be met by the proposal for thirty minutes of physical therapy every two weeks.

The mother balked. The girl was making progress, and her mother feared that she would regress unless this level of therapy was maintained. She rejected the school department's plan, triggering the appeals process. The school district forwarded the rejected plan to the regional mediator and the state's Bureau of Special Education Appeals. A mediation conference ensued.

The mother, shy and reserved, was accompanied to mediation by an advocate from the state's Office for Children. The special education director was accompanied by the physical therapist who had prepared the school's therapy recommendations and who would provide the therapy. The nursery school teacher was also present.

The mediator, a state employee, opened the session by explaining the process and emphasizing its confidentiality and informality and his desire that the parties reach a settlement acceptable to all. The mother's advocate spoke first, outlining the child's history and the mother's requests for more frequent consultation between the school district and the nursery school program and the provision of therapy (both occupational and physical) throughout the summer. The special education director then stated the school's position that the child did not need one hour of physical therapy per week and that thirty minutes every two weeks was adequate. She said that the school district already had agreed to greater consultation with the nursery school and that a summer program probably could be worked out, although the school district's summer plans were not yet final.

The mediator then separated the parties, moving the special education director and the therapist to another office. For the remainder of the three and one-half hour session, the mediator shuttled from one room to the other. The mother refused to modify her position. She believed that the child needed one hour of physical therapy a week; independent assessments had recommended it, and she thought that the school should provide it. Although initially maintaining that the child did not need an hour each week of physical therapy, the school officials conceded in a private caucus with the mediator that there was a more critical hurdle: The school district had one physical therapist (who was present), and she simply did not have the time in her schedule to provide this child with a full hour each week.

At the conclusion of one round of private sessions, the case appeared stalemated. The mother (who initially had been too nervous to speak but gradually was participating) appeared to be unyielding. The therapist was aggrieved at having her judgment questioned and her already overbooked schedule potentially swamped. The special education director believed that she had done all she could.

The mediator changed the subject. The school already had agreed in principle to the mother's request for greater consultation and a summer program; the details were then worked out. At about this time, the teacher, who had said very little, told the mediator she felt she might have been misleading in her earlier remarks. She said she was nervous, had never participated in mediation before, and had not known what to say. She then described in some detail the child's physical condition and the modifications the nursery school staff had made to enable her to participate in the regular daily program of activities.

Then the mediator reconvened the group. Agreements regarding consultation and the summer program were ratified. The teacher gave the. school department personnel her view of the child's condition and the special attention and program modification she required; the mother spoke up to say that one reason she wanted the hour of therapy a week was to help maintain the child's determination and her sense that it was important she do her exercises, even though she often did not want to.

The mediator separated the disputants again, caucusing first with the school representatives. The therapist said that she might be able to find a half hour each week. The special education director told her that she did not have to disrupt her schedule. The therapist offered a specific half-hour slot.

The mother rejected the thirty minutes per week. It was clear that she would go to a hearing rather than accept anything less than the hour she had requested.

After much juggling of her schedule, the therapist eventually "found" an hour each week. The resulting agreement provided for one hour per week of individual physical therapy, together with bimonthly consultations and a summer program of physical and occupational therapy.

Although they are not always pleased with a particular mediator or a particular outcome, parents of handicapped children and representatives of school districts have been overwhelmingly enthusiastic in their evaluation of mediation. Parents are satisfied with the process for several different reasons:

The school district cannot walk all over us.

The mediator knew our rights and wouldn't let the school ignore them.

The mediator made things a lot easier by being a neutral third party and taking in both sides.

The mediator helped us to feel at ease and took the mystery out of the process.

We were able to settle the case and learned a lot.

It kept us out of a hearing and helped us apply pressure to the district.

The mediator listened to me.

We got what we wanted.

Even parents who hired lawyers and condemned the expense, who felt outnumbered by a phalanx of school officials, or who disliked not knowing what was going on in the other room when the mediator met separately with school officials reported that they thought the mediator was fair and they would use the process again.[26] Despite this support, some of the state-run programs have fallen victim to budgetary shortfalls. Ironically, the Massachusetts program, which saved parents and schools significant amounts of time and money as well as satisfying participants on all sides, no longer exists.

Whether the successful use of mediation in special education can be transferred to other types of disputes between individuals and public institutions remains to be seen. Disagreements over special education include a number of features that may or may not be present in other contexts:

- A continuing relationship between the disputants—parents and school districts—that lasts for as long as the child is in school (potentially 18 years)
- Multi-issue disputes, in which there is much room for judgment, disagreement, and creativity—and thus for negotiation
- Disagreements over plans for the future, as opposed to actions in the past

- In the states with the most active mediation programs, well-trained, skillful mediators who are knowledgeable about both legal and educational issues
- Active advocacy groups, which educate parents about their rights under the law and, on occasion, represent them at both mediations and hearings
- Individuals who come from all socioeconomic and ethnic groups
- A complex yet clear framework of laws, which have been enforced consistently
- Federal and state statutes, which created extensive new entitlements for individuals and gave them the right to demand specific procedures annually
- A burdensome alternative to mediation—the formal due process hearing
- A community of interest between the disputants: the education of a child who has needs with which all the parties can sympathize.

Perhaps, ultimately, the reason that mediation is so successful in this arena is that the process nurtures rather than destroys the trust and cooperation needed among people with an interest in the education of children with special needs.

Public institutions other than schools or prisons have even fewer ways of resolving conflicts informally. Hospitals, facilities for the mentally ill or retarded, and nursing homes all face special problems in settling disputes among patients, between patients and staff, or between patients and administrators. Added to the power imbalance between individuals and the institutions that house them are questions of whether patients are competent to participate in resolving their own disagreements.

Problems are acute in both public and private nursing homes because of the large numbers of Americans (close to 2 million at last count) who spend their last years in them, their extended stays, and the frequently crippling costs, which often leave residents with no resources and no place else to go. In addition to day-to-day disputes over the quality of care, food, clothing, and recreation, there are allegations of neglect and abuse by staff and loss or mismanagement of property or money. Disagreements arise over medical treatment or payment. Finally, disputes over denial of admission, involuntary discharge, or forced transfers to less desirable facilities produce extremely serious situations.

The Older Americans Act of 1965 requires each state to establish a "long-term care ombudsman" to investigate complaints in nursing homes. The ombudspeople, frequently aided by cadres of retired volunteers, are supported by state and federal funds. The system has limited resources and varies significantly from state to state.

All the ombudspeople investigate complaints by nursing home residents or their relatives of egregious mistreatment. Beyond this statutory function, some offices view their function as one of advocacy on behalf of individual residents, while others function strictly as investigators or fact-finders. So far they have not attempted to involve residents and nursing home staff in solving problems. Supplementing the ombudspeople either with outside mediators (as in the special education disputes) or with residents and staff taught to mediate internally (as in the high school programs) is an idea the ombudspeople themselves, as well as outside organizations of dispute resolvers, are beginning to explore.

Whatever the ultimate shape of health care reform in the United States, it seems likely to include dispute resolution options for addressing questions of access to care and payment for treatment and apportioning liability for professional malpractice.

Disputes over Enforcing Laws

Government agencies with responsibility for enforcing laws increasingly are turning to mediation (or "conciliation," as they often label it) to handle private citizens' charges that another citizen or business has broken a law. Numerous federal, state, and local statutes, for example, prohibit decisions about hiring, firing, promotion, or furnishing services from being based on a long list of illegitimate distinctions: race, sex, national origin, handicap, age, and (sometimes) sexual orientation or marital status. For people with complaints, it often has proved even more difficult to get relief under these laws than it was to get them passed in the first place. From the point of view of the businesses complained about, the process can be burdensome and expensive.

Investigations by agencies given responsibility for enforcing anti-discrimination laws frequently are slow and frustrating. Waiting periods can drag on for years. By then the relief sought, such as a promotion, reinstatement, or admission to a government-funded program, long since has become moot. In terms of time and expense, going to court may be even worse.

Reacting to these pressures, federal and local enforcement agencies have devised a variety of informal ways of settling complaints of discrimination. In some, investigators combine mediation with an early attempt to discover the facts behind each complaint. Thus, for example, the investigator will invite an employee complaining of being illegally passed over for promotion, together with a representative of the employer, to discuss the situation and attempt to settle. The federal Equal Employment Opportunity Commission, which began such a program in the 1970s under the leadership of Eleanor Holmes Norton, reported settling approximately 60 percent of its cases in this fashion. The EEOC was criticized by a variety of constituencies for combining its investigatory and dispute resolution functions and de-emphasized its settlement role. It is now experimenting with referring complaints to outside mediators soon after they are filed.

Independent agencies (such as the Federal Mediation and Conciliation Service) or private organizations (such as the Center for Dispute Settlement in Washington, D.C., or the Minneapolis, Minnesota, Mediation Center), also mediate cases referred by agencies responsible for dealing with discrimination. The Center for Dispute Settlement implemented an eighteen-month pilot program under the EEOC's auspices to use private mediators to resolve cases referred by the EEOC. Mediators in each of four field offices (in Houston, New York, Philadelphia, and Washington, D.C.) worked with volunteering parties alleging discriminatory discharge, discipline, or terms and conditions of employment. The cases were screened so that those that seemed to indicate a pattern of discrimination were kept out of mediation. Agreements had the same force as any settlement reached through the EEOC; if an agreement was not reached, the case was referred back to the EEOC's normal investigative process. Preliminary figures indicated that slightly more than half of all cases in which the parties chose to mediate were settled through the process.

Lacking the clout of those who ultimately decide which complaints have merit, mediators who are independent of the agencies have an easier time avoiding the use of actual or implied threats—or "muscle mediation." (They also may settle fewer cases.)

In one interesting but short-lived experiment, the Federal Mediation and Conciliation Service sent complaints of age discrimination from half of its regions to its professional staff labor mediators, while sending complaints from the other half to trained community mediators. The community mediators, most of whom had prior experience as volunteers mediating interpersonal disputes or working with the elderly, helped parties to settle almost twice the proportion of complaints as the professional labor mediators.[27]

Some critics have condemned the use of informal settlement techniques to resolve complaints brought under laws governing important public policies such as discrimination, consumer protection, or housing. Fears that settlements will pacify legitimate complaints, thus hiding them from public scrutiny, battle against the recognition that perhaps the majority of these complaints cannot be resolved at all if they are not settled promptly. Yet the few test cases provide the impetus to settle the thousands of others. Those of us who have worked with individuals complaining of discrimination or consumer abuse know only too well that they often prefer getting faster, less expensive, and private relief to becoming test cases. The reality is that the overwhelming majority of lawsuits, including those brought by governmental enforcement agencies or private civil rights plaintiffs, are settled prior to a full trial. Thus, the question in most instances is not whether but how to settle—how soon, how effectively, and at what cost. For some complainants, whose disputes involve continuing relationships with employers or colleagues (denial of tenure at a university, for example), some sort of mediation may provide the only possibility of keeping critical relationships intact while settling the immediate dispute.

A few government agencies have begun to experiment with mediation as a way of administering government benefit programs. A Massachusetts law, for example, provides for voluntary "conciliation" by employees of the agency that decides on claims for workers' compensation. The conciliators have no decisionmaking functions. Their settlement sessions are private, and (unlike in many of the discrimination agencies) most of the information developed is protected from later use in formal hearings if no settlement is achieved.

The Challenge of Public Dispute Resolution

Disputes over using land and natural resources, spending government money, devising rules, or managing public institutions often risk impasse if no way can be found to achieve consensus. The issues are often diffuse and technically complex, the parties unorganized. Except in the rare cases of legislatively created procedures, such as those for disputes over discrimination or (in a few states) over siting hazardous waste facilities, there may be no deadlines or alternatives (such as court) for reaching resolution.

To many of us, the challenge is also the promise: We are attempting to devise ways outside of the usual bureaucratic structure, which so often produces stalemate, to create consensus by satisfying the interests of the people most concerned with the outcome.

8

ADR and
the Legal System

A MOVEMENT BEGUN SCARCELY TWENTY YEARS ago by a few pioneers has become an integral part of the legal system. As we have seen, growing numbers of courts, in different types of cases, now encourage or require litigants to participate in some variation of mediation or arbitration before they may go to trial. Almost every federal district court already has adopted or is in the process of adopting some form of alternative dispute resolution. Even in responding to appeals of district court decisions, most of the federal circuits now have programs that require significant numbers of litigants to participate in mediation, either in person or by telephone conference call. According to a survey by the National Center for State Courts, approximately 1,200 state and local courts now have some sort of ADR program.

Recent federal legislation has encouraged the increasing reliance on dispute resolution techniques by trial courts. In 1990, Congress passed the Civil Justice Reform Act (CJRA), which requires every federal district court to design and implement its own plan to reduce the expense and delay of civil litigation. The CJRA specifically encourages courts to include alternative dispute resolution programs in their plans "where appropriate." Almost all have done so.

Although many of the federal programs involve judicial persuasion of parties to participate in mediation, participation increasingly is made mandatory. Regardless of the degree of their coercion into mediation, about half the parties settle in mediation at the federal trial court level, somewhat fewer (one-third to 40 percent) in the courts of appeals. One exception is the Southern District of New York, headquartered in Manhattan, where a cadre of trained volunteer lawyers, meeting an average of three sessions per case with parties ordered into mediation by the court, settles close to 80 percent of all cases assigned to mediation. Fifty-one percent of the mediation cases were resolved within a year of filing, as compared with 31 percent of the cases that were eligible for mediation (prisoners, social security, and tax cases are not) but not sent for purposes of evaluation.

In 1988, Congress enacted the Court-Annexed Arbitration Act, which established a five-year pilot program in twenty federal districts. Ten of the districts were authorized to include mandatory arbitration, while the other ten were not. A study conducted by the Rand Institute revealed that cases assigned to mandatory court-annexed arbitration in North Carolina cost litigants 20 percent less than a similar control group.[1]

States also have discovered settlement-oriented processes. Through legislation and court rule they rapidly are encouraging, requiring, or regulating various procedures for settling disputes ranging from determining child custody to siting hazardous waste facilities or foreclosing against farm property. A 1990 survey of state laws lists over 300 statutes from the 50 states and the District of Columbia concerning alternative dispute resolution.[2] Of these, more than 200 deal with areas other than traditional labor-management negotiations. Two-thirds of the laws outside the labor field have been enacted since 1980.

At least twenty states have passed comprehensive legislation to define and encourage the development of alternative dispute resolution. In Texas, Florida, and Indiana, laws go beyond encouragement and authorize judges to require that virtually any civil case be sent to mediation or nonbinding arbitration. (Referral to binding arbitration requires the parties' consent.) Courts in several large cities, with the encouragement of the American Bar Association, have also instituted "multidoor courthouse" programs, modeled on a suggestion made by Harvard law professor Frank Sander at the Roscoe Pound Conference in 1976, to offer litigants a choice of nonlitigative processes.

Despite these steps, which generally are considered to be improvements, practitioners share growing concerns over the quality of alternative dispute resolution programs designed by courts, sometimes hastily, without adequate planning or resources. Warns Margaret Shaw, former director of the Institute of Judicial Administration, "Ultimately, the real issue is how we can insure that the experiments are going to take place with quality, especially in light of tremendous fiscal cutbacks."[3]

Without waiting for legislation, some judges, having grown tired of trying long, drawn-out cases, regularly adopt the role of "mediator" in an effort to bring about faster, more satisfactory solutions. Federal Judge Robert C. Zampano and Connecticut Superior Judge Frank S. Meadow, for example, jointly mediated a $41 million settlement of all legal claims involved in the collapse of a high-rise construction project in Bridgeport, Connecticut. Reacting enthusiastically to their experiences, some of these judges have become the most ardent boosters of settlement alternatives.

As lawyers, from corporate to domestic relations, become increasingly sophisticated about settlement processes, they are writing them into their contracts. Growing numbers of agreements require parties to engage in mediation or arbitration should a dispute arise between them in the future. The most sophisticated of these agreements structure multitiered processes, which progress from negotiation to mediation, or occasionally a minitrial, and culminate in arbitration or litigation only where the nonbinding processes are unable to produce agreement. On the international level, the United States–Canada Free Trade Agreement, which went into effect at the beginning of 1988, calls for the use of a variety of procedures, including mediation, arbitration, and panels of neutral experts, to resolve most of the disputes that may arise over the agreement's interpretation or application.

Some insurance companies, together with manufacturers of allegedly defective or injury-producing goods, have decided that using mediation or arbitration not only lowers their transaction costs but reduces the uncertainties that can shut off whole areas of insurance business (insuring swimming clubs with diving boards, for example). Consequently, several insurers have started to make wholesale referrals of disputed claims to certain dispute resolution providers. Similar arrangements exist between several car manufacturers and the Council of Better Business Bureaus for warranty complaints about new cars. The Manville Personal Injury Settlement Trust, which was created by the bankruptcy court to settle or litigate all claims of death or injury to workers exposed to asbestos manufactured by the Johns Manville Corporation, negotiated with claimants' attorneys a whole array of settlement possibilities, to be provided by private mediators, arbitrators, and neutral experts. Similar structures were crafted for the multiple claims that stemmed from injuries allegedly caused by the Dalkon Shield.

Some professionals in the field are growing increasingly uncomfortable with the relationship between such large users of dispute resolution services and particular mediators, arbitrators, or private programs whose business may come largely or even exclusively from a single customer. They question whether people who rely on obtaining business solely or primarily from an institution that is a party to a continuing stream of disputes can remain impartial concerning the outcomes of those disputes.

In the early days of alternative dispute resolution, efforts relied heavily—sometimes exclusively—on volunteers or a few private dispute settlers with substantial support from foundations. Now, although community and some court programs still make heavy use of volunteers, the field is becoming increasingly professionalized and, in some cases, commercialized. This development has caused considerable ambivalence among practitioners. Indeed, futurist Paul Shay questions whether the sense that conflict resolution is a "calling" has prevented many dispute resolvers from charging clients what their services are worth and thus retarded the development of a cadre of professional neutrals.[4] Similarly, Harvard law professor Frank E.A. Sander, creator of the multidoor courthouse concept, warns that overreliance on volunteer mediators by financially strapped states and localities not only inhibits the professionalization of the field but also the increased use of mediation in large-scale commercial and public policy disputes.[5]

Some of the emerging businesses have no such ambivalence. One national franchise of arbitrators and mediators recently projected annual revenues of $30 million; its chief competitor projects revenues of $10 million. Meanwhile, the legal establishment has embraced dispute settlement alternatives. The American Bar Association's committee on dispute resolution began in the 1970s as the Special Committee on the Resolution of Minor Disputes, evolved into the Special Committee on Dispute Resolution, then, ultimately, because of widespread interest by attorneys and others, it was designated the Section on Dispute Resolution. A few large law firms have established negotiation or ADR departments alongside their still-burgeoning litigation departments. A considerably larger number of law firms and corporate legal departments are providing training in ADR for all their attorneys.

As recently as 1982, the New Jersey Bar tried to prevent a lawyer from acting as a divorce mediator, asserting that in so doing the lawyer was committing malpractice. Some legal scholars, who subsequently predicted that it would be considered malpractice for a lawyer to fail to discuss alternatives to litigation when advising clients on the most effective ways of resolving their disputes, have been proved correct. In New Jersey, the state bar association recently adopted a resolution in which it urges New Jersey lawyers to inform their clients about ADR. Colorado instituted an ethical rule that requires all of its attorneys to advise their clients of alternative forms of dispute resolution in any matter "involving or expected to involve litigation." The "Texas Lawyer's Creed: A Mandate for Professionalism," which was adopted by the state's Supreme Court, includes a pledge by lawyers to advise clients regarding the availability of mediation, arbitration, and other forms of alternative settlement techniques. In Missouri, some state courts mail information about ADR options to all clients who are involved in litigation, bypassing their attorneys.

The institutionalization of alternative dispute resolution as a recognized component of the legal system raises a number of questions about the regulation and professionalism of both the process and the dispute resolvers—the very sorts of questions many of the people who began the movement were anxious to avoid.

Who Is Qualified to Settle Disputes?

For good reasons and bad, dispute resolution has attracted practitioners of a wide variety of backgrounds. The movement's antilegal implications, coupled with the enthusiasm of the early pioneers, have attracted dissatisfied practitioners from related professions—primarily law and mental health—and people with no particular professional background. Hardly a day goes by when I do not get a call from someone seeking advice on how to break into the field.

Many of the new additions are talented, sincere people, disillusioned with the monotony or adversarial nature of their existing jobs. Some seek entry into a new field because they have been unable to succeed elsewhere. A few see ADR as a way to make a fast buck.

Until recently, dispute resolution was virtually unregulated. Anyone, regardless of lack of knowledge or skill, could hang out a shingle and offer to mediate or arbitrate anyone's dispute. Furthermore, poorly trained and inexperienced neutrals offered (for a fee) to train others.

In some settings, such as mediating between neighbors or friends, this situation may be perfectly appropriate. In others, such as labor-management or commercial disputes, the parties themselves may be sufficiently sophisticated and knowledgeable about various practitioners not to need the outside imposition of standards. In still others, such as court-imposed settlement procedures, there may be no substitute for regulation.

Some dispute resolvers have become increasingly concerned about protecting both consumers and the integrity of the processes we use in ADR. Yet many practitioners still point to the relative youth of the field and the lack of consensus about which type of people make the best neutrals. Some of us also worry about creating inappropriate barriers to entry into a rapidly changing area and hampering the innovative quality that has made conflict resolution so exciting. For example, some judges select only retired judges as neutrals, despite the fact that their experience may be neither the only nor the most appropriate preparation for mediating. The *Wall Street Journal* article describing the increasing demand for regulation quotes a Dallas mediator on the difficulty of identifying desirable mediation skills: "How do you judge a good mediator?" ... "Is it the percentage of your cases that settle? Is it the fact that you settled at 4 o'clock instead of 8 o'clock?"[6]

Regardless of these concerns, outsiders are preempting those in the field and defining minimum qualifications for serving as a neutral, at least in programs sponsored or referred to by courts or administrative agencies. These rules easily could spread to programs without court or agency

connections. Among the states that recently have legislated, by statute or
court rule, minimum qualifications for those who may practice as mediators or arbitrators are California, Florida, Iowa, Michigan, Minnesota,
New York, Oklahoma, Texas, Virginia, and Wisconsin. The Administrative Conference of the United States has compiled a roster of 350 neutrals
from whom federal agencies may select and is reviewing 200 more names
to add to it.

So far, the result of regulation has been a hodgepodge of requirements
of training, experience, or degrees in related professions. Regulations promulgated by the Florida Supreme Court, for example, list three different
areas of qualifications. In order to receive court referrals of family law
cases, mediators must have any one of the following credentials: a master's degree in social work, mental health, behavioral or social sciences, or
be a psychiatrist, attorney, or certified public accountant. A family mediator must hold a degree in one of these fields and have at least four years of
experience in one of them; however, those with eight years of mediation
experience (with at least ten mediations per year) are excused from this requirement. To mediate civil cases, mediators must be members of the Florida Bar with at least five years of practice (unless they are retired judges
from any state) and must observe and conduct two circuit court mediations under the supervision of a certified mediator. For both of these areas, the Florida rules also require at least forty hours of training by a program approved by the state's Supreme Court. In county courts, which
handle cases of lower value, mediators need only complete a certified
training program of at least twenty hours. They also must observe and
conduct four mediations under the supervision of a court-certified mediator, unless they are certified as a family or circuit court mediator. Final
certification of mediators is up to the local courts.

Oregon court rules eliminate occupational status or degrees as requirements for mediators or arbitrators. In domestic relations cases the Oregon
rules require mediators to complete at least five hours of substantive
training in both alcohol/drug abuse and domestic violence/child abuse in
addition to six hours of training in the court system, a minimum of forty
hours of training in family mediation, or a fifty-four-hour combination of
thirty hours of basic mediation training and twenty-four hours of family
mediation. Oklahoma combines training requirements with observation
by an experienced mediator, independent case experience, and continuing
education. (Because mediation generally is agreed to be so much more difficult to perform well than arbitration, most of the training and experience
requirements relate only to mediation.)

On the federal level, the U.S. Department of Justice has issued qualifications guidelines as part of its implementation of the Administrative Dispute Resolution Act. These guidelines recommend that mediators have

demonstrated experience as third-party neutrals or, alternatively, some formal training as neutrals. Unlike several state regulations, these guidelines do not include academic or occupational prerequisites. Other qualifications are impartiality, which can be satisfied by disclosure of all interests that may create actual or apparent bias, and sufficient general knowledge of the subject matter of the dispute.

In response to the call for development of qualifications standards, I chaired the first Commission on Qualifications of the Society of Professionals in Dispute Resolution (SPIDR). The commission developed recommendations to guide legislatures and other policymakers in what we considered the inevitable imposition of qualification requirements. Attempting to walk the thin line between excluding talented people from a relatively new field and protecting the public from shoddy practice, we hinged our recommendation of mandated qualifications on the degree of choice the parties have over the dispute resolution process, the use of a particular dispute resolution program, and the identity of the actual dispute resolver. The greater the degree of choice, the less mandatory should be the requirements.

In other words, we decided that despite its limitations, the free market should continue to be relied on where the parties have free choice of whether to use a settlement alternative in the first place and, if so, which people to use as their dispute resolvers. (The single caveat requires that consumers be provided with complete and accurate information about the background of the people from whom they choose.) On the other hand, where courts, public agencies, or private organizations operate programs that do not offer the parties a choice of processes, programs, or neutrals the parties must use to engage in ADR, standards governing the qualifications for such programs and neutrals are appropriate and necessary.

As for specifics, the commission chose to emphasize qualifications that demonstrate competent performance (such as neutrality, demonstrated knowledge of relevant procedures, ability to listen and understand what is being heard, and—for mediators—ability to help parties develop their own solutions) over the way in which people achieve such qualifications (such as formal degrees, specialized 'training, or experience). In other words, the field should develop a way to find out who is a good neutral and not restrict itself to examining a mere collection of degrees or professional licenses.

Behind this somewhat unorthodox approach is the recognition that there is no evidence (at least at present) that any particular background or degree is required to be a competent neutral. Indeed, there is impressive evidence that some individuals who possess no particular credentials make excellent dispute resolvers. Furthermore, the requirement of graduate degrees would create a significant barrier to the entry of many talented individuals into this fledgling occupation, whether as professionals or volunteers. Consequently, the commission recommended that no degree should be considered a prerequisite for service as a neutral. Instead, it emphasized the development of performance criteria or, in the alternative, the reliance on experience and on well-designed training and apprenticeship programs that provide significant personal observation and feedback.[7]

In response to the recommendations of the SPIDR Commission on Qualifications, a Test Design Project was formed to work with professionals from the testing field on the development of a scheme to test mediators' performance.[8] Pending the development of performance-based testing of neutrals, courts and agencies that wish to certify mediators have taken a variety of approaches to selecting or certifying mediators. Some require a common core of training and rely on the informal judgment of the trainers concerning who can perform adequately. A growing number of states, including Oklahoma, Texas, Florida, and Utah, have adopted the general approach of the SPIDR Commission and require the successful (albeit subjectively evaluated) completion of an apprenticeship in addition to mediation training.

Other programs, especially in contexts where substantive knowledge or significant experience as a negotiator or mediator seems desirable, have attempted to assess and quantify neutrals' prior experience in order to establish which candidates possess the desired threshold of experience. The FDIC, working with a few mediators as consultants, has promulgated a rating scale in an effort to quantify diverse experiences and assess the amount and the degree of difficulty of each candidate's experience in resolving complex, frequently multiparty disputes. Points are given for such criteria as time spent (as opposed to number of cases) mediating complex cases (akin to a pilot's "flying time"), with fewer points for training, teaching, and ethnic and gender diversity.

Decisions to be made over the next few years by courts, legislatures, and administrative agencies concerning the qualifications of dispute resolvers may well affect the ability of the hundreds of programs that successfully use volunteers to remain in business. They also will govern the development of new careers in the field and the flexibility of people from other professions to include dispute resolving as part of their practices.

In the meantime, those who engage mediators or arbitrators or who hire ombudspeople have incomplete guidance. Although the SPIDR Commission report lists skills considered necessary for competent performance as a neutral, at present very few programs test mediators or arbitrators for all (or any) of these qualities. As the field grows, stories proliferate of occasional mediators who use inappropriate pressure to convince parties to settle. Others act as simple dealmakers or auctioneers, paying scant attention to the parties' needs or to possibilities for creating a variety of options for settlement, some of which may maximize the gains of all concerned. Yet these possibilities are the very reasons that many people choose mediation in the first place.

In the absence of clear credentials, those who use dispute resolution services or seek training in dispute resolution processes should be alert to some danger signals:

- A mediator who focuses only on the dollar amounts involved in a dispute or repeatedly pushes the parties to "split the difference"
- A family mediator who does not meet separately with each of the parties or find some other way of discovering their fears or concerns about dealing directly with each other
- A commercial mediator who speaks only to the parties' attorneys, ignoring the disputants themselves
- An arbitrator who knows nothing about the substance of the dispute being arbitrated
- A person who has not mediated a substantial number of cases but offers mediation training to others

A good arbitrator should be decisive, comfortable running a hearing, capable of distinguishing facts from opinions, and, where required, able to write reasoned decisions. A good mediator has a broader range of skills but at a minimum should be a good listener, be a clear communicator, be able to identify and separate the issues involved in a dispute, and be sensitive to the disputants' values and priorities. A mediator needs to learn how to move the parties toward an agreement while still allowing them to make their own informed decisions concerning particular outcomes.

"Anything You Say in Here Is Confidential"

Traditionally, most settlement alternatives have operated in private. Particularly in mediation, mediators want to assure parties that whatever is told to them will be held in strictest confidence. This is so for several reasons. First, one of a mediator's essential tasks is to learn enough about the parties' needs and priorities to be able to help them to develop satisfactory solutions. In order to obtain such information, a mediator often speaks with parties (and their counsel, if they are represented) individually and attempts to create an atmosphere in which they feel free to tell the mediator what they would not tell each other. Second, disputants should be free to create a variety of settlement options without the concern that they could be made public. Third, parties may need protection from abuse by those who might use a procedure only to gain admissions or information about their opponents' case or to make headlines about positions taken or concessions gained. Fourth, parties have an interest in ensuring that what they say in mediation does not come back to haunt them in a later proceeding regarding the same or a different matter. Fifth, practitioners are well aware that some people choose settlement options because they prefer to keep their personal or business affairs private. Finally, both mediators and arbitrators worry that their reputation for neutrality will be damaged if they are required to act as a witness for one party or the other.

Despite the arguments for confidentiality, judicial response to any effort to require a neutral to testify in court about information learned during negotiations necessarily involves a balancing of the value of confidentiality in bringing about settlement against the need of courts for evidence and their disinclination to create new exceptions to the general rule that anyone can be required to give evidence. Courts faced with the issue generally have concluded that mediators need not testify. They have based their reasoning either on the long tradition (often incorporated into court rules) providing confidentiality for settlement offers or on the threatened danger to neutrality if the mediator should be forced to testify for one of the parties.[9]

Growing numbers of states have enacted comprehensive legislation to provide immunity from required disclosure of confidential communications made in mediation. Even these laws offer less protection to the mediator than the broad "privilege" not to testify commonly granted to lawyers, psychiatrists, and ministers. For example, California's statute is limited to testimony sought for civil trials and Massachusetts' protection extends only to those mediators who have prescribed amounts of training and experience.

In a few states, mediators are permitted by statute to refuse to testify about confidential communications made in mediation; however, only those mediators who work under the auspices of state or court-established programs may be protected. Other states have laws preserving confidentiality, but limit their coverage to particular forms of mediation. Virtually all of the states providing legislatively for the mediation of certain types of family disputes, for example, protect mediators from forced disclosure of confidential communications. The federal Administrative Dispute Resolution Act contains its own confidentiality protection for processes that fall within its coverage.[10]

In the absence of specific statutory protection, some court programs and many private mediators ask parties to sign agreements stating that they will not disclose outside the mediation what was said in a mediation session, nor will they attempt to subpoena the mediator or any documents produced by or for the mediator. There is no recorded case of a court's failing to honor these agreements. Although they do not offer complete protection against an attempt by someone who is not a party to the agreement to force disclosure, they appear to provide the best protection currently available for keeping private any confidences divulged during mediation.

The Ethical Standards of Dispute Resolvers

Just as legal standards governing the qualifications of neutrals and the confidentiality of communications made during mediation are in flux, so too are ethical standards governing the behavior of those who mediate or arbitrate. Even lawyers acting as neutrals have little outside guidance. The American Bar Association's *Model Rules of Professional Conduct*, which forms the basis of the codes most states use to police the legal profession, barely mentions the lawyer who acts as mediator or arbitrator, and then only in the relatively rare circumstance in which the lawyer attempts to resolve a dispute between two or more existing clients.[11] The more usual situation—the lawyer-mediator or -arbitrator who represents neither party—is not discussed.

The American Bar Association did enact standards to govern lawyers serving as family mediators. The standards took a significant step in acknowledging that an attorney ethically may act as a mediator. They left many difficult questions unanswered, however, relying on the mediator's obligation to refer parties to independent attorneys to deal with most difficulties.[12] More recently the ABA joined with the Society of Professionals in Dispute Resolution and the American Arbitration Association to produce more explicit standards of conduct for mediators.[13]

Growing numbers of state courts have adopted ethical standards for mediators to whom they refer cases; many have a limited focus, however, and do not address such important concerns as impartiality, fees, advertising, and the role of mediators in achieving settlement—all of which are concerns the National Standards on Court-Connected Mediation Programs have recommended that courts' codes of ethics address.[14] Only Florida's ethical code provides explicit sanctions for violations, which include costs, oral admonishment, written reprimand, additional training, or suspension and decertification.

California recently adopted rules to regulate privately funded dispute resolvers, but the rules apply only to those who have been appointed under court auspices and whose decisions have the force of judicial rulings. The rules do not touch private mediators or even arbitrators who handle cases without court appointment.

Although a few federal courts have issued some ethical standards for mediators through court rules or ADR program procedures, none has established comprehensive standards of practice for those who mediate under the courts' auspices.

Several organizations of neutrals have developed their own standards. The Ethical Standards of Professional Responsibility adopted by the Society of Professionals in Dispute Resolution stress the need for impartiality, the parties' informed consent, maintaining confidentiality, and avoiding conflicts of interest.[15]

The most debated ethical questions about ADR concern mediation: whether the mediator has a duty to ensure that everyone with an interest in the outcome of a dispute is represented at the bargaining table; whether the mediator has any responsibility for the fairness of an agreement; and whether it is appropriate to mediate at all when the parties have significantly different knowledge, resources, or power. The SPIDR standards take a middle ground concerning the mediator's responsibility for absent interests, charging the neutral with ensuring that any unrepresented interests are considered by those who are present. Many mediators would go further, asking whether anyone is missing whose participation is necessary either to reaching a complete agreement or to having the agreement fully implemented. If so, they would explore the possibility of including the missing parties or decline to mediate.

On the question of the mediator's responsibility for the ultimate agreement, the SPIDR standards state that the mediator must inform the parties of any concern he or she may have about the possible consequences of a proposed agreement. The mediator then has the option of educating the parties, referring one or more for outside advice, or withdrawing from the case in extreme circumstances (while maintaining confidentiality). In labor-management mediation, responsibility for the fairness of the final agreement traditionally has been thought to belong solely to the parties. In other contexts, most mediators would agree that it is inappropriate to assist parties in entering an agreement that is patently unfair or based on misleading or inaccurate information. Court rules in Florida go further, by providing that mediators also should terminate unproductive mediation sessions that would result in emotional or monetary costs to the parties.[16]

Deciding where to draw the line between the mediator's duty to be impartial and his or her accountability for an obviously unfair or unworkable agreement can be extremely difficult. Divorce mediation provides an example: If one spouse confides to the mediator that income or assets have not been fully disclosed, the mediator first should attempt to convince the person to make full disclosure. If the spouse refuses, the mediator should figure out how to withdraw from the mediation without breaking the promise of confidentiality.

As for refusing to mediate at all when parties are grossly unequal in sophistication or resources, philosophies differ. Negotiating power is not unitary: one party may have a dominant personality, for example, while another has access to superior information, advice, or alternatives to agreement. Mediators constantly work with the parties in an attempt either to minimize the effect of power imbalances or to help them assess realistically the effect of relative negotiating power on their choices.

In extreme cases, however, there are legitimate concerns about whether it is useful—or even appropriate—to attempt to mediate when resources, knowledge, or political power clearly is unequal (in a dispute between a car owner and General Motors, for example). In these circumstances, two questions need to be answered: whether it is possible to educate the less savvy parties about the process (some of us train novice negotiators before undertaking a complex mediation); and whether some access to expertise (legal or technical advice, for example) can be furnished to those who do not have it otherwise available.

The difficulty with declining to mediate in a situation of power imbalances is that mediation may be as well or better suited to the task as are any other available alternatives. Where legislation is an alternative (as in the siting of locally unwanted projects), it should be clear that legislatures often respond to the political power of lobbyists and interest groups. Nor do the courts, with their complicated procedures and costly assistance, generally favor the less powerful. And, as Honorable Wayne Brazil, a federal magistrate-judge, recently reminded a gathering of federal judges, ADR processes usually serve as an alternative not to obtaining a judicial decision on the merits (the overwhelming majority of civil cases are disposed of without a trial), but to settlement negotiations between two lawyers, a lawyer and an insurance claims adjuster, or an unrepresented client and a lawyer or claims adjuster.[17]

Courts are the most appropriate forum for protecting legal rights and distinguishing guilt from innocence. But many disputes that involve parties with multiple needs or ongoing relationships may be resolved most appropriately through a process that can take account of these needs or relationships. Finally, in some situations involving parties of unequal power locked in battle, many of us believe that persuading them to try mediation may be preferable to leaving them to their own devices.

With the focus shifted from the mediator to the court, the question of the judicial role in settlement is receiving increased attention. Many people question the propriety and effectiveness of judges deciding cases that they previously attempted and failed to settle through a form of judicial "mediation." Although judges admittedly are the most familiar with their own cases, they may become too familiar. Having spoken candidly with the parties, sometimes in separate sessions, and used techniques to encourage settlement that would not be used in adversarial proceedings, judges often become privy to information that may unfairly influence their subsequent decisions. A recent decision by a Florida appellate court questioned this situation and, despite a prior agreement by the parties not to challenge the trial judge's neutrality should his attempt to mediate fail, reversed the trial judge's criminal contempt order against the party who had nonetheless raised such a challenge. According to the reviewing court, the roles of mediator and judge are "conceptually different," and mediating should be left to the mediators.[18]

Law professor Judith Resnik, the leading critic of judges' attempts to become actively involved in settling cases before trial, has raised additional concerns:

> Disengagement and dispassion supposedly enable judges to decide cases fairly and impartially. The mythic emblems surrounding the goddess Justice illustrate this vision of the proper judicial attitude: Justice carries scales, reflecting the obligation to balance claims fairly; she possesses a sword, giving her great power to enforce decisions; and she wears a blindfold, protecting her from distractions.[19]

Resnik and others fear the unchecked power and threat to judges' potential impartiality that are involved in holding informal, sometimes private meetings between judges and litigants. As yet, however, the criticisms do not seem to have deflected the trend toward increased judicial involvement in settlement efforts. Judges could (and some do) avoid these potential pitfalls by using other court personnel or private dispute resolvers as neutrals. Although this practice shields individual judges from appearances of bias, judges' referrals to specific individual dispute resolvers or organizations outside the courts raise other concerns. In response to concerns over the appearance of impropriety, the chief administrative judge of Massachusetts Trial Courts recently instituted a courtwide prohibition on referrals by court personnel to specific private, for-profit dispute resolvers.

In an effort to insulate the judge from this type of situation, even when private neutrals or court staff serve as the mediator, the National Standards for Court-Connected Mediation Programs recommend limits on the content and mode of communications between mediators and the judges assigned to their cases. According to the standards, judges who will preside over the trial of a case if no settlement is reached should be informed only of a party's failure to comply with a court order to mediate, requests by the parties for additional time, procedural actions to which the parties consent, or the mediator's assessment that the case is inappropriate for mediation. Upon conclusion of a mediation, judges should be informed only of the lack of an agreement or, if agreement is reached, its terms, in a manner consistent with the reporting of other settlement agreements. Finally, the standards strongly recommend that the parties, not the mediator, make all of the communications to the judge whenever possible and, when not, that the mediator communicate with the judge in writing or through administrative personnel.[20]

A somewhat different—but also troubling—development has taken place in Connecticut, where the state legislature authorized sitting judges to moonlight for a private, nonprofit mediation service called Sta-Fed (for state and federal) ADR, Inc. The idea, according to the judges who masterminded it, is to keep judges on the bench and off the rolls of the large profitmaking organizations that have been wooing them with salaries that the public courts cannot match. The judges, on their own time (if there is such a thing) mediate cases referred by other judges. Parties are given a choice between Sta-Fed and other private dispute resolution organizations. Despite this unassailable motive, the potential for dealing on a confidential and paid basis with the same parties in mediation that also come before the judges in court (albeit in different cases) raises troubling prospects of conflicts of interest.

Neutrals' Liability

Whenever people undertake to offer a new service, it is inevitable that questions will arise concerning their liability should they provide the service inadequately. The question of mediators' and arbitrators' liability is slowly being resolved. Ironically, for a field that exists to provide alternatives to courts, the answers probably will come from the courts, as a result of lawsuits brought by dissatisfied disputants.

As recommended by the National Standards for Court-Connected Mediation Programs, however, several states have addressed the issue by statute. Some of the statutes provide mediators with limited immunity from civil liability. Under these laws, mediators who are appointed by the court or employed by the state are liable for their errors only if they act in bad faith, with a malicious purpose, or with a willful disregard of human rights, safety, or property. Eight states provide absolute immunity; in Florida, for example, court-appointed mediators enjoy full judicial immunity "in the same manner and to the same extent as a judge."

It is highly questionable whether professional mediators, who charge a fee for their services, should be protected from liability for their own mistakes to a greater extent than other professionals, such as lawyers or doctors. Another approach to protecting court-appointed mediators while permitting compensation of any victims of a mediator's malpractice is that followed by most mediators in private practice. Courts may purchase malpractice insurance for volunteer mediators while requiring mediators who practice for a fee to protect themselves (and their clients) through insurance. The District of Columbia Superior Court purchases group insurance for all of its mediators. The New Jersey Supreme Court Task Force on Dispute Resolution recommended that the state underwrite the defense of any mediator sued as a result of participating in a court-annexed program and indemnify any mediator found liable.

To date, arbitrators have been afforded fairly broad immunity from attack on their decisions. They have been held liable for their failure to decide a case once they have accepted it, however. Mediators rarely have been sued and never (at least to public knowledge) held liable for malpractice.

Choosing a Process

An array of processes for settling disputes has become part of the legal landscape. Although choosing one is often difficult, people who know about alternative dispute resolution processes say that they prefer them to traditional litigation.[21] Yet most people still know little about available alternatives. "L.A. Law" and "The People's Court" do not have their counterparts in "Minneapolis Mediation" or "The People's Peacemaker." Perhaps they never will. Because of their emphasis on privacy, most alternative processes consciously are shielded from public view. In any case, the settlement of conflict, as opposed to its escalation, generally makes dull press.

In addition to the lack of public awareness, several significant impediments to choosing settlement-oriented processes remain. The first is the psychology of the disputants themselves. As a lawyer attempting to establish a dispute resolution program in a large law firm confided to me: "By the time that clients reach our litigation department, they want to kill, not to settle. We have been unable to convince many people to put their long-term interest in a resolution ahead of their immediate desire for revenge."

Of course, there are answers to this phenomenon. Some of them can be found in the educational role that lawyers should play, others in the way in which law firms are structured. (Perhaps some day litigation departments will be restructured as dispute resolution departments.) Furthermore, the economic structure of law practice, in which most billing is by the hour, frequently keeps some lawyers from even informing clients of alternatives to litigation. Such a failure would violate lawyers' ethical codes in a few places today; perhaps soon this information will be required throughout the country.

Less obvious than the economic disincentive is the effect of lawyers' philosophical orientation toward advocacy and decisionmaking and away from interest-based negotiation. As law professor Leonard Riskin has recognized:

> The philosophical map employed by most practicing lawyers and law teachers ... differs radically from that which a mediator must use. What appears on this map is determined largely by the power of two assumptions about matters that lawyers handle: (1) that disputants are adversaries—*i.e.*, if one wins, the others must lose—and (2) that disputes may be resolved through application, by a third party, of some general rule of law. ... [M]oreover, on the lawyer's standard philosophical map, quantities are bright and large while qualities appear dimly or not at all. When one party wins, in this vision, usually the other party loses, and, most often, the victory is reduced to a money judgment. ... [Nonmonetary] interests—which may in fact be the principal motivations for a lawsuit—are recognizable in the legal dispute primarily to the extent that they have monetary value or fit into a clause of a rule governing liability.[22]

This summary of what it traditionally has meant to "think like a lawyer"—a world view that still underlies what future attorneys learn in law school—helps to explain why many lawyers resist nonlitigative approaches. And even when lawyers are willing to suggest alternatives to court, the alternatives they think of are more likely to consist of arbitration or a type of mediation that focuses exclusively on monetary results rather than on a search for ways of meeting the parties' nonmonetary as well as financial needs.

Finally, lawyers may fear losing their traditional monopoly over most forms of dispute resolution. There is some basis to the fear. As long as litigation (or even most arbitration) remains the archetypical way of resolving conflict, only lawyers have the expertise necessary to navigate the system. (The possession of unique expertise, in fact, is the mark of a profession.) To the extent that the parties themselves are enabled to resolve their disagreements—albeit with the help of their attorneys and/or the assistance of outside neutrals—some of the lawyers' mystique is lost. The best among our profession are counselors as well as technicians, advisors as well as advocates.

What in fact is the best process for particular parties with a particular dispute varies with both the people and the situation. Obviously, the time, money, and psychic stress associated with each of the alternatives is a significant consideration. However, it may take some time to understand the parties' interests and to involve them in an exploration of options. Consequently, the quickest and the cheapest way may not always be the best.

Other than transaction costs, the following considerations should govern the choice of a process:

- The extent to which a creative, perhaps not strictly monetary, result is possible or desirable
- The value placed by the parties on their future relationship
- The need for the parties to cooperate in implementing or complying with a solution
- The parties' desire to be listened to, to participate actively in the process, and to retain control over the outcome
- The need for finality (and thus the avoidance of appeals or other challenges to the result)
- The desirability of establishing a principle to govern the resolution of future disputes and the suitability of the particular dispute for deriving such a principle
- The parties' preference for an objective standard of what is a fair result versus their own notion of fairness

We are approaching a time when the legal landscape no longer will feature litigation as the sole or even the primary way to resolve a dispute. The answers to questions such as the courts' role in managing alternative processes, the quality and ethical standards of dispute resolvers, the legal protection given to confidentiality, and the enforceability of alternative processes will influence significantly both the characteristics and the usefulness of ADR.

Afterword

As I was finishing this manuscript, the telephone rang. It was a middle-aged lawyer who had been part of a bar association group that Michael Lewis and I trained to mediate two years earlier in preparation for a court-sponsored Settlement Week. He wondered whether one of us would be interested in mediating a partnership conflict. Two of his clients and a third party were involved in several businesses at partners and stockholders. The third partner, in his seventies, had been promising to retire for five years, but was insisting that his interests be bought out for what the younger partners considered a princely sum. Recognizing that the remedies available to his clients through a lawsuit could result in destroying their complex holdings, not to mention their long relationship, our former trainee had persuaded the retiring partner's attorney to try an alternative.

Two weeks later I spent a ten-hour marathon session in a hotel conference room mediating the dispute with the partners and their lawyers. They settled on terms for the retiring partner's withdrawal, accompanied by a buyout of his shares, to be redeemed partly for a much smaller amount of cash, to be paid over several years, and partly in real estate. The real estate had been owned by the partnership and coveted by the retiring partner, who wanted something tangible to show for all his years of effort. In case we had overlooked anything, the parties agreed on their own dispute resolution provision to deal with any remaining contingencies: "The parties agree to execute whatever documents are required to effectuate these agreements and to resolve through good-faith negotiation (with a mediator if they desire) any additonal issues that may arise between them."

As I was leaving, one of the partners brought his wife in to meet me. All three partners hugged one another and the mediator. I remembered to congratulate the two who were not retiring on their new partnership.

*   *   *

Word travels slowly; the revolution is a quiet one. But word does travel.

Americans have been raised to believe that the only way to settle important issues is to take them to court. We consider it part of our birthright to sue if we are injured, fleeced, or aggrieved. Novels, movies, television, and anecdotes about end-of-the-rainbow, court-ordered pots of gold reinforce the assumption that "see you in court" is the only acceptable response to simmering conflicts.

But the last fifteen years have seen a gradual expansion of this birthright. We still can threaten to sue. But we also can choose from a growing menu of other procedures, some lodged at the courthouse and some available outside the formal legal system. With schools beginning to teach conflict resolution, our children (or our children's children) will be raised to understand that there are many ways to settle disputes.

The growth of dispute settlement options is consistent with other emerging signs of interest in collaboration. In business, highly technological industries require sharply increased levels of coordination and teamwork. A new line of computer software, called "groupware," allows different people to work on the same document at the same time. Firms increasingly are organized internally into task forces and externally into joint ventures with other firms.

As the European Community becomes a reality, the United States is entering into arrangements with other nations for increasing trade and conserving resources. Representatives of twenty-four countries recently called on the United Nations to go further and organize worldwide protection of the earth's threatened environment.

In our private lives, even divorces often lead not to complete separation but to coparenting and newly extended families. Not surprisingly, one of the fastest growing branches of therapy today attempts to treat couples or entire families together.

Former Harvard president (and former law school dean) Derek Bok predicts that society's greatest opportunities in the next generation "will lie in tapping human inclinations toward collaboration and compromise rather than stirring our proclivities for competition and rivalry. If lawyers are not leaders in marshalling cooperation and designing mechanisms which allow it to flourish, they will not be at the center of the most creative social experiments of our time."[1]

Every American will continue to have the right to a day in court. But there also will be available the equally useful alternative of a morning at the mediator's office or an afternoon before an arbitration panel. Most valuable among the processes available to resolve disputes will be those that involve the people with a stake in the outcome in deciding for themselves what that outcome should be.

Notes

Chapter 1

1. Alexis de Tocqueville, *Democracy in America* (1835).
2. Marc Galanter, "The Debased Debate on Civil Justice" (U. of Wisconsin DPRP Working Paper, 1992).
3. Speech to National Institute on ADR, Harvard Law School, Cambridge, Massachusetts, November 12, 1993.
4. Jerold Auerbach, *Justice Without Law?* (1983).
5. Joel Rogers and Terence Dunsworth, Symposium at the University of Wisconsin, Institute for Legal Studies, cited in Milo Geyelin, "Suits by Firms Exceed Those by Individuals," *Wall Street Journal*, December 3, 1993, p. B1.
6. David Trubek, Austin Sarat, William Felstiner, Herbert Kritzer, and Joel Grossman, "The Costs of Ordinary Litigation," 31 *U.C.L.A. Law Review* 72 (1983).
7. Barbara A. Curran, *The Legal Needs of the Public: The Final Report of a National Survey* (1977).
8. William L.F. Felstiner, "Influences of Social Organization on Dispute Processing," 9 *Law and Society Review* 63 (1974).
9. Derek C. Bok, "A Flawed System of Law Practice and Training," 33 *Journal of Legal Education* 530 (1983).
10. Laurence Tribe, "Too Much Law, Too Little Justice," *Atlantic Monthly* 25 (July 1979).
11. George Nicolau, "Grievance Arbitration in a Prison: The Holton Experiment," 1 *Resolution of Correctional Problems and Issues* 1 (Spring 1975).
12. Warren E. Burger, "Isn't There a Better Way?" 68 *ABA Journal* 274 (March 1982).
13. Joel Rogers and Terence Dunsworth, Symposium at the University of Wisconsin, Institute for Legal Studies, cited in Milo Geyelin, "Suits by Firms Exceed Those by Individuals," *Wall Street Journal*, December 3, 1993, pp. B1, B3.
14. 5 U.S.C. §571 et seq. (1990).
15. Negotiated Rulemaking Act of 1990, 5 U.S.C. §561 (1990).
16. 28 U.S.C. §471 et seq. (1990).
17. "How the Secret Oslo Connection Led to the Israeli-P.L.O. Pact," *New York Times*, September 5, 1992, pp. 1, 10.
18. Christopher W. Moore, "'Have Process, Will Travel': Reflections on Democratic Decision Making and Conflict Management Practice Abroad," *NIDR Forum* (Winter 1993), p. 1.
19. The National Institute for Dispute Resolution and the Wirthlin Group, *Dispute Resolution Focus Group Results* (1992).

Chapter 2

1. David A. Lax and James K. Sebenius, *The Manager as Negotiator: Bargaining for Cooperative and Competitive Gain* (1986).

2. Roger Fisher, Bruce Patton, and William Ury, *Getting to Yes* (2d ed., 1992); see also Howard Raiffa, *The Art and Science of Negotiation* (1982); William Ury, *Getting Past No: Negotiating with Difficult People* (1991).

3. Robert B. Mnookin, "Why Negotiations Fail: An Exploration of Barriers to the Resolution of Conflict," 8 *Ohio State Journal on Dispute Resolution* 2 (1993).

4. Sandford Jaffe, paper prepared for the "Fitting the Forum to the Fuss" National Workshop, Harvard Law School, Cambridge, Massachusetts, March 27–28, 1992.

5. *Washington Post*, August 26, 1987.

6. William E. Simkin, *Mediation and the Dynamics of Collective Bargaining* (1971).

7. "How the Secret Oslo Connection Led to the Israeli-P.L.O. Pact," *New York Times*, September 5, 1992, pp. 1, 10.

8. Fair Housing Amendments Act of 1988, 42 U.S.C. §3601; Family Support Act, 42 U.S.C. §682(h); 45 C.F.R. §250.36.

9. David A. Lax and James K. Sebenius, *The Manager as Negotiator* (1986).

10. John W. Cooley, "Arbitration vs. Mediation—Explaining the Differences," 69 *Judicature* 263 (1986).

11. Robert Coulson, *Business Arbitration—What You Need to Know* (1980); letter from Robert Coulson, President, American Arbitration Association, January 20, 1987.

12. Herbert M. Kritzer and Jill K. Anderson, "The Arbitration Alternative: A Comparative Analysis of Case Processing Time, Disposition Mode, and Cost in the American Arbitration Association and the Courts," 8 *Justice System Journal* 6 (1983).

13. Ellen Joan Pollock, "Arbitrator Finds Role Dwindling as Rivals Grow," *Wall Street Journal*, April 28, 1993.

Chapter 3

1. Speech to Workshop on Identifying and Measuring Quality in Dispute Resolution Processes and Outcomes, University of Wisconsin–Madison Law School, July 13, 1987.

2. Sally Engle Merry and Ann Marie Rocheleau, *Mediation in Families: A Study of the Children's Hearings Project* (1985).

3. Gerald J. Stahler and Joseph DuCette, *Final Evaluation Report on the Use of Family Mediation to Prevent and Treat Adolescent Neglect* (1987).

4. *McGuire v. McGuire*, 157 Neb. 226, 59 N.W. 2d 336 (1953).

5. Kenneth Kressel, *The Process of Divorce* 7 (1985).

6. *Id.* at 9.

7. *Id.* at 11.

8. Judith S. Wallerstein, "Children of Divorce," 57 *American Journal of Orthopsychiatry* 199 (1987).

9. Kenneth Kressel, *The Process of Divorce* 13 (1985).

10. Judith A. Avner and Susan Herman, *Divorce Mediation: A Guide for Women* (1984).

11. Lincoln Clark and Jane Orbeton, "Mandatory Mediation of Divorce: Maine's Experience," 69 *Judicature* 310 (1986).

12. Margaret Shaw, Linda R. Singer, and Edna A. Povich, *National Standards for Court-Connected Mediation Programs* (1993).

13. Hugh McIsaac and Mary A. Duryee, "Mandatory Mediation—Pro," unpublished paper, 1991.

14. Michael Fix and Phillip J. Harter, *Hard Cases, Vulnerable People: An Analysis of Mediation Programs at the Multi-Door Courthouse of the Superior Court of the District of Columbia* (Urban Institute, 1992).

15. Jessica Pearson and Nancy Thoennes, *A Preliminary Portrait of Client Reactions to Three Court Mediation Programs* (1982).

16. Joan B. Kelly, "Parent Interaction After Divorce: Comparison of Mediated and Adversarial Divorce Processes," 9 *Behavioral Sciences and the Law* 387 (1991).

17. Joan B. Kelly, "Is Mediation Less Expensive? Comparison of Mediated and Adversarial Divorce Costs," 8 *Mediation Quarterly* 15 (1990).

18. Joan B. Kelly and Mary A. Duryee, "Women's and Men's Views of Mediation in Voluntary and Mandatory Mediation Settings," 30 *Family and Conciliation Courts Review* 34 (1992).

Chapter 4

1. Erik D. Green, "Corporate Alternative Dispute Resolution," 1 *Ohio State Journal on Dispute Resolution* 203 (1986).

2. Marc Galanter and Joel Rodgers, "The Transformation of American Business Disputing? Some Preliminary Observations," unpublished manuscript, University of Wisconsin at Madison, 1988.

3. William Nelson, "Contract Litigation and the Elite Bar in New York City, 1960–1980," 39 *Emory Law Review* 413 (1990).

4. Ronald J. Gilson and Robert H. Mnookin, *Cooperation and Competition in Litigation: Can Lawyers Dampen Conflict?* working paper, presented at the New Theoretical Perspectives on Dispute Resolution conference, Stanford University, February 1993.

5. Connecticut ADR Project, Inc., *Final Report* (1988).

6. Some of the examples in this chapter are described more fully in Bureau of National Affairs, *Alternative Dispute Resolution Report;* Center for Public Resources, *Alternatives to the High Cost of Litigation;* or James F. Henry and Jethro K. Lieberman, *The Manager's Guide to Resolving Legal Disputes* (1985).

7. Robert H. Gorske, panel presentation at Workshop on Identifying and Measuring Quality in Dispute Resolution Processes and Outcomes, University of Wisconsin-Madison Law School, July 13, 1987.

8. Richard Enslen, *Ibid.*

9. Thomas D. Lambros, *Ibid.*

10. *Strandell v. Jackson County*, 838 F.2d 884 (7th Cir. 1988); *In re N.L.O., Inc.*, 5 F.3d. 154 (6th Cir. 1993).

11. See *Arabian American Oil Co. v. Scarfone*, 685 F. Supp. 1220 (M. D. Fla. 1988); *Federal Reserve Bank of Minneapolis v. Carey-Canada, Inc.*, 123 F.R.D. 603 (D.Minn. 1988); *McKay v. Ashland Oil Co., Inc.*, 120 F.R.D. 43 (E.D. Ky. 1988).

12. Conversation with James E. McGuire, Boston, Mass., November 11, 1988.

13. James F. Henry and Jethro K. Lieberman, *The Manager's Guide to Resolving Legal Disputes* (1985).

14. Conversations with Michael K. Lewis, Washington, D.C., 1988.

15. Stephen B. Goldberg, "Meditations of a Mediator," 2 *Negotiation Journal* 234 (1985).

16. *Ibid.*

17. Florida §44.302; Indiana A.D.R. Rule 2; North Carolina §7A-38, §50-13.1(b); and Texas §152.003.

18. Rule 16 of the Superior Court Rules of the District of Columbia.

19. Talk by Professor Barry C. Dorn to Society of Professionals in Dispute Resolution, Pittsburgh, Pennsylvania, October 9, 1992.

20. DPIC Companies, *Mediation* (undated report).

21. *Ibid.*

22. Letter from Jay Adam, October 2, 1988.

23. Jim Carlton, "No Wonder Rome Wasn't Built in a Day—No Facilitators," *Wall Street Journal*, February 10, 1993, p. A1.

24. *De Valk Lincoln Mercury, Inc. v. Ford Motor Co.*, 811 F.2d 326 (7th Cir. 1987); *AMF, Inc. v. Brunswick*, 621 F. Supp. 456 (E.D. N.Y. 1985).

Chapter 5

1. *Patterson v. ITT Consumer Financial Corp.*, No. A057729 (Ct. Appl., 1st Dist., 4th Div., April 19, 1993).

2. *Shearson/American Express, Inc. v. McMahon*, 482 U.S. 220 (1987).

3. Center for Public Resources, "Arbitration Doesn't Favor Brokers, GAO Finds," 10 *Alternatives to the High Cost of Litigation* 97–98 (1992).

4. A. Best and A.R. Andreasen, "Consumer Responses to Unsatisfactory Purchases: A Survey of Perceiving Defects, Voicing Complaints and Obtaining Redress," 11 *Law and Society Review* 701 (1977).

5. Marc Galanter, "Delivering Legality: Some Proposals for the Direction of Research," 11 *Law and Society Review* 225 (1977).

6. Bureau of National Affairs, *Alternative Dispute Resolution Report* 166 (1987).

7. Consumer Dynamics International, *Auto Arbitration Panels: Are They Working?* (1986).

8. Mark Budnitz, "Consumer Dispute Resolution Forums," *Trial* 45 (December 1977).

9. Barbara P. Gregg, "Characteristics of a Model Consumer Dispute Resolution Mechanism," in American Bar Association, Special Committee on Alternative Dispute Resolution, *Consumer Dispute Resolution: Exploring the Alternatives* (1982).

10. Bureau of National Affairs, *Alternative Dispute Resolution Report* 205–206 (1987).

11. Quoted in *ibid*. The *ADR Report* contains a number of articles between 1986 and 1989 covering the development of farmer-lender mediation.

12. Food Agriculture Conservation and Trade Act of 1990, Pub. L. No. 101–624; Agricultural Credit Improvement Act of 1992.

13. Leonard L. Riskin, *The Farmer-Lender Mediation Program: Implementation by the Farmers Home Administration* (Administrative Conference of the United States, November 1991); *see also* Leonard L. Riskin, "Two Concepts of Mediation in the FmHA's Farmer-Lender Mediation Program," 45 *Administrative Law Review* 21 (Winter 1993).

14. Jeanne M. Brett and Stephen B. Goldberg, "Grievance Mediation in the Coal Industry: A Field Experiment," 37 *Industrial & Labor Relations Review* 49 (1983).

15. Alan F. Westin and Alfred G. Feliu, *Resolving Employment Disputes Without Litigation* 2 (1988).

16. *Fregara v. Jet Aviation*, 764 F.Supp. 940 (1991).

17. *Gilmer v. Interstate/Johnson Lane Corp.*, 500 U.S. 20 (1991).

18. Roberta V. Romberg, "The Counselor System at National Broadcasting Company," in *Resolving Employee Disputes Without Litigation* 176 (1988).

19. Confidential communication from a corporate ombudsperson, McLean, Virginia, November 1986.

20. Mary P. Rowe, "The Corporate Ombudsman: An Overview and Analysis," 3 *Negotiation Journal* 127 (1987).

21. Craig A. McEwen, "An Evaluation of the Equal Employment Opportunity Commission's Pilot Mediation Program," working paper, Center for Dispute Settlement, Washington, D.C., 1994.

Chapter 6

1. Quoted in Daniel McGillis, *Community Dispute Resolution—Programs and Public Policy* (1986).

2. Quoted in "How Community Justice Centers Are Faring," National Institute for Dispute Resolution, *Dispute Resolution Forum* (December 1988).

3. Richard Danzig, "Towards the Creation of a Complementary, Decentralized System of Criminal Justice," 26 *Stanford Law Review* 1 (1974).

4. Daniel McGillis, *Community Dispute Resolution—Programs and Public Policy* (1986).

5. George Nicolau, *Community Mediation: Progress and Problems* (1986).

6. Jessica Pearson, Nancy Thoennes, and Lois Vander Kooi, "Mediation of Contested Custody Disputes," 11 *Colorado Lawyer* 336 (1982).

7. Robert C. Davis, "Mediation: The Brooklyn Experiment," in Roman Tomasic and Malcolm M. Feeley (eds.) *Neighborhood Justice: Assessment of an Emerging Idea* 154 (1982).

8. Daniel McGillis, *Community Dispute Resolution—Programs and Public Policy* (1986).

9. Sally Engle Merry and Susan S. Silbey, "What Do Plaintiffs Want?" 9 *Justice System Journal* 151 (1984).

10. George Nicolau, *Community Mediation: Progress and Problems* (1986).

11. Craig McEwen and Richard Maiman, "Small Claims Mediation in Maine: An Empirical Assessment," 33 *Maine Law Review* 237 (1981).

12. Mark S. Umbreit and Robert B. Coates, *Victim Offender Mediation: An Analysis of Programs in Four States of the U.S.* (1992).

13. David P. Mesaros, "The Oklahoma Department of Corrections: Assisting Crime Victims Through Post-Conviction Mediation," 1 *Ohio State Journal on Dispute Resolution* 331 (1986).

14. William R. Drake and Michael K. Lewis, "Community Justice Centers—A Lasting Innovation," in National Institute for Dispute Resolution, *Dispute Resolution Forum* (December 1988).

Chapter 7

1. Quoted in Stephen Gillers, "New Faces in the Neighborhood: Mediating the Forest Hills Housing Dispute," in *Roundtable Justice: Case Studies in Conflict Resolution* (Robert B. Goldmann, ed.) 85 (1980).

2. "MOVE/Philadelphia Bombing: A Conflict Resolution History," *CR Notes* 2 (1986).

3. Lawrence Susskind & Jeffrey Cruikshank, *Breaking the Impasse: Consensual Approaches to Resolving Public Disputes* 3 (1987).

4. *Washington Post*, November 25, 1986, B1–2.

5. William O. Vose, speech to a seminar sponsored by the American Institute of Architects, the American Council of Consulting Engineers, the American Society of Engineers, and the National Realty Committee, Washington, D.C., January 7, 1987.

6. *Ibid.*

7. William O. Vose, "View from the Top: Peace on Wisconsin Avenue Believe It or Not!" 14 *Pipeline* 1–2 (July 1987).

8. *Washington Post*, November 25, 1986, B1–2.

9. Lee Dembart and Richard Kwartler, "The Snoqualmie River Conflict: Bringing Mediation into Environmental Disputes," in *Roundtable Justice: Case Studies in Conflict Resolution* (Robert B. Goldmann, ed.) 39 (1980).

10. Gail Bingham, *Resolving Environmental Disputes: A Decades of Public Experience* (1986).

11. Bureau of National Affairs, 3 *Alternative Dispute Resolution Report* 267 (1989).

12. Phyllis N. Segal and Denise R. Madigan, "Federal ADR Update: DOL Completes ADR Initiatives," *Consensus*, January 1993, p. 2.

13. Cathy Costantino, *Summary of FDIC ADR Creditor Claims Pilot Project* (April 1993).

14. Philip J. Harter, "Negotiating Regulations: A Cure for Malaise," 71 *Georgetown Law Journal* 1 (1982).

15. "Regulatory Negotiation: Four Perspectives," in National Institute for Dispute Resolution, *Dispute Resolution Forum* (January 1986).

16. *Ibid.*

17. Stephen D. Baruch, "The Dawning of a New Era of Cooperation," *Legal Times*, May 17, 1993, pp. 29, 31.

18. Bureau of National Affairs, 2 *Alternative Dispute Resolution Report* 117 (1988).

19. "Regulatory Negotiation: Four Perspectives," in National Institute for Dispute Resolution, *Dispute Resolution Forum* (January 1986).

20. *Ibid.*

21. *Ibid.*

22. Bureau of National Affairs, 1 *Alternative Dispute Resolution Report* 133, 54 (1987).

23. *Ibid.*

24. Philip H. Harter, speech to Fannie Mae Research Roundtable Series, "Building Consensus for Affordable Housing," Washington, D.C., November 29, 1993.

25. Julie Liam, *The Impact of Conflict Resolution Programs on Schools: A Review and Synthesis of the Evidence* (1988).

26. Linda R. Singer and Eleanor A. Nace, *Mediation in Special Education* (1985).

27. Linda R. Singer and Ronald A. Schechter, *Mediating Civil Rights: The Age Discrimination Act* (1986).

Chapter 8

1. E. Allan Lind, *Arbitrating High Stakes Cases: An Evaluation of Court Annexed Arbitration in a United States District Court* (1990).

2. American Bar Association, Standing Committee on Dispute Resolution, *State Legislation on Dispute Resolution* (1988).

3. Panel discussion, CPR Legal Program Spring Meeting (June 1993); see also Margaret Shaw, Linda R. Singer, and Edna A. Povich, *National Standards for Court-Connected Mediation Programs* (1992).

4. Speech to the Annual Conference of the Society of Professionals in Dispute Resolution, Los Angeles, California, October 21, 1988.

5. Frank E.A. Sander, "Who Should Pay for Court-Connected ADR?" *American Bar Association Journal* 105 (February 1992).

6. Wade Lambert, "Calls Increase for Guidelines on Mediation," *Wall Street Journal*, October 23, 1993.

7. Society of Professionals in Dispute Resolution, *Qualifying Neutrals: The Basic Principles* (1989).

8. Christopher Honeyman, *Interim Guidelines for Selecting Mediators* (NIDR, 1993).

9. *NLRB v. Macaluso*, 18 F.2d 51 (9th Cir. 1980).

10. 5 U.S.C. §574. (1990).

11. American Bar Association, *Model Rules of Professional Conduct*, Rule 2.2 (1983).

12. American Bar Association, "Standards of Practice for Lawyer Mediators in Family Disputes," 18 *Family Law Quarterly* 363 (1984).

13. American Arbitration Association, American Bar Association, and the Society of Professionals in Dispute Resolution, "Standards of Conduct for Mediators" (final draft, unpubl., April 8, 1994).

14. Margaret Shaw, Linda R. Singer, and Edna A. Povich, *National Standards for Court-Connected Mediation Programs* (1992).

15. Society of Professionals in Dispute Resolution, *Ethical Standards of Professional Responsibility* (1986).

16. Florida Rules for Certified and Court-Appointed Mediators, Fla SupCt No. 78, 943, May 28, 1992.

17. Speech to the National ADR Institute for Federal Judges, Harvard Law School, Cambridge, Massachusetts, November 12, 1993.

18. *Evans v. Florida*, Fifth District, Case No. 91-1729.

19. Judith Resnik, "Managerial Judges," 96 *Harvard Law Review* 376 (1982).

20. Margaret Shaw, Linda R. Singer, and Edna A. Povich, *National Standards for Court-Connected Mediation Programs*, Section 9 (1992).

21. The National Institute for Dispute Resolution and the Wirthlin Group, *Dispute Resolution Focus Group Results* (1992).

22. Leonard Riskin, "Mediation and Lawyers," 43 *Ohio State Law Journal* 29 (1982).

Afterword

1. Derek C. Bok, "What Are America's Law Schools Doing Wrong? A Lot," 12 *Student Lawyer* 46 (1983).

Selected Bibliography

American Bar Association. "Standards of Practice for Lawyer Mediators in Family Disputes." 18 *Family Law Quarterly* 363 (1984).

_____. *Legislation on Dispute Resolution: 1990/1991 Addendum to the 1989 Federal and State Dispute Resolution Legislative Monograph* (1992).

American Bar Association, Special Committee on Alternative Dispute Resolution. *Consumer Dispute Resolution: Exploring the Alternatives* (1982).

American Bar Association, Standing Committee on Dispute Resolution. *Legislation on Dispute Resolution: Federal and State Laws and Initiatives Pertaining to ADR* (1990).

Auerbach, Jerold. *Justice Without Law?* New York: Oxford Press, 1983.

Avner, Judith A., and Susan Herman. *Divorce Mediation: A Guide for Women.* New York: National Organization for Women, 1984.

Best, A., and A. R. Andreasen. "Consumer Responses to Unsatisfactory Purchases: A Survey of Perceiving Defects, Voicing Complaints and Obtaining Redress." 11 *Law & Society Review* 701 (1977).

Bingham, Gail. *Resolving Environmental Disputes: A Decade of Experience.* Washington, D.C.: Conservation Foundation, 1986.

Brazil, Wayne D. *Effective Approaches to Settlement: A Handbook for Lawyers and Judges.* Clifton, N.J.: Prentice-Hall Law and Business, 1988.

Brett, Jeanne M., and Stephen B. Goldberg. "Grievance Mediation in the Coal Industry: A Field Experiment." 37 *Industrial & Labor Relations Review* 49 (1983).

Budnitz, Mark. "Consumer Dispute Resolution Forums." *Trial* 45 (December 1977).

Bureau of National Affairs. *Alternative Dispute Resolution Report* (published bi-weekly).

Bush, Robert Baruch. "Efficiency and Protection, or Empowerment and Recognition? The Mediator's Role and Ethical Standards in Mediation." 41 *Florida Law Review* 253 (1989).

Carpenter, Susan, and W.J.D. Kennedy. *Managing Public Disputes.* San Francisco: Jossey-Bass, 1988.

Center for Public Resources. *Alternatives to the High Cost of Litigation* (published monthly).

_____. *Mainstreaming: Corporate Strategies for Systematic ADR Use* (1989).

Clark, Lincoln, and Jane Orbeton. "Mandatory Mediation of Divorce: Maine's Experience." 69 *Judicature* 310 (1986).

Cochran, Robert F., Jr. "Legal Representation and the Next Steps Toward Client Control: Attorney Malpractice for the Failure to Allow the Client to Control Negotiation and Pursue Alternatives to Litigation." 47 *Washington & Lee Law Review* 821 (1990).

Connecticut ADR Project, Inc. *Final Report* (1988).

Consumer Dynamics International. *Auto Arbitration Panels: Are They Working?* (1986).

Cooley, John W. "Arbitration vs. Mediation—Explaining the Differences." 69 *Judicature* 263 (1986).

Cuomo, Mario. *Forest Hills Diary: The Crisis of Community Low-Income Housing.* New York: Random House, 1974.

Danzig, Richard. "Towards the Creation of a Complementary Decentralized System of Criminal Justice." 26 *Stanford Law Review* 1 (1974).

Deis, Michelle. "California's Answer: Mandatory Mediation of Child Custody and Visitation Disputes." 1 *Ohio State Journal on Dispute Resolution* 149 (1985).

Edelman, Peter. "Institutionalizing Dispute Resolution Alternatives." 9 *Justice System Journal* 134 (1984).

Emery, Robert E., and Melissa M. Wyer. "Divorce Mediation." 42 *American Psychologist* 472 (1987).

Fisher, Roger, William Ury, and Bruce Patton. *Getting to Yes.* New York: Penguin, 1991.

Fix, Michael, and Phillip J. Harter. *Hard Cases, Vulnerable People: An Analysis of Mediation Programs at the Multi-Door Courthouse of the Superior Court of the District of Columbia.* Washington, D.C.: Urban Institute, 1992.

Folberg, Jay, and Alison Taylor. *Mediation: A Comprehensive Guide to Resolving Conflicts Without Litigation.* San Francisco: Jossey-Bass, 1984.

Galanter, Marc. "Delivering Legality: Some Proposals for the Direction of Research." 11 *Law & Society Review* 225 (1977).

Goldberg, Stephen B. "Meditations of a Mediator." 2 *Negotiation Journal* 345 (1985).

_____. "The Mediation of Grievances Under a Collective Bargaining Contract: An Alternative to Arbitration." 77 *Northwestern University Law Review* 270 (1982).

Goldberg, Stephen B., Frank E.A. Sander, and Nancy H. Rogers. *Dispute Resolution: Negotiation, Mediation, and Other Processes*, 2d ed. Boston: Little, Brown, 1992.

Goldmann, Robert B. (ed.) *Roundtable Justice: Case Studies in Conflict Resolution.* Boulder: Westview, 1980.

Green, Eric D. "Corporate Alternative Dispute Resolution." 1 *Ohio State Journal on Dispute Resolution* 203 (1986).

Grillo, Trina. "The Mediation Alternative: Process Dangers for Women." 100 *Yale Law Journal* 1545 (1991).

Handcock, William A. (ed.) *Corporate Counsel's Guide: Alternative Dispute Resolution in the Employment Context* (1993).

Harter, Philip J. "Negotiating Regulations: A Cure for Malaise." 71 *Georgetown Law Journal* 1 (1982).

Haynes, John. *Divorce Mediation: A Practical Guide for Therapists and Counselors.* New York: Springer, 1981.

Henry, James F., and Jethro K. Lieberman. *The Manager's Guide to Resolving Legal Disputes.* New York: Harper and Row, 1985.

Kelly, Joan B. "Is Mediation Less Expensive? Comparison of Mediated and Adversarial Divorce Costs." 8 *Mediation Quarterly* 15 (1990).

_____. "Mediation and Psychotherapy: Distinguishing the Differences." 1 *Mediation Quarterly* 33 (September 1983).

_____. "Parent Interaction After Divorce: Comparison of Mediated and Adversarial Divorce Processes." 9 *Behavioral Sciences and the Law* 387 (1991).

Kelly, Joan B., and Mary A. Duryee. "Women's and Men's Views of Mediation in Voluntary and Mandatory Mediation Settings." 30 *Family and Conciliation Courts Review* 34 (1992).

Kressel, Kenneth. *The Process of Divorce.* New York: Basic Books, 1985.

Lax, David A., and James K. Sebenius. *The Manager As Negotiator: Bargaining for Cooperative and Competitive Gain.* New York: Free Press, 1986.

Liam, Julie. *The Impact of Conflict Resolution Programs on Schools: A Review and Synthesis of the Evidence.* Unpubl., Albany, N.Y.: State University of New York, 1988.

McCarthy, William. "The Role of Power and Principle in Getting to Yes." 1 *Negotiation Journal* 59 (1985).

McEwen, Craig A. *An Evaluation of the Equal Employment Opportunity Commission's Pilot Mediation Program.* Working paper, Washington, D.C.: Center for Dispute Settlement, 1994.

McEwen, Craig, and Richard Maiman. "Small Claims Mediation in Maine: An Empirical Assessment." 33 *Maine Law Review* 237 (1981).

McGillis, Daniel. *Consumer Dispute Resolution: A Survey of Programs.* Washington, D.C.: National Institute for Dispute Resolution, 1987.

_____. *Community Dispute Resolution—Programs and Public Policy.* Washington, D.C.: National Institute for Justice, 1986.

Merry, Sally Engle, and Ann Marie Rocheleau. *Mediation in Families: A Study of the Children's Hearings Project.* New York: Grant Foundation, 1985.

Merry, Sally Engle, and Susan S. Silbey. "What Do Plaintiffs Want?" 9 *Justice System Journal* 151 (1984).

Mnookin, Robert H. "Why Negotiations Fail." 8 *Ohio State Journal on Dispute Resolution* 2 (1993).

Moore, Christopher W. *The Mediation Process.* San Francisco: Jossey-Bass, 1986.

"MOVE/Philadelphia Bombing: A Conflict Resolution History." *CR Notes* 2 (1986).

Murray, John, Alan Rau, and Edward Sherman. *Processes of Dispute Resolution: The Role of Lawyers.* New York: Foundation Press, 1989.

National Institute for Dispute Resolution. *Dispute Resolution Forum* (published several times a year).

National Institute for Dispute Resolution and the Wirthlin Group. *Dispute Resolution Focus Group Results* (1992).

Nicolau, George. *Community Mediation: Progress and Problems* (1986).

Note. "The Dilemma of Regulating Mediation." 22 *Houston Law Review* 841 (1985).

Note. "The Sultans of Swap: Defining the Duties and Liabilities of American Mediators." 99 *Harvard Law Review* 1876 (1986).

Pearson, Jessica. "The Equity of Mediated Divorce Agreements." 9 *Mediation Quarterly* 179 (1991).

_____. "An Evaluation of Alternatives to Court Adjudication." 7 *Justice System Journal* 420 (Winter 1982).

Pearson, Jessica, Nancy Thoennes, and Lois Vander Kooi. "Mediation of Contested Custody Disputes." 11 *Colorado Lawyer* 336 (1982).

Pirie, Andrew J. "The Lawyer as Mediator: Professional Responsibility Problems or Profession Problems?" 63 *Canadian Bar Review* 378 (1985).

Plapinger, Elizabeth, and Margaret Shaw. *Court ADR: Elements of Program Design.* New York: Center for Public Resources/CPR Legal Program, 1992.

Potapchuk, William R., and Caroline G. Polk. *Building the Collaborative Community.* Working paper, National Institute for Dispute Resolution, National Civil League, and Program for Community Problem Solving, 1992.

Project on Equal Education Rights. *Final Report: An Analysis of the Use of Mediation to Resolve Civil Rights Complaints* (1980).

Provine, D. Marie. *Settlement Strategies for Federal District Judges.* Washington, D.C.: Federal Judicial Center, 1986.

Raiffa, Howard. *The Art and Science of Negotiation.* Cambridge: Harvard, 1982.

Resnik, Judith. "Managerial Judge." 96 *Harvard Law Review* 376 (1982).

Riskin, Leonard. "Toward New Standards of the Neutral Lawyer." 26 *Arizona Law Review* 329 (1984).

———. "Mediation and Lawyers." 43 *Ohio State Law Journal* 29 (1982).

Riskin, Leonard, (ed.) *Divorce Mediation: Readings.* Washington, D.C.: American Bar Association, 1985.

———. "The Represented Client in a Settlement Conference: Lessons of G. Heileman Brewing Co. v. Joseph Oat Corp." 69 *Washington University Law Quarterly* 1059 (1991).

Rogers, Nancy H., and Craig A. McEwen. *Mediation: Law, Policy, Practice* (supplement). Rochester, N.Y.: Lawyers Co-operative, 1989, 1992.

Rogers, Nancy H., and Richard A. Salem. *A Student's Guide to Mediation and the Law.* New York: Bender, 1987.

Rowe, Mary P. "The Corporate Ombudsman: An Overview and Analysis." 3 *Negotiation Journal* 127 (1987).

Rowe, Mary P., and Michael Baker. "Are You Hearing Enough Employee Concerns?" 62 *Harvard Business Review* 127 (1984).

Sander, Frank E.A. "Alternative Methods of Dispute Resolution: An Overview." 37 *University of Florida Law Review* 1 (1985).

———. "Varieties of Dispute Resolution." 70 F.R.D. 111 (1976).

Sander, Frank E.A., and Stephen B. Goldberg. "Making the Right Choice." *ABA Journal* (November 1993).

Sander, Frank E.A., and Michael Prigoff. "Professional Responsibility: Should There Be a Duty to Advise of ADR Options?" 76 *American Bar Association Journal* 50 (November 1990).

Schoenbrod, David. "Limits and Dangers of Environmental Mediation: A Review Essay." 58 *New York University Law Review* 1453 (1983).

Shaw, Margaret, Linda R. Singer, and Edna A. Povich. *National Standards for Court-Connected Mediation Programs.* Washington, D.C.: Center for Dispute Settlement, 1992.

Siemer, Deanne C. "Perspectives of Advocates and Clients on Court-Sponsored ADR," in *Emerging ADR Issues in State and Federal Courts.* Chicago: American Bar Association, 1991.

Simkin, William E. *Mediation and the Dynamics of Collective Bargaining*. Washington, D.C.: Bureau of National Affairs, 1971.

Singer, Linda R., Michael K. Lewis, Alan Houseman, and Elizabeth A. Singer. "Alternative Dispute Resolution and the Poor, Part I: What ADR Processes Exist and Why Advocates Should Become Involved." 26 *Clearinghouse Review* 142 (1992).

Singer, Linda R., Michael K. Lewis, Alan Houseman, and Elizabeth A. Singer. "Alternative Dispute Resolution and the Poor, Part II: Dealing with Problems in Using ADR and Choosing a Process." 26 *Clearinghouse Review* 288 (1992).

Singer, Linda R., and Eleanor Nace. *Mediation in Special Education*. Washington, D.C.: National Institute for Dispute Resolution, 1985.

Singer, Linda R., and Ronald A. Schechter. *Mediating Civil Rights: The Age Discrimination Act*. Washington, D.C.: National Institute for Dispute Resolution, 1986.

Slaikeu, Karl A. "Designing Dispute Resolution Systems in the Health Care Industry." 4 *Negotiation Journal* 395 (1989).

Society of Professionals in Dispute Resolution. *Ethical Standards of Professional Responsibility* (1986).

————. *Mandated Participation and Coercion: Dispute Resolution as It Relates to the Courts* (1990).

————. *Qualifications Sourcebook Compendium* (1993).

————. *Qualifying Neutrals: The Basic Principles* (1989).

Solomon, Lewis D., and Janet Stern Solomon. "Using Alternative Dispute Resolution Techniques to Settle Conflicts Among Shareholders of Closely Held Corporations." 22 *Wake Forest Law Review* 105 (1987).

Stahler, Gerald J., and Joseph DuCette. *Final Evaluation Report on the Use of Family Mediation to Prevent and Treat Adolescent Neglect*. Washington, D.C.: Center for Dispute Resolution, 1987.

Stulberg, Joseph B. *Taking Charge: Managing Conflict*. Lexington, Mass.: D. C. Heath, 1987.

Susskind, Lawrence. "NIDR's State Office of Mediation Experiment." 2 *Negotiation Journal* 323 (1986).

Susskind, Lawrence, and Jeffrey Cruikshank. *Breaking the Impasse: Consensual Approaches to Resolving Public Disputes*. New York: Basic Books, 1987.

"Symposium: Critical Issues in Alternative Dispute Resolution." 12 *Seton Hall Legislative Journal* 1 (1988).

"Symposium on Critical Issues in Mediation Legislation." 2 *Ohio State Journal on Dispute Resolution* 1 (1986).

Thoennes, Nancy, Jessica Pearson, and Julie Bell. *Evaluation of the Use of Mandatory Divorce Mediation*. Denver: Center for Policy Research, 1991.

Tomasic, Roman, and Malcolm M. Feeley (eds.) *Neighborhood Justice: Assessment of an Emerging Idea*. New York: Longman, 1982.

United Nations. *Handbook on the Peaceful Settlement of Disputes Between States*. New York: United Nations, 1992.

Ury, William. *Getting Past No: Negotiating with Difficult People*. New York: Bantam Books, 1991.

Ury, William L., Jeanne M. Brett, and Stephen B. Goldberg. *Getting Disputes Resolved: Designing Systems to Cut the Costs of Conflict.* San Francisco: Jossey-Bass, 1988.

Wallerstein, Judith S. "Children of Divorce." 57 *American Journal of Orthopsychiatry* 199 (1987).

Wallerstein, Judith S., and Joan Berlin Kelly. *Surviving the Break Up: How Parents and Children Cope With Divorce.* New York: Basic Books, 1980.

Westin, Alan F., and Alfred G. Feliu. *Resolving Employment Disputes Without Litigation.* Washington, D.C.: Bureau of National Affairs, 1988.

Wheeler, Michael. "Regional Consensus on Affordable Housing: Yes in My Backyard?" 12 *Journal of Planning Education and Research* 139 (1993).

Wilkinson, John H. (ed.) *Donovan Leisure Newton & Irvine ADR Practice Book.* New York: Wiley, 1990.

About the Book
and Author

Within the past few years, innovative methods have been developed not only to settle disputes out of court but to supplement or replace the means by which legislatures, businesses, communities, therapists, and schools handle conflicts that once could be resolved only by litigation or force. *Settling Disputes* serves as an essential guide to the new settlement alternatives. This second edition, updated in response to the rapid changes of the past five years, includes substantial new material that describes recent transformations in the way that courts and public agencies respond to disputes. The book discusses alternative dispute resolution from the viewpoints of potential participants and offers advice to those who are involved in disputes to help them analyze their situations and goals. Finally, it provides suggestions for professionals involved in dispute resolution and for those whose jobs in law, business, government, or health are affected by the new options for settling disputes.

The dispute resolution movement continues to offer the most hopeful, powerful alternative to the business and personal costs of litigation or, worse, of violence. It has tremendous implications for the professional lives of Americans, for their private lives—as parents, spouses, neighbors, and consumers—and for their role as citizens.

Linda R. Singer is a partner in the law firm of Lichtman, Trister, Singer & Ross. Since 1971, she has directed the Center for Dispute Settlement, one of the most active organizations in the dispute resolution field. She now handles an active mediation and arbitration practice as a principal in ADR Associates in Washington, D.C.

Index